Writing Historical Fiction

Writing Historical Fiction

A Writers' and Artists' Companion

Celia Brayfield and Duncan Sprott

Series Editors: **Carole Angier and Sally Cline**

B L O O M S B U R Y

LONDON • NEW DELHI • NEW YORK • SYDNEY

Bloomsbury Academic

An imprint of Bloomsbury Publishing Plc

50 Bedford Square
London
WC1B 3DP
UK

1385 Broadway
New York
NY 10018
USA

www.bloomsbury.com

Bloomsbury is a registered trademark of Bloomsbury Publishing Plc

First published 2014

British Library Cataloguing-in-Publication Data
A catalogue record for this book is available from the British Library.

ISBN: PB: 978-1-7809-3785-4
         ePub: 978-1-7809-3577-5
         PDF: 978-1-7809-3838-7

Library of Congress Cataloging-in-Publication Data
Brayfield, Celia.
    Writing historical fiction : a writers' and artists' companion / Celia Brayfield and Duncan Sprott.
        pages cm
    Summary: "With advice from leading international and bestselling writers, this book provides all the practical advice you need to write historical fiction succesfully"-- Provided by publisher.
    Includes bibliographical references and index.
    ISBN 978-1-78093-785-4 (pbk.) -- ISBN 978-1-78093-577-5 (epub) -- ISBN 978-1-78093-838-7 (epdf) 1. Historical fiction--Authorship--Handbooks, manuals, etc. 2. Authorship. I. Sprott, Duncan, 1952- II. Title.
    PN3377.5.H57B73 2013
    808.06'69--dc23

                                                                                      2013026675

Typeset by Fakenham Prepress Solutions, Fakenham, Norfolk NR21 8NN
Printed and bound in India

Celia Brayfield's previous books
Fiction
Wild Weekend
Mister Fabulous and Friends
Heartswap
Sunset
Getting Home
Harvest
White Ice
The Prince
Pearls
Non-Fiction
Deep France: A Writer's Year in the Béarn
Bestseller: Secrets of Successful Writing
Arts Reviews
Glitter: The Truth About Fame

Duncan Sprott's previous books
Fiction
The Clopton Hercules
Our Lady of the Potatoes
The Ptolemies: The House of the Eagle
Daughter of the Crocodile
Kleopatra's Shadow (forthcoming 2014)
Non-Fiction
1784
Sprottichronicon

Celia Brayfield

To M. B., who kindly encouraged my love of history at a time when this
was not fashionable.

Duncan Sprott

To Deborah Rogers

Contents

Part 2: Tips and tales – guest contributions

Part 3: Write on

Preface

Historical fiction has been popular for much longer than most of us imagined, as the history of it in these pages will show. In modern times its popularity soared, until today – with writers like Hilary Mantel, Philippa Gregory and many others – it is not only one of the most popular literary genres, but one of the most admired. We are in a golden age of historical fiction.

This book is the fifth is a series of Writers' & Artists' Companions to writing. Like all the others, it is written by two eminent practitioners: in this case one specialist in the ancient world and one in the modern. Between them they cover the field, from the Epic of Gilgamesh to e-publishing. We are confident that you will not find a more complete, scholarly, entertaining and altogether fascinating guide to the writing of historical fiction anywhere.

The authors, Celia Brayfield and Duncan Sprott, provide their own personal reflections on their genre in Part One and a practical writing guide in Part Three. In between is a dazzling array of guest writers, including Hilary Mantel and Philippa Gregory – and Orhan Pamuk and Rose Tremain – who add their experiences and advice. Writing is an art as well as a craft: the craft can be taught, or at least shared, but the art is up to you. The best we can all do is to join in the conversation, and listen to as many voices as we can.

Historical fiction has long since graduated from the romantic doldrums in which it languished for several decades. Today we recognise that many literary novels – perhaps most – are historical, i.e. set in the past; and accordingly that many of our literary novelists – perhaps most – are historical novelists too. Thus the very meaning of 'historical novel' has changed; and in writing one (or many) you will be joining not a tributary but the mainstream. *Writing Historical Fiction* hopes to be an invaluable Companion on your way.

Carole Angier and Sally Cline, series editors

Introduction

Once upon a time. Legends, myths and fairy tales, the earliest stories humankind has told, are all set in the past, the Dreamtime, the age of giants, elves, fairies, Titans, nymphs and talking animals, when the roads were paved with bread. The past is the natural habitat of fiction.

For us, the authors of this book, the question is not why historical fiction is so popular but why fiction ever left the past at all. Literary critics think of historical fiction as a genre, but in what system of thought can *Midnight's Children* be likened to *Forever Amber*, or *The Celebrated Cases of Judge Dee* to *War and Peace?* Perhaps we can think of historical fiction as a supergenre which can embrace all others, but also extend to the boldest, most dazzling experimental writing.

Today we can read Joan of Arc's speeches on-line and refight the battles of Alexander the Great in a digital game. We know so much about the past and still so little about ourselves, and so historical fiction searches for the truth that is beyond the historian's evidence. As Ezra Pound wrote, "We do not know the past in chronological sequence. It may be convenient to lay it out anaesthetised on the table with dates pasted on here and there, but what we know we know by ripples and spirals eddying out from us and from our own time."

Wherever authors fix their ambitions, historical fiction poses the same challenges: how to balance accuracy with credibility; how to give your characters their voices; how much research to do; how much research to leave out. This book will guide writers through these decisions but that is not the real reason we wrote it. We wrote this book because we love historical fiction, in all its fascinating, rich and unresolvable complexity, and we want more of it, and better.

Celia Brayfield
Duncan Sprott

Part 1:
Historical fiction

Reflections 1

by Duncan Sprott

On being stuck fast

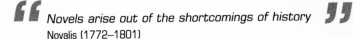

Novels arise out of the shortcomings of history
Novalis (1772–1801)

I suppose there was never any doubt that I would make my living out of the dead: from the start it was going to be the past, the whole past, and nothing but the past. Among the epigraphs for my first book, a cuttings job on the newspapers of the year 1784,[1] I put some lines from *1984*, in which George Orwell had Winston Smith propose a toast – not to the confusion of the Thought Police, not to the death of Big Brother, not to humanity or the future, but to the past. O'Brien agrees gravely, 'The past is more important'.

Thirty years on, I am still writing about the past, and the past still seems more important. Where should we be without it? Without the past there would be no laws, no government, no infrastructure, no religions, no books and no words to describe anything. As Edward Said put it, 'The condition of being modern and European... neither of those two categories has any true meaning without being related to an earlier alien culture and time'.[2] Apart from today, now, the fleeting moment, history is all we have. As for tomorrow, we have no hold on the future except through dreams and imagination. This is also partly true of our hold on the past – most of it is lost, except fragments. One function of historical fiction is to retrieve those fragments and build them up into a coherent whole; to make it all live again. To reconstruct what was lost is by no means impossible. The historical novelist can go where the historian fears to tread. We have to imagine and dream and research it back into existence: to restore, revive, rebuild what is lost. And that makes me think of T. S. Eliot:

'These fragments I have shored against my ruins.'[3]

Without the past, we are nothing.

The Essex village where I was born was not where we belonged: both my parents had come from elsewhere in England. But my birthplace managed to give me my first taste of the past: a Norman castle mound (I had to imagine the building itself) with a moat, and a boat for rowing across. Also a Norman church, the antiquity of which impressed me, even at five years old. Inside there were old tombs and an old language, declaimed by hieratic figures amid a vague earthy aroma of antiquity. We moved, when I was six, just as I was getting my bearings, to a town where I definitely didn't belong. I was always looking back, at how things used to be, and then, at the past of everything. My generation was the last that could sit in church and hear the resonant words of the King James Bible (1611), and the 1662 Book of Common Prayer, the very voice of the past. Looking back has had its disadvantages ever since Lot's wife, but I did look back. I always have looked back instead of forward. And I was aware, very young, of the dangers, because one of the first poems echoing round my empty head was:

'Do diddle di do,
Poor Jim Jay,
Got stuck fast in yesterday.'[4]

I knew it, even then: I was stuck myself. Unlike Jim Jay, I wanted to be stuck. 'Stuck fast in yesterday' could be the epigraph to my life.

Our family was ordinary enough, but we had exotic, bizarre things: a stuffed crocodile, for instance, dangled from the picture rail in the hall. Just a baby, two foot long, but still a crocodile, brought back from nobody-knew-where by my seafaring grandfather, a man I never met. In the cupboard under the stairs was that same grandfather's telescope, heavy, brass-bound, four feet long (to look through the narrow end felt like looking into history). And we had a giant tortoise shell, brought back from (I suppose) the Galápagos, and an array of glittering brass from India. My mother, so very good at throwing things away, sent all these treasures, one by one, to the jumble sale. The best things were always the lost things, defined by their absence. What didn't get chucked out was a small leatherbound family Bible with a copperplate page of ancestors going back to 1770. When I was 12 I wrote to Great Aunt Mary to ask one or two questions. She told me we were related to Mrs Gladstone (great, it meant I was descended from William the Conqueror – if only I could prove it); and that her father's family built stagecoaches and carried the Irish mail from Chester to Holyhead. I was hooked. Genealogy meant the excitement of being a detective, but also the frustration of not being able to find the right clue. Where the facts fizzled out, imagination took over.

The Egyptologist Jan Assmann has written: 'History has two faces, one turned towards us, the other averted. The face turned towards us is the sum total of event, remembrance. It is history recalled by those involved in it, as shapers or witnesses, doers or sufferers. The hidden face of history is not what we have forgotten, but what we have never remembered, those products of imperceptible change, extended duration, and infinitesimal progression that go unnoticed by living contemporaries and only reveal themselves to the analytic gaze of the historian.'[5]

From the start, I was interested in the hidden face of history, what was lost, what could be gotten back from the past.

There were books, of course. First and best was *Gates of Horn and Ivory*,[6] which also went to the jumble sale, though I found a replacement copy last year. The front endpapers show Sir Edward Poynter's *Israel in Egypt* (1867) with sepia pyramid, obelisk, temple pylons, and Hebrew slaves hauling a stone lion. The back endpapers show a Greek theatre, with a sepia audience, and the advice to 'Notice how keenly they seem to listen'. Inside are 'Little Bright Eyes the Cave Boy', 'Nefret, A Little Princess of Egypt', and the stories of Minos and Daedalus, Achilles, Odysseus, Solomon, Prince Gautama, and Alexander the Great. Strange but true, between the covers of *Gates of Horn and Ivory* lay the whole of my later life – from Prehistory to Classical Hebrew, from Ancient Greek to Alexander, Ptolemaic Egypt and Buddhism. And the stories happen to be fictionalised history for kids. That book must have sown the seeds, but they nearly didn't sprout. School history killed dead my early interest in ancient Egypt. Medieval times were seldom mentioned. The Victorians stood for unspeakable boredom: the Corn Laws, Bismarck, Italian Unification, and the Causes of the First World War. History was kept alive not by learning dates at school but by reading in bed at home, by stories. All the key ingredients, then, were present from the start: the exotic, the bizarre, genealogy, and stories of the lost past.

When I (self-)published a skeleton history,[7] the result of some 35 years of intermittent, if not manic, geneaology, that felt like the full stop. There was nothing left in the records to find: the info was lost that might connect up the dangling wires of the story into a coherent electric whole. Later on, though, I found I could access the very deepest past via a simple DNA test. The experts couldn't say for sure whether I was a Viking or an Ancient Briton, but they did tell me that my mitochondrial DNA – passed down from mother to daughter all the way back to Mitochondrial Eve, who lived in Africa 150,000 years ago – showed that I belonged to the U haplogroup (Brian Sykes's 'Uma' family).[8] In Spencer Wells' book, *The Journey of Man*,[9] I found the map that shows the men's side of things: the snail-slow spread of Y-chromosome lineages across the world that allows us to plot the different routes taken by early man. My DNA markers – M68, M89, M9, M45, M173[10] – show which way my hunter-gatherer ancestors walked out of Africa perhaps 50,000 years ago – north out of the Great Rift Valley, across the Red Sea at low water (during the Ice Age) into the Arabian peninsula, up through the Zagros Mountains into what is now Iraq, and as far as the Hindu Kush. Somewhere near Kabul one branch of the family turned right and went off to become Indians. Our lot turned left, trekked across northern Europe, ending up, aeons later, in what is now southern Denmark. Somewhere around here, as Angles, and/or Saxons, we picked up a surname. In the eleventh century we appeared in the north of England, and got a mention in Domesday Book (1086). By the 1260s we were in southern Scotland and hung on there, Not-Quite-Scots, for six hundred years until my grandfather shot south to Norfolk, England. That is how I ended up being 'English'. During that journey of some 44,000–50,000 years, shifting maybe one mile every ten years, my dark-skinned forebears lost their colour, going through all the shades of brown until they were the pale pink that white men like to call white in order to set themselves apart from the black men who are all our cousins, however distant.

Finding out about roots: how could that not be the most interesting and important thing in the world? History is how we got to where we are – the story of the journey. History is who we are, and why we are what we are; why I am what I am – white, but not quite English, or Scottish, or British, because how do you define race or nationality when you realise where your journey started? Some of my early ancestors must have stayed in Africa, becoming, later on, ancient Egyptians; others will have become Ethiopians, Kushites, Arabs, Israelites, Assyrians, Sumerians, Hittites, Persians, Greeks and Romans – all of which peoples have to be my relatives. But my ancestors did not stop: they kept moving on, leaving behind them family branches which would, in time, become Scyths, Steppe people, then Huns, and Goths, and Vandals – the barbarians who resisted Rome. The story of all this, built upon a saliva sample, is one great conjectural emendation. What does all this have to do with historical fiction? For one thing, the story of the journey *is* historical fiction. It's also about horizons, about everything and everybody being connected. The incredible journey is not just mine but everybody's. And as it happens, the one sure thing these people took out of Africa was story. You don't know where you're going until you know where you come from.

On myth and historical fiction

" *History often resembles 'Myth', because they are both ultimately made of the same stuff.* "
J.R.R. Tolkien[11]

Story must have existed from the start, as oral tale-telling: tales of the ancestors. We could pinpoint where it started by looking at the San, in modern Namibia, one of the hunter-gatherer tribes that never went anywhere but stayed home, who are descended from our earliest African ancestors.

Historians and anthropologists get excited when they find parallels between the myths of different peoples, as if this is proof of trading contact, a sign of influence. Multiple trade contacts did exist, and from a very early date.[12] But stories must have survived from the deep past, and the proof is not so much of trading contact as proof that stories change, are embellished in the telling, adapted and improved, because a story that contains something new, something made-up, will always be a better story. From the start, storytellers shaped their material, cutting and polishing, improving.

> *Ultimately literature is nothing but carpentry... Both are very hard work. Writing something is almost as hard as making a table. With both you are working with reality, a material just as hard as wood. Both are full of tricks and techniques. Basically very little magic and a lot of hard work are involved.*
>
> Gabriel García Márquez[13]

And the magic goes right back to the beginning. What remains of this early body of story, our first attempts at *history*, is what we have called myth: episodes or stories handed down through the generations, continually retold or referred to for their resonant meaning.[14] In early times stories will have been based on real people, who grew in the telling: brave men became heroes (e.g. Heracles, Odysseus, Jason) and kings (e.g. Horus, Osiris, Oedipus, Midas); some heroes and kings became gods, or demi-gods, took on a life – or an afterlife – of their own.

It should be no surprise that an ancient Sumerian story like *Gilgamesh* has elements in common with a Greek story like the *Odyssey*, or with Persian stories, or with the *Arabian Nights*: a good story circulates, is remembered and retold, kept alive, made better, and passes down through the generations. People who travel – sailors, merchants, colonisers – take not only articles of trade, and handsome greeting-gifts, but also good stories. Stories help to make potential enemies into allies; stories build bridges between men. The storyteller is a welcome guest, not an enemy but a friend.

Story may be the most powerful thing in the world.

If 'Historical fiction is a kind of modern myth', as Jan Assmann says,[15] should we not regard myth as a kind of ancient historical fiction? Yes, partly true, partly invented, its purpose to entertain, but also, perhaps to instruct, full of dialogue that couldn't possibly be authentic, but above all full of suspense; a story that holds the hearer spellbound until the last word is spoken.

'Mythology', as determined by Gottlob Heyne and Gottfried Herder in the eighteenth century, dealt with the origin of the world and the many creatures in it, the vicissitudes of vegetation, weather, eclipses, the discovery of fire, and the mystery of death.[16] Mythology has an aetiological function, explaining away the mystery of how things came to be how they are, and why. Much of it has been lost, of course, and some of it was deliberately destroyed. The earliest Irish and Welsh texts were written down by Christian scribes, people who were often hostile to the so-called pagan traditions that preceded them. Gods and goddesses of the older religion were deprived of their power, reduced to shadowy phantoms, or historicised into kings, queens or heroes (divinisation can be a two-way process). In fact, *most* of myth must be lost. Even with the named divinities of the ancient Gauls or Britons (e.g. Epona, Cernunnos, Maponos) not one word of narrative survives in the native language: we have only brief remarks by Greek and Latin writers to go on, and whatever physical evidence survives in the way of statues, or votive offerings. It seems significant, though, that the narratives from early Irish and Welsh traditions contain countless parallels in motif, theme, and character with other Indo-European traditions that we usually call 'mythology', not only Greek and Roman but also Norse, Slavic, Iranian, and Indian.[17] These are the last pathetic survivors, the mangled, garbled remains of what must once have made a good deal more sense; the only vestiges of prehistoric story handed down from the deep past.

> *We lose track of everything, and of everyone, even ourselves. The facts of my father's life are less known to me than those of the life of Hadrian... What is ever left but crumbled walls, or masses of shade?*
>
> Marguerite Yourcenar *Reflections on the Composition of Memoirs of Hadrian*[18]

The truth is that nobody can remember anything. Not now, not then, not ever. We had to make it all up: not only myth but most of history too.

Asked about the banana fever in *One Hundred Years of Solitude* (1978), Gabriel García Márquez said:

> The banana fever is modelled closely on reality... I've used literary tricks on things which have not been proved historically. For example, the massacre in the square is completely true, but while I wrote it on the basis of testimony and documents, it was never known exactly how many people were killed. I used the figure three thousand... obviously an exaggeration... What's really surprising is that now they speak very naturally in the Congress and the newspapers about the 'three thousand dead'. I suspect that half of all our history is made in this fashion.[19]

From the beginning, the past was lost, until people realised that not having a past made them feel insecure, and started worrying, and began to ask the big questions: Who are we? Where did we come from? Where are we going? Story managed to answer every question. Story kept the tribe quiet and happy, because stories provoke laughter and provide comfort. Stories dispel fear, give hope and resssurance in difficult times, and courage to keep going, or to fight the next enemy. Hero stories set an example before the young: what it means to be a warrior and a man. All stories came out of the past. We had to pretend, in the beginning, that we could remember what happened.

From the very beginning there will have been mythmakers, bards, story-tellers, wise men (and women) licensed to embroider. While a myth does not come from nowhere, at some point somebody has made up a story, with gods and heroes as characters, and his listeners swallowed it whole. Even if we have lost those stories, it's not difficult to guess what they were about. Christopher Booker's *The Seven Basic Plots*[20] provides the clues: Overcoming the Monster, The Quest, Voyage and Return... At first story was oral, all done from memory, and memory can play tricks. From the start they will have indulged in the faking of forgotten facts. This was the past rearranged, restructured and reinterpreted, revised and rebuilt: a re(-)vision. And this is exactly what goes on in historical fiction. Far from being the invention of Sir Walter Scott, as Georg Lukács[21] would have us believe, the so-called 'genre' of historical fiction existed before any of the others. It has to be the oldest genre. We should see myth for what it really is.

In the beginning was historical fiction.

On the historical novel as metaphor

> *Mes personnages, je ne suis aucun d'eux et je suis chacun d'eux.*
> Henri de Montherlant

In 1935, the German Jewish novelist Lion Feuchtwanger published an interesting essay, 'The Purpose of the Historical Novel',[22] in which he came to the conclusion that the historical novel is a metaphor. Feuchtwanger asked whether the great historical works of literature presented history or mythology for their own sake; whether their authors were merely enticed by colourful costumes and locations; and whether they intended to give shape to contemporary or historical subject matter. In every case, he found that the writer's sole purpose was to voice his own (contemporary) attitudes and a subjective (but in no sense historical) view of the world, and that the reader was definitely meant to notice. The point of using historical wrappings was to lift the subject out of the personal and private sphere, set it on a platform and achieve some degree of distance – on the analogy that it's easier to see the shape of a mountain from several miles away than when you are up close. Tolstoy, Feuchtwanger says, did not really want to write a history of Napoleon's campaigns: he wanted to present contemporary ideas about war and peace. He pushed everything back in time to give the reader a better perspective.

Feuchtwanger says that in his own historical novels he meant the content to be just as modern as in the contemporary ones. He never wrote about history for its own sake; he never used period costumes and historic trappings except as a means of stylisation, the simplest way of creating an illusion of reality. Some writers put their stories in a distant place, maybe some exotic place, for greater clarity; for the same purpose Feuchtwanger shifted his stories to a distant time.

His point, then, is that when you write a story with a historical setting it's a means of achieving distance, a way of rendering your own thoughts and feelings, your own era, your own philosophy, and yourself. It's all a metaphor.

Wanting to show 'the path of a man from deed to indolence, from action to contemplation', Feuchtwanger was tempted to use a contemporary figure – Walter Rathenau.[23] He tried to make this work, but failed. When he shifted the subject 200 years back in time and related the idea to the Jew Josef Süss Oppenheimer, he felt he had come much closer to his goal.[24] Later on, interested in the conflict between nationalism and internationalism in the heart of a single individual, Feuchtwanger was afraid that if he tackled that theme it 'would be overshadowed and contaminated by personal grudges and resentment'. He moved the setting to 75 BC, and gave the conflict to Flavius Josephus, the historian of the Jews, instead. Feuchtwanger felt he could make a more convincing job of the people who torched Nero's Rome than of those who, in 1933, set fire to the Reichstag in Berlin.[25] Feuchtwanger says he always tried to render every detail accurately, but never paid much attention to getting the historical facts right. He confesses to altering documentary evidence if it interfered with his plans. Unlike the scientist, Feuchtwanger says, the historical novelist has the right to choose a lie that enhances illusion over a reality that distracts from it. Homer, the authors of the Bible, Shakespeare, and countless other historical works, he notes, have all been bold and cavalier in their handling of documented reality, but their fictional characters and imaginary deeds, their 'lies' have more life in them than the bare facts sifted by historians. 'In most cases', Feuchtwanger says, 'a good legend or a good historical novel is more believable, gives a truer picture, is livelier... than a precise rendering of historical facts.'

So, however the historian assembles his materials, the fact that the facts are *arranged*, given a shape, will always result in a view of history that is subjective. The historian is no different from the novelist; they are both producing Art.

As John Lewis Gaddis notes, historians can select from the cacophony of events *what they think* is really important: they can be in several times and places at once; they can zoom in and out between macroscopic and microscopic levels of analysis. In the historian's method of time travel it's the historian who imposes significances on the past, not the other way round.[26]

Hayden White, the philosopher of history, noted that events recorded in strict order of occurrence get rearranged almost at once into a story with a discrete beginning, middle and end. These then become histories.[27] Whereas the historian's evidence is always incomplete, and his perspective always limited,[28] contrast the position of the historical novelist, who knows everything; who can, quite literally, go anywhere, any time; who, by filling in all the gaps with plausible fictions, can make things complete, and perfect. Like Tolstoy in *War and Peace*, the historical novelist can render the past more real than present reality.

In the movie *Being John Malkovitch* (Spike Jonze, 1999) the historian's process of getting into and back out of somebody else's mind can actually be seen happening.[29] The plot features an entrepreneur who finds himself by accident inside the actor's brain, seeing and feeling whatever Malkovitch sees and feels. He hatches a plan to let other people inside the brain at $200 a trip. Critics saw the film as a parody of postmodernism.[30] In fact, I think what you see in this movie is what it feels like to be a novelist, particularly a historical novelist, one who takes up residence inside somebody else's head, perhaps that of a well-known historical figure who died hundreds of years ago. You think that person's thoughts, you fight his battles, you put your words into his (her) mouth; you look out on the world through his (her) eyes, you share the agony as she gives birth to her children and you die his horrible death at Thermopylae (and it's all faintly creepy, if you think about it, no?)

In effect, your book is the world in miniature, the microcosm, over which you have total and perfect control; and in which you play at being God. You create the world and the characters in it; you make them move; you can kill them off any time you like. You also have the power to destroy that world. You may be constrained by the facts of history, but you don't actually *have* to stick to them: you can still do more or less what you like. You are the All-powerful One yourself. You are also a magician.

Cue to quote Talleyrand: 'Nothing is easier to arrange than the facts.'

And also Lytton Strachey: 'Compilations of facts are no more history than butter, eggs, salt and herbs are an omelette.' The texture and taste of this famous omelette will vary depending on who is mixing the ingredients...

But to go back to Feuchtwanger: If the historical novel is a metaphor, are all historical novelists, in truth, labouring with metaphors? If I write about Kleopatra and Antony am I really making a comment on the twenty-first century? The knee-jerk response is no, of course not. Sure, I may find the idea of monarchy interesting, and the fact that brother-sister incest was *de rigueur* in the Ptolemaic royal family, and that the Ptolemies were free to do *just what they liked*. I may be interested in Lord Acton's 'Power corrupts and absolute power corrupts absolutely'. But I'm not covering up any message by using 'historical wrappings'. I'm interested in the story for itself, to retrieve and reconstruct a history that has been lost for 2,000 years.

On the other hand, there is a different kind of metaphor that Feuchtwanger doesn't mention (I'm thinking of Robert Graves *being* Claudius; of Marguerite Yourcenar *becoming* Hadrian.) I could say it's very deep-rooted, but I may be presenting the Ptolemies as a family in which there appears to be a collective denial of love. There is a level on which I am aware that the Ptolemies are, to some degree (though there was no incest, and we are not [yet] gods in our own lifetime) a metaphor for my own family, and that, at bottom, this book is about affection, and the absence of affection, about kindness, and the absence of kindness; about the presence and absence of love. And also about anger, fear, jealousy, hatred; but also, of course, it's about the bizarre, the exotic, the wonderful; it's about the gods, belief and unbelief, and a hundred or so other things. And I know very well that all this is really why the subject grabbed me in the first place. So, yes, there will be some lights in which my novel may be regarded as a metaphor. *Though I would never tell anybody.*

In a book every father is in some sense one's own father, every mother one's own mother, and every child an aspect of oneself. Probably also every hero. Consciously or unconsciously one identifies with the characters, identifies them as emanations of the archetypal characters who inhabit one's own microcosm, the world in miniature that is one's own family, one's own home. Any book is a metaphor, in that case; a metaphor not only of the writer's existence but also of the reader's. And if I can't 'get on' with a book, maybe that is because I don't 'belong' in it; because none of the characters 'click' with any of the prototypes or paradigms from my past.

So is historical fiction just one great ego trip? Are we refugees from reality pouring our camouflaged private concerns into a different – and public – mould? Is what I do for a living just a weird disguised form of public self-analysis? I am myself the mixer of the ingredients in my novel. I am the one who imposes order on the chaos of history. I am the one who brings things to life. I am the god in my story (literally, inasmuch as in *The Ptolemies* my narrators are Thoth, Egyptian god of Wisdom, and Seshat, goddess of the Library). So, on the one hand, yes, my book may be about me. But I'm also with Flaubert, striving after objectivity, the whole truth, in the sense that, having undertaken exhaustive (and exhausting) researches there is nothing that I do not know about my characters, period, and chosen location, and the result is that whatever I make up about them will be true, down to the last word of dialogue. *Word for word.* Even the ultra-objective Flaubert, however, is visible in his own creation – at least in *Salammbô*. The sex and violence of Flaubert's Carthage will not be found in Polybius' *History*: Flaubert made it all up, and one cannot help but note his special interest in the Marquis de Sade.[31] (And that, surely, is the fundamental reason why Flaubert wrote *Salammbô*.)

Never to be forgotten, Flaubert's *Madame Bovary, c'est moi.*

 We go to fiction for many reasons – to be entertained, instructed, diverted, enlightened, entranced... What we are really in search of is not fiction, but life itself. Like the figures in our dreams, the characters we encounter in fiction are really us, and the story we are told is the story of ourselves. And therein lies the delightful paradox that the novelist's transcendent lies are

> eminently more truthful than all the facts in the
> world, that they are... 'true lies'
> John Banville[32]

On being not quite proper

In *The True History of the Novel*,[33] Margaret Anne Doody laments the decline of the historical novel from its former glory:

> A number of important nineteenth-century novels are historical novels, like Manzoni's *I Promessi Sposi*... and *War and Peace*. It took a while to bring this genre down, but we had done it by the early twentieth century, largely by decrying it for falseness to history and for 'sensationalism' (but battle, executions, sieges, etc., may very well evoke sensations). The moving pictures' fondness for the historical novels' scenes and effects only proved that this kind of novel was 'low' – lowbrow and disreputable. The only kind of historical novel acceptable now is one set in a past within living memory. Everything else of the kind is considered 'trash.'[34]

Even Margaret Drabble's august *Oxford Companion to English Literature* (1985)[35] notes under *Historical Novel*, 'The attraction of the form has now greatly declined, except in the popular market, where G[eorgette] Heyer succeeded such writers as [Baroness] Orczy, [Stanley] Weyman and [Maurice Henry] Hewlett', though the entry does concede 'the form has also been successfully used' by writers as diverse as Mary Renault, Naomi Mitchison, William Golding, and J. G. Farrell'.[36]

Despite the very wonderful things going on at the top end – and one could add a host of august names to the roll of honour, such as Giuseppe Tomasi di Lampedusa (*The Leopard*), Robert Graves (*Claudius*), Marguerite Yourcenar (*Memoirs of Hadrian*), Alejo Carpentier (*The Kingdom of this World*), Hermann Broch (*The Death of Virgil*), Herman Hesse (*Siddhartha; Narziss and Goldmund*), Thornton Wilder (*The Bridge of San Luis Rey*), John Fowles (*The French Lieutenant's Woman; A Maggot*), Gabriel García Márquez (*The General in His Labyrinth*) for example – the rubbish down at the bottom seems to have gotten the illustrious genre in which we all belong – *or pretend not to* – a very bad name.

Andrew Miller, writing in *The Guardian* in 2011,[37] said, 'There are still critics out there who insist that novels with historical settings are not quite proper. Novels should be about the Now, should have a whiff of last week's headlines – or next week's.' Miller says that, for him, history was 'always a rattle-bag of wonderful stories... not something apart from us, sealed off. It is in our blood, our music, our language, the building we pass on the way to work. And at its best, historical fiction is never a turning away from the Now but one of the ways in which our experience of the contemporary is revived. Janus-like, such books look both to the past and to the present...'

A discredited class of novel? What, indeed, is so wrong with Now? Flaubert hated Now. Robert Graves hated Now. Italo Calvino too. In *Six Memos for the Next Millennium*,[38] Calvino says, 'When I began my career, the categorical imperative of every young writer was to represent his own time. Full of good intentions, I tried to identify myself with the ruthless energies propelling the events of our century... I tried to find some harmony between the adventurous, picaresque inner rhythm that prompted me to write and the frantic spectacle of the world, sometimes dramatic and sometimes grotesque. Soon I became aware that between the facts of life that should have been my raw materials, the quick light touch I wanted for my writing, there was a gulf that cost me increasing efforts to cross. Maybe I was only then becoming aware of the weight, the inertia, the opacity of the world – qualities that stick to writing from the start, unless one finds some way of evading them.'[39]

Here is Calvino again: 'What many consider to be the vitality of the times – noisy, aggressive, revving and roaring – belongs to the realm of death, like a cemetery for rusty old cars.'[40] The fact is that we know far too much about the present, and the things we do know are not the ones we want to know. Lytton Strachey said the history of the Victorian Age will never be written – because we just know too much about it. It is simply unmanageable. The history of the twentieth century will be even more difficult. And as for us, in the twenty-first century, we don't know what will happen next, or where we are going any more than the folks shivering in a cave somewhere in Northern Spain at the end of the last Ice Age. The paradox is that the past, about which we know much less, is more manageable: there is less information to plough through, it's easier to research, easier to grasp.

I'm with Calvino about the 'frantic spectacle'. It's as if the world of now is spinning too fast for anyone to see what's going on. Everything is out of focus. We need the distant view in order to see the range of mountains. The past, at least, will keep still long enough for us to take a proper look. In the past one does know, up to a point, what happens next. One can get a reasonable perspective on things in a way that, for the present, is impossible. At least, one can *impose* that perspective on the past, where order, and arrangement are possible.

Calvino talks of the contemporary novel as an encyclopedia,[41] as a method of knowledge. I think the novel is the place for total history. Details should not be left out; the richness of the past is a vital part of making the reader believe, in making the old, lost world live again. Sure, the only art is leaving things out. Sure, less is more. Sometimes. But sometimes more is more. Sometimes more is better.

To paraphrase Edmund White (who was talking about autobiography): History shows us formal long-shot panoramas of crowds – especially armies – historical fiction gives us the individual in all his glowing detail.[42]

But the past has always been with us in fiction. And though the press squawk when the Man Booker shortlist contains nothing but historical fiction, demanding to know what is wrong with now, really the historical novel is nothing to get hysterical about. As Edmund White noted, back in 2003, 'Many books of fiction, even most books, are historical novels, whether we call them that or not.'[43] And Margaret Atwood has said, 'All novels are historical novels – the present never really exists in fiction.'[44]

Not everybody has been quite so dismissive of historical fiction, or its usefulness. Sir Steven Runciman, author of *A History of the Crusades*, was asked by a writer for the *New Yorker* if he had ever thought about writing a historical novel. 'Oh yes', he replied, 'I deeply wanted to do so in order to say what I know to be true, but cannot prove.'[45]

We think historical fiction is very proper, utterly proper.

On writing about antiquity

> *One can contract the distance between centuries at will.*
>
> Marguerite Yourcenar[46]

Gabriel García Márquez once said in an interview, 'Most people don't realise that a novel like *One Hundred Years of Solitude* is a bit of a joke, full of signals to close friends.'[47] Other things, too, I suspect, were 'a bit of a joke'. Herodotus' *Histories*, for example, and Apollonius Rhodius' *Argonautica*, may be other works that the 'modern' world takes far too seriously. I sometimes think that the Pliny's *Natural History* must have been the ancient equivalent of *Private Eye*, so stuffed is it with the absurd and the bizarre. But the ancient sense of humour was quite different from ours. In fact everything about antiquity is different, and difficult. That, of course, is (a) all part of the challenge, and (b) all part of the fun. Time travel is the ultimate trip, the ultimate *interior* journey. Tackling the Ptolemies, Hellenistic Egypt, a Greek dynasty, plus an excursion into Republican Rome, felt more like my own particular trip to Hades to interrogate the dead.

Antiquity has caused many authors a great deal of trouble. Amelia Edwards, co-founder of the Egypt Exploration Society (1885) and author of *A Thousand Miles up the Nile* (1876), and herself a novelist, said nobody ever wrote about Egypt quickly. She was right. Everything you touch is open to doubt and complicating factors, whether it's the gods, pinning down what the Egyptians believed, dodgy translations, what happened when, and where, and whether a fact is reliable or not. 'History has been called an enormous jigsaw with a lot of missing pieces.'[48] Egypt is that jigsaw, indeed, writ very large.

As for the Ptolemies, the subject is one of extreme complexity. At the bottom of things is Egypt, knowable only by painstaking reconstruction. On top, pile the Greeks in Egypt, a whole extra civilisation, the reconstruction of the city of Alexandria, and a family that must be the most convoluted and inbred in the whole of history. Bizarre and wonderful, yes, but the tangled genealogy has to be unravelled. What takes time is reconstructing a coherent psychology, piecing together the family dynamic, having it all interlock and make plausible sense. Did they really hate each other? How did they react to being obliged to marry their own sisters? What were their feelings? Were they a bunch of psychopaths? And so on. There are no materials in history to tell, and no models anywhere else in history. It all has to be invented. Did they, I ask myself so often, love each other after all? And yet, there is so much death, so much bloodshed. How could Kleopatra have *loved* her brother-husbands Ptolemy XIII and XIV if she could put them to death? Did she not have a heart at all? On the other hand, so much of history is garbled story, it is not impossible that one is wrestling not so much with the history of the Ptolemies as with the myth. For sure, one uses the zoom lens, makes things up, but everything has to start from a germ of truth, some fact that can be built on, or made to grow. On top of all that, while we know a great deal about quite a few of the Ptolemies, there are huge gaps where there is no information. Papering over the cracks is not difficult, but who knows whether what Polybius wrote was true? References to Ptolemy VIII Physkon, for example, may be biased, the malicious work of his enemies, the Museum scholars he chucked out of Alexandria. Who knows whether Plutarch – writing some 150 years after the event – told the truth about Kleopatra? A cursory glance at C.B.R. Pelling's commentary on Plutarch's *Life of Antony*[49] will turn up the words 'creativity', 'invention', 'fabrication'. Plutarch did not set out to tell the whole truth in his *Parallel Lives*: he wanted to draw moral lessons. And yet, thanks to Shakespeare, the world has swallowed Plutarch's myth whole, and the 'movie' Cleopatra of Joseph Manciewicz and others is more alive and real to us than almost any other character in history. I happen to believe that Plutarch got Antony and Kleopatra wrong, completely and magnificently wrong.

The real Kleopatra was quite different.

Flaubert wrote *Salammbô* (1862) [50] only with great pain and tribulation. His vast researches are legendary. He claimed to have read – and probably did – more than 200 books. He made trips to Tunis and Carthage, gathering exotic details. His letters are full of his struggle: 'In order for one's book to *sweat* truth, one has to be stuffed to the ears with its subject.'[51] He imagined that, after all the trouble *Madame Bovary* (1856) caused, *Salammbô* would be a piece of cake. No chance. It took just as long – five years, and caused him the same blood, sweat and tears.[52] His letters make it sound as though *Salammbô* was driving him mad. But although Salammbô was a fictional character, she was real enough for Flaubert, modelled on Kuchuk Hanem, an Egyptian dancer and courtesan he met in Wadi Halfa.

Salammbô would be exotic and richly coloured, an imaginative recon-struction of a vanished civilisation: Carthage, and the bloody revolt and annihilation of unpaid mercenaries at the end of the First Punic War. All was based on Polybius's *History* (second century BC). Flaubert told the Goncourt brothers he wanted to write something purple.[53] And he sure did.

The choice of an exotic subject was deliberate: he wanted to escape from his own life and times. '*Bovary* inspired me with a long disgust for bourgeois ways,' he wrote. 'Now I'm going to live... in a splendid subject, far from the modern world I'm fed up with.'[54] 'The narration and description of a battle in antiquity is no small task... I'm overwhelmed with fatigue. I'm carrying two entire armies on my shoulders – thirty thousand men on one side, eleven thousand on the other, not counting the elephants ... the camp followers, and the baggage! Let's be ferocious... Let's pour brandy on to this century of sugar water... My men have already begun to *eat* each other... '[55]

The Goncourts put their finger on what is wrong with *Salammbô*. In their journal for 1861, having listened to Flaubert reading from the manuscript, they wrote: 'Immensely fatiguing are the eternal descriptions, the minute button-by-button itemisations of every character and every costume, which destroy any possibility of grand group effects. All the effects are minuscular... faces are obscured by trappings, feelings are lost in landscapes.' Immense effort, infinite patience, and rare talent had gone into Flaubert's attempt to reconstruct ancient Carthage, but they thought the project doomed: Flaubert had not been able to *illuminate*.[56] Flaubert himself wrote, '*Carthage* will make me die of fury yet. I am now full of doubts about the ensemble... I think there are too many soldiers... I'm lost in battle engines – ballistae and scorpions – and it all passes my understanding as well as everybody else's... It's taking a long time, and the *writing* is becoming more and more impossible. In short, I'm like a toad squashed by a paving stone, like a dog with its guts crushed out by a shit-wagon... The military art of the ancients makes my head swim; I'm stuffed with it; I vomit catapults, have a hoisting machine up my arse, and piss scorpions....'[57]

Flaubert was proud of his 'Carthaginian girl', but she had a mixed reception. Victor Hugo and Berlioz, among others, were full of praise. The critics proclaimed their disgust at its bloodiness, eroticism, 'obscenity' and pictorial extravagance. Others cast doubt on its authenticity.[58] But *Salammbô* was authentic: Polybius had provided the framework and much of its detail, and the book was a wild success.

Flaubert had shown the proofs to Sainte-Beuve, saying, 'Now I have nothing further to do except discover printers' errors, mistakes in style, mistakes in grammar, etc. – in short, undergo the usual humiliations.' In the margin of that letter Sainte-Beuve scribbled: 'Grammatical mistakes not very important! The essential is that a book should have life and interest, catch hold of the reader, *bite* him – be absorbingly real, or magic.'[59] But Sainte-Beuve hated Flaubert's subject, objected to his method and thought he had failed.[60] Above all, he felt that *Salammbô* did not BITE the reader. Flaubert wrote a long letter defending himself. He gave sources for elephants' ears painted blue, for men who daub themselves with vermilion and eat apes and vermin; for Lydian men in women's dress; for the carbuncles formed by lynxes' urine, the crucified lions, right down to the ankle chainlet... everything.[61] He cared very much about his reputation as a painstaking, if amateur scholar. Victor Hugo, in *Notre-Dame de Paris* (1831) shows a cavalier disregard for fact: in this respect Flaubert is Not Guilty. He claimed that there was no detail in his book without documentary authority. For Flaubert, a historical novel had to be as historically accurate as possible, and in that belief he broke decisively with the Romantic tradition.[62]

Remarkable achievement though *Salammbô* is, Flaubert did not quite let go of his research and allow the fiction to take off. He had done *too much* research. He failed to cast it away and let fiction take priority.

Robert Graves, on the other hand, flew through antiquity, writing both *I, Claudius* and *Claudius the God*[63] (250,000 words in all) in eight months flat. He said he wrote *I, Claudius* only to make money. (He was £4,000 in debt). 'I got so close to [Claudius]', he said, 'that I was accused of doing a lot of research that I had never done at all.' 'If you only use the main sources, and you know the period, a book writes itself.' Asked why he chose the historical novel, Graves said, 'I had noted in my diary a year or two before, that the Roman historians... especially Tacitus, had obviously got Claudius wrong, and that one day I'd have to write a book about it.'

Graves said, 'I didn't think I was writing a novel. I was trying to find out the truth of Claudius. And there was some strange feeling between Claudius and myself. I found out that I was able to know a lot of things that happened without having any basis except that I knew they were true. It's a question of reconstructing a personality.'[64] Graves had always disliked ancient Rome, but the idea of writing about Claudius had been growing on him. In the end, it *was* 'pleading for execution'. Scholars tended to ignore Claudius, but he happened to have written a lost autobiography, and that is what Graves produced. In short, Graves found a gap, and filled it. He read hundreds of books, soaking himself in the atmosphere of the Rome of Claudius' time, genning up on everything, including brutal murders, until he knew as much as any academic. The moral – or amoral – atmosphere is all authentic.[65]

The two Claudius books are far from academic or 'historical' though. Graves applied his own idiosyncratic view to the facts. And yet classical students always glean from these books an important picture of ancient Rome. Although he referred to *I, Claudius* as a potboiler, and said it was rubbish, it is really nothing of the kind. Despite the fact that he did not much enjoy reading historical fiction, he brought Claudius triumphantly to life. *The Times Literary Supplement* later called *I, Claudius* the *only* successful historical novel of the twentieth century.[66]

Viewers of the BBC TV version of *I, Claudius* did not believe that the events they watched really took place in history, but they were convinced of the essential truth. *I, Claudius* satisfies Aristotle's dictum (in *Poetics*)[67] that fiction (something not historically true) may be more satisfying than the real. Aristotle said that fiction could present the *general* truth about something more effectively – indeed, more truthfully – than could some *particular* (or even unique) historical record. Graves claimed that he had no imagination, meaning that he was no use at writing novels with contemporary settings.[68] But if he had a bunch of historical facts to make sense of, and if they engaged his interest by setting him a puzzle to solve – then he could produce a fine novel. In the case of *I, Claudius* he proved that he had plenty of 'imagination', although he called it 'reconstruction'. Like Tolstoy with *War and Peace*, he said that it wasn't a novel at all. Graves's Claudius was in fact an oblique caricature (but not a portrait) of himself. Even the stutter was Graves's. Since the character of the historical Claudius is lost for ever, for millions of readers Graves's fictional Claudius has turned into the real one.[69]

Marguerite Yourcenar spent one third of her life trying to define, and then trying to portray, the Emperor for *Memoirs of Hadrian* (1951).[70] She first had the idea for a book about Hadrian on a visit to Rome in 1924. It was not published until 27 years later. As she wrote, later, 'There are books which one should not attempt before having passed the age of forty.'[71] And again, 'It took me years to calculate exactly the distances between the emperor and myself.'[72] She wrote, 'The writer must soak up the subject completely, as a plant soaks up water, until the ideas are ready to sprout.'[73] Her meticulous attention to detail was such that, for example, she watched in the Pantheon for the 'exact spot where sunlight would fall on a morning of April 21...'[74] To get closer to Hadrian she would spend a few hours before starting work writing Greek.[75] Truly to recapture an earlier time, she said, needed years of research (just how much research may be seen in her 15-page bibliographical note)[76] and an almost mystical act of self-identification. She did both and wrought a kind of transhistorical miracle.[77] Though one does wonder just how much of this was strictly necessary.

Although Yourcenar claimed she was trying to efface the personal in this book, there are signs that her identification with Hadrian was total. Sometimes she denied it, but once she said it would be truer to say not 'Hadrian is my own self' or 'I am Hadrian' but '*I became Hadrian...*'.[78]

Yourcenar's prose is often described as 'marmoreal' – which I take to mean smooth and sparkling, like marble, but heavy. I find it impossible to read it with any speed. Although one early version of the book was wholly in dialogue, the finished work has none. Nobody opens the mouth to speak. And all is very chaste between Hadrian and Antinous. Even so, by any standards, *Memoirs of Hadrian* is a masterpiece.

Some saw *Memoirs of Hadrian* as a fictionalised biography, but it has most often been read as a historical novel.[79] Like Tolstoy and Graves before her, Yourcenar denied it. She said, 'Hadrian is not, strictly speaking, a novel, but a meditation or a narrative situated on the limit of history...'.[80] As for other people's historical novels, she regarded them as 'merely a more or less successful costume ball'.[81] In her *Reflections on the Composition of Memoirs of Hadrian*, Yourcenar makes some perceptive remarks about her craft. About time, for example, she says: 'The problem of time foreshortened in terms of human generations: some five and twenty aged men, their withered hands interlinked to form a chain, would be enough to establish an unbroken contact between Hadrian and ourselves.'[82] And about her method: 'One foot in scholarship, the other in magic arts, or, more accurately and without metaphor, absorption in that sympathetic magic which operates when one transports oneself, in thought, into another's body and soul.'[83] Yourcenar knows, has *worked out*, everything that can be known about Hadrian. It is perfectly possible to do this, though – as her own example proves – it may take some time. Diane Middlebrook's biography of Ovid was interrupted by her death, and will probably never be published, but those who heard her read from the drafts of the book felt as if she knew everything about him.[84] Just so: it is possible to know *all*, even about a remote historical figure like Ovid, for whom no biography exists. In his case, it is the works that, scrutinised and meditated upon, yield up the life story. You learn to read between the lines, to connect up things that are not connected, to put two and two together to make 22. And it's as good as plugging the characters into the mains: they light up, all-electric, like magic. Thus Yourcenar, like Robert Graves, is able to *know* what Hadrian is thinking. She *knows* when Hadrian is lying. Flaubert, above all, noted this odd phenomenon of *knowing* the unknown. For the researcher who has done his stuff, who knows every last fact about his subject, every last detail about his era, everything he invents will be true.

Here is a story from the *Inner Chapters* of Chuang Tzu (c.369–286 BC), the Daoist Chinese philosopher. Among many other skills he was an expert draftsman:

> The king asked him to draw a crab. Chuang Tzu replied that he
> needed five years, a country house, and twelve servants. Five years
> later the drawing was not begun. 'I need another five years,' Chuang

Tzu said. The king granted them. At the end of these ten years, Chuang Tzu took up his brush and, in an instant, with a single stroke, he drew a crab, the most perfect crab ever seen.[85]

Like drawing the perfect crab, writing a novel can take a long time, and the deep thinking you do is just as important as the actual writing. Any novel takes time, of course, but the historical kind can take for ever. *Memoirs of Hadrian* took only a third of a lifetime to write; for the writing of *The Leopard*[86] Giuseppe Tomasi di Lampedusa spent literally his whole life in preparation, and he was dead before publication day.[87] A novel can – probably should – take a lot of mulling over. The time it takes includes time spent doing nothing. It may even take its own time, and demand to go at its own speed. It's the journey that matters, not the arrival. Which reminds me of *Ithaca*:

> " *As you set out for Ithaca*
> *hope that the road is a long one,*
> *filled with adventures, filled with discoveries...* "
> C. P. Cavafy[88]

On the heart

What is it, then, that the historical novel has that is missing from history? Perhaps the shaping of story into a narrative arc with drama and tension, all within the constraints of historical fact. Perhaps the in-depth exploration of character. Not much has survived from the past about people's feelings, except in diaries and letters, but the novel can restore feelings, can infer, deduce, and reconstruct the landscape of the heart. Yes, what is missing from history is the heart. Call it love, if you like. This is, of course, dangerous ground. The Greeks thought it most unwise to get mixed up with Eros: to fall in love, they thought, was to be mad. The historical novelist must also keep Eros on a tight leash, under control, or things may slide headlong into slushy romance, and a different category of fiction altogether. So, there is a fine line to be drawn. On the one hand, feelings did exist in the past, we want to recover them, and we can. This may sound like a farewell to Flaubertian rigour, but feelings are important, human kindness is important (the lack of it means death, war, devastated lands...). Flaubert himself wrote, in a letter to Mlle Leroyer de Chantepie, dated 1859: 'The anatomy of the human heart is as yet uncharted.'[89] Have we made any progress with the charting of the heart since then?

In *The Historian's Craft*, Marc Bloch said that history is a whole and that no period and no topic can be understood except in relation to other periods and topics. He wanted to see a 'wider, more human history', which described how and why people live and work together.[90] That sounds to me rather like what historical fiction ought to do. Bloch saw life as a whole, as a complicated interplay of ideals and realities. He wanted history to examine the hidden forces which determine behaviour and the structure of society. He wanted to understand and explain things like state of mind and habits of life. And he wanted history to use new types of source material: he thought written records were not enough.

History cannot recover the secrets of the heart – though that is what Marc Bloch wanted history to do. He underscored the historian's obligation to explore what he called 'the secret needs of the heart': but he intended the exploration he envisioned to remain on the surface of awareness: 'In the last analysis it is human consciousness which is the subject matter of history.'[91]

In *Paris and its Provinces, 1792–1802*, Richard Cobb wrote, 'There must be a wide element of guess work in social history. It is like attempting to sound the unsoundable and to penetrate the secrets of the human heart.'[92] Peter Gay says 'historians grow nervous before those "secret needs of the heart" – more secret even than Bloch imagined'. Many historians have found Bloch's proposal too rash. Gay thought it didn't go far enough.[93] Exactly. We want to know everything about the heart. William Skidelsky, writing in the *Observer* in 2011,[94] noted a growing belief that it is in personal relationships and feelings that the important truths about the world will be found. Most people, he says, feel that the important stuff happens behind closed doors, or inside people's heads.

Stephen Crane, author of *The Red Badge of Courage* (1895), asked why he wrote his story as fiction rather than history, said he wanted to feel the situations of the war not from the outside, but as a protagonist. He could only do this in a novel. Historical fiction makes us feel, as a protagonist, what would otherwise be lost to us. It transports us into the past. The very best historical fiction presents to us a truth of the past that is not the truth of the history books but a bigger and more important truth – a truth of the heart.[95] Edmund White has written, 'The job of the enlightened historical novelist is to show that the sun never sets twice on the same human sentiments. Each period has its own character, and no sentiment is natural, uninflected by the prevailing social forces.'[96] White says that if historical fiction is to be given the same weight we admire in the best novels of modern life, we must kick out the picturesque and trace out the consequences of moral choices – but only those that were genuine options at the time. We must forget modern ideas of fairness and erotic appeal, and happy marriages between sharing and loving partners of the same age and station; we must dig up the buried shapes of long-forgotten values and social arrangements. He says, 'The new historical novel must not sanitise the past for contemporary tastes.'[97] We want to know what it was really like, and it is not difficult to reconstruct 'how it was'.

White stresses the importance of little true facts – what the French call *les petits faits vrais* – that make a narrative convincing and bring it to life. Such historical facts, he says, derive from the inner as well as the outer world, and to such a degree that we can talk about an archaeology of feelings, an archaeology of sentiment.[98]

Historical fiction is the beating heart of history. Or, to juggle the words, history *with a beating heart* – that is to say, alive, restored to life; history with the feeling(s) put back in, if not the history *of* emotion. But it's more than that: it's the history of love, the history of fear, the history of hope, the history of longing, all mixed up together.

It was Lucien Febvre (1878–1958) who lamented the historian's failure to write histories of love and death, the history of pity, the history of cruelty, and the history of joy. Emotional and melodramatic, always the self-conscious fighter for a new history, Febvre wanted his profession to bathe in the past.[99] He wanted a grasp, firmer than ever, on the totality of human experience.

These might well be goals at which the historical novelist should aim.
The past may be a foreign country, *but you can learn the language*.
The borders are not closed.
The historical novel is both passport and visa.
In fact, the historical novel may be the *bridge*.

In Thornton Wilder's *The Bridge of San Luis Rey* the last words lay stress on love. Whatever happens in a life, the important thing is to have been loved:

'But soon we shall die and all memory of these five will have left
the earth, and we ourselves shall be loved for a while and forgotten.
But the love will have been enough; all those impulses of love
return to the love that made them. Even memory is not necessary
for love. There is a land of the living and a land of the dead, and
the bridge is love, the only survival, the only meaning.'[100]

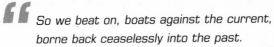

So we beat on, boats against the current,
borne back ceaselessly into the past.
F. Scott Fitzgerald *The Great Gatsby*[101]

Notes

1. Duncan Sprott, *1784*, George Allen & Unwin, London, 1984.
2. Edward Said, *Orientalism: Western Conceptions of the Orient*, Penguin, 1995, p. 132.
3. T. S. Eliot, *The Wasteland*, in *Collected Poems 1909–1962*, Faber, London, 1970, p. 79.
4. Walter de la Mare, *Jim Jay*, in *Peacock Pie*, Faber, London, 1913.
5. Jan Assmann, *The Mind of Egypt: History and Meaning in the Time of the Pharaohs*, p. 3, Harvard University Press, 2003.
6. Katharine Murray, *Gates of Horn and Ivory*, Collins' Biographical Histories, London and Glasgow, 1932.
7. Duncan Sprott, *Sprottichronicon: A Millennium Cracker*, Duncan Sprott, 2000.
8. Brian Sykes, *The Seven Daughters of Eve*, Bantam, London, 2001. 'Uma' was one of 36 women, 'clan mothers', who lived thousands of years ago, from whom almost everyone on earth is descended through the maternal line. Her clan has

been found mainly in Western Eurasia, particularly in Turkey, Armenia, Syria and Iraq. Personal communication, Oxford Ancestors: www.oxfordancestors.com

9. Spencer Wells, *The Journey of Man: A Genetic Odyssey*, Penguin, 2002.

10. Wells, op. cit., 182–3

11. J. R. R. Tolkien, Andrew Lang Lecture, 8 March 1939, 'On Fairy Stories'. Published in *Essays Presented to Charles Williams*, 1945, and in *The Tolkien Reader*, 1966.

12. See the map in E. H. Warmington, *The Commerce Between the Roman Empire and India*, (1928). 2nd edn. Curzon/Octagon, London and New York, 1974.

13. George Plimpton (ed.), *Writers at Work: The Paris Review Interviews*, 6th Series, Penguin, 1985.

14. James MacKillop, *Dictionary of Celtic Mythology*, p. xvii, Oxford University Press, 1988.

15. Jan Assman, *The Mind of Egypt: History and Meaning in the Time of the Pharaohs*, Harvard University Press, 2003.

16. MacKillop, op. cit., xviii.

17. MacKillop, op. cit., xviii.

18. Marguerite Yourcenar, *Reflections on the Composition of Memoirs of Hadrian*, in *Memoirs of Hadrian*, p. 276, Penguin Classics, 2000.

19. George Plimpton (ed.), *Writers at Work: The Paris Review Interviews*, 6th series, Penguin, 1985, pp. 325–6.

20. Christopher Booker, *The Seven Basic Plots: Why We Tell Stories*, Continuum, London, 2004.

21. Georg Lukács, *The Historical Novel* (1962), Pelican, 1981, p. 15.

22. Lion Feuchtwanger, 'Von Sinn des historischen Romans', in *Das Neue Tage-Buch*, 1935. Trans. by John Ahouse as 'The Purpose of the Historical Novel', avaialble at: www.usc.edu/libraries/archives/arc/libraries/feuchtwanger/writings/historical.html [accessed 15 March 2013].

23. Walter Rathenau (1867–1922), German industrialist and statesman; Foreign Minister of Germany during the Weimar Republic.

24. Lion Feuchtwanger, *Jud Süss*, 1925, Eng. trans. *Jew Süss*, 1927.

25. Lion Feuchtwanger, *The Josephus Trilogy*, 1932–42.

26. John Lewis Gaddis, *The Landscape of History: How Historians Map the Past* (2002), p. 22, Oxford University Press, New York, 2004.

27. Gaddis, op. cit., p. 19.

28. Gaddis, op. cit., p. 26.

29. Gaddis, op. cit., p. 126.

30. Gaddis, op. cit., p. 113.

31. A. J. Krailsheimer (ed. and trans.), Gustave Flaubert, *Salammbô*, p. 10, Penguin Classics, 1977.

32. John Banville, 'The Prime of James Wood', review of James Wood, *How Fiction Works*, *New York Review of Books*, 20 November 2008.
33. Margaret Anne Doody, *The True Story of the Novel* (1997) Fontana, London, 1998.
34. Doody, op. cit., pp. 295–6.
35. Margaret Drabble, (ed.), *The Oxford Companion to English Literature*, Oxford University Press, 1985.
36. Drabble, op.cit., p. 463.
37. Andrew Miller, *The Guardian*, 29 June 2011.
38. Italo Calvino, *Six Memos for the Next Millennium*, Jonathan Cape, London, 1992.
39. Calvino, op. cit., p. 4.
40. Calvino, op. cit., p. 12.
41. Calvino, op. cit., p. 105.
42. Edmund White, 'Today the artist is a saint who writes his own life', *London Review of Books*, 9 March 1995.
43. Edmund White, 'More history, less nature', *Times Literary Supplement*, 25 July 2003.
44. Erica Wagner, 'Back to the future', *The Times*, 1 November 2000.
45. David Plante, *New Yorker*, 3 November 1986, p. 53.
46. Marguerite Yourcenar, *Reflections on the writing of Memoirs of Hadrian*, in *Memoirs of Hadrian*, Penguin Classics, 2000, p. 276.
47. Plinio Apuleyo Mendoza and Gabriel García Márquez, *The Fragrance of Guava* (1982), Verso, London, 1983, p. 70.
48. E. H. Carr, *What is History?* (1961), Penguin, 1971, p. 13.
49. C. B. R. Pelling (ed.), *Plutarch: Life of Antony* (1988), Cambridge University Press, 1994.
50. A. J. Krailsheimer (ed. and trans.), Gustave Flaubert, *Salammbô*, Penguin Classics, 1977.
51. Francis Steegmuller (ed. and trans.), *The Letters of Gustave Flaubert*, Volumes I and II, Picador, London, 2001, p. 337.
52. Enid Starkie, *Flaubert: The Making of the Master*, p. 385, Penguin, 1971.
53. Steegmuller, op. cit., pp. 332–3.
54. Steegmuller, op. cit., p. 346.
55. Steegmuller, op. cit., p. 362.
56. Steegmuller, op. cit., p. 365.
57. Steegmuller, op. cit., p. 366.
58. Steegmuller, op. cit., p. 375.
59. Steegmuller, op. cit., pp. 376–7.
60. Steegmuller, op. cit., p. 390n. 25.

61. Steegmuller, op. cit., p. 398.

62. Krailsheimer, op. cit., p. 9.

63. Robert Graves, *I, Claudius* (1934), *Claudius the God* (1934), Penguin, 1977.

64. George Plimpton (ed.), *Writers at Work: The Paris Review Interviews*, 4th Series (1977) p. 56, Penguin, 1982.

65. Martin Seymour-Smith, *Robert Graves: His Life and Work*, p. 229, Bloomsbury, London, 1995.

66. Seymour-Smith, op. cit., p. 229.

67. In T. S. Dorsch (ed.), *Aristotle, Horace, Longinus: Classical Literary Criticism*, Penguin, 1965.

68. Seymour-Smith, op. cit., p. 230.

69. Seymour-Smith, op. cit., pp. 231–2.

70. Marguerite Yourcenar, *Memoirs of Hadrian* (*Memoires d'Hadrien*, 1951), Penguin Classics, 2000.

71. Yourcenar, *Reflections*, p. 270.

72. Josyane Savigneau, *Marguerite Yourcenar: Inventing a Life*, p. 178, University of Chicago Press, London, 1993.

73. Savigneau, op. cit., p. 181.

74. Yourcenar, *Reflections*, p. 288.

75. Savigneau, op. cit., p. 193.

76. Yourcenar, *Memoirs of Hadrian*, pp. 251–65.

77. Joan Acocella, 'Becoming the Emperor', *New Yorker* 14 and 21 February, 2005.

78. Savigneau, op. cit., p. 219.

79. Savigneau, op. cit., p. 220.

80. Savigneau, op. cit., pp. 249–50.

81. Acocella, op. cit.

82. Yourcenar, *Reflections*, p. 270.

83. Yourcenar, *Reflections*, p. 275.

84. Sally Cline and Carole Angier, *The Arvon Book of Life Writing*, pp. 36–7, Methuen, London, 2010.

85. Chuang Tzu, quoted in Italo Calvino, *Six Memos*, p. 54.

86. Giuseppe Tomasi di Lampedusa, *The Leopard* (*Il Gattopardo*, 1958), Harvill Press, London, 1996.

87. See, *passim*, David Gilmour, *The Last Leopard: A Life of Giuseppe Tomasi di Lampedusa* (1988), Collins Harvill, 1990.

88. C. P. Cavafy, *Complete Poems* (ed.), Daniel Mendelsohn, Knopf, New York, 2012, p. 13. Cavafy's poems, of course, may be read not only as poetry but also as one long historical novel made up of multiple micro-texts.

89. Steegmuller, op. cit., p. 350.
90. Joseph R. Strayer, Introduction to Marc Bloch, *The Historian's Craft* (1954), pp. ix–x, Manchester University Press, Manchester, 1967.
91. Marc Bloch, *The Historian's Craft*, quoted in Gay, op. cit., p. 7.
92. Richard Cobb, quoted in Gay, op. cit., p. 7n. 1.
93. Peter Gay, *Freud for Historians* (1985), Oxford University Press, Oxford, 1986, p. 8.
94. William Skidelsky, 'It's time to stop this obsession with works of art based on real events', *Observer* 23 January 2011.
95. Richard Lee, www.historicalnovelsociety.org/historyis.htm [accessed 24 December 2012].
96. Edmund White, 'More history, less nature', *Times Literary Supplement*, 25 July 2003.
97. Edmund White, *Times Literary Supplement*, 25 July 2003.
98. Edmund White, *Times Literary Supplement*, 25 July 2003.
99. Peter Gay, op. cit., p. 208.
100. Thornton Wilder, *The Bridge of San Luis Rey* (1927), Penguin Modern Classics, 2000, p. 128.
101. F. Scott Fitzgerald, *The Great Gatsby*, (1925), Penguin Modern Classics, 1989, p. 176.

Reflections 2

by Celia Brayfield

The past polemical

> **❝** *Who controls the past, controls the future.*
> *Who controls the present, controls the past.* **❞**
> Slogan of The Party, from *1984* by George Orwell

We can learn history to learn about human nature. We can learn about the past to help us understand the present. But if we want any experience of freedom in that present, individual or national, we must also understand the process by which we have learned about the past. We must ask who taught us what we think we know, and why. We must ask who kept the records, what they left out and whose voices they ignored. Historical fiction fills the voids, illuminates the shadows and redraws the picture. If we, as writers, are to be honest, we must ask ourselves what we want to believe and how we're making the facts fit our own story.

Orwell depicted the process of history being written by the winners. The regime of The Party in *1984* had largely effaced memory in its citizens and reconstituted the past in official history that rationalised total civil obedience. In his *The Use and Abuse of History, or, How the Past is Taught to Children*, the historian Marc Ferro argues that plurality is the hallmark of democracy.[1] Historians can only be the children of their own times, constructing narratives according to their own agendas, but 'the essence of a democratic society is that alternative histories are, at least in principle, possible'.[2]

History, as many of our guest contributors have observed, is speeding up, running faster. Documentary records of significant events are created on smartphones in an instant and posted on YouTube within seconds. The past is almost out of control entirely and the present will not be subjugated. Journalism has becomes so blatantly partial that it has lost its role as the first draft of history. If you doubt this, watch the Fox News coverage of the US elections in 2012.

The victors' view is challenged increasingly fast, often within their lifetimes. Creating a historical record, however, is still only the beginning of a long and complex process. Events happen, a record is created, then forgotten, then rediscovered and reinterpreted, a process in which historical fiction has more power over a society than historical fact. The cycle is repeated until events are completely obscured by fiction, at which point they are consigned to mythology – until a crazed archaeologist on the Discovery Channel demonstrates that, on the balance of what can be proved from rocks and remains, there is probably some truth in the legends of Atlantis, the siege of Troy and Noah's flood.

The trouble with history is that it is so useful to the mighty. Clio, the muse of history, gives her followers such authority, such irrefutable arguments. The idea that something is right because it is natural, and natural because it has happened before, is absurd but irresistible. Ferro, as a historian of the twentieth century, cited the rise, fall and forgetting of Nazi Germany as an example. Adolf Hitler, as a young political prisoner, turned to a romanticised, anti-industrial interpretation of history in his book *Mein Kampf* to define his ideal of a *volkisch* state, in which cause he was to justify war, genocide and ethnic cleansing. He derived his ideas from the nineteenth-century philosopher Johann Gottlieb Fichte, who had cherry-picked Tacitus to define the Aryan ideal. Tacitus had no first-hand knowledge of the tribesmen of Magna Germania who, like the rest of northern Europeans at the time, have left no written records. The literate are the true victors in history, as their accounts are preserved and venerated.

Our time is the post-post era – post-postcolonialism, post-postmodernism. Learning history in school is now less about learning about the events of the past than learning about the creation of the historical record of them.

The lesson is worth taking. A good historian goes back to primary sources, but what to do if those sources were never created? And how primary is primary? The records created from the manuscripts by conscientious nineteenth-century scholars omit much.

Plural history may be politically correct but it doesn't speak to the geek in us. The obsessional concern with authenticity and the profound desire for certainty and truth that underlies it is not satisfied in the process of discussing if Mary Seacole made a greater contribution to the development of nursing than Florence Nightingale. The inner geek re-emerges in new media, immersed in the detail of a digital game such as *Rome: Total War.*

Ferro identified two impulses in learning history, the militant and the therapeutic. In fiction, militant history tells the story of a people. It is the history of Salman Rushdie, Chinua Achebe and Dai Si-je and before them of James Fenimore Cooper, Walter Scott and Shakespeare. Therapeutic history seeks to heal old wounds, to expose old wrongs and create a process of reconciliation; this is the history of Toni Morrison, of Margaret Atwood and Charles Frazier, and before them of Thomas Hardy, Victor Hugo and Leo Tolstoy.

Post-millennial readers are suspicious of winners, and historical fiction in the twenty-first century is written about the losers. Many of the most resonant recent works of historical fiction were prompted by the authors' determination to create a voice for people who have been marginalised by traditional history. *Beloved*, by Toni Morrison, published in 1987 and awarded the Pulitzer Prize among many others, was inspired by the story of an African slave in America after the Civil War, who killed her own daughter rather than let her be recaptured by slave owners. The historical narrative had become over-familiar, and the task of the historical novelist then is to de-familiarise the territory. Morrison has described being interested more in the feminist themes of the book than in evoking a time when slavery still existed in America.

'Slavery is very predictable. There it is, and there's some stuff about how it is, and then you get out of it or you don't. It can't be driven by slavery. It has to be the interior life of some people, a small group of people, and everything that they do is impacted on by the horror of slavery, but they are also people.'[3]

Imagining the world from the viewpoint of a non-dominant character or society is the driving force in post-colonial writing. It brings the gift of empathy, in that readers are more ready to relate to an ordinary citizen than a general in triumph or an enthroned monarch. Very clearly, in *Wide Sargasso Sea* (1966), Jean Rhys sought to challenge the picture that Charlotte

Bronte evoked in *Jane Eyre* of the depersonalised 'mad' wife of Jane's employer and later husband, Mr Rochester. On a much wider canvas and with documentary, as well as literary, motives, Salman Rushdie's *Midnight's Children* (1980) depicts India after it leaves what was then the British Empire through Indian eyes.

Sarah Waters found the title of her first novel, *Tipping the Velvet* (1998), while researching her PhD thesis on lesbian and gay themes in historical fictions, and continued to draw on this work for several later novels which she has called her 'lesbo historical romps.'[4] Madeline Miller, discussing her novel *The Song of Achilles*, winner of the 2012 Orange Prize for Fiction, was motivated not so much by wanting to define the characters as lovers as by thinking of Patroclus as one of the millions of ordinary people whom history regards as insignificant. 'Patroclus is not an epic person, the way Achilles is. He's an "ordinary" man. But he has more power than he thinks, and the moments where he reaches out to others and offers what he sees as his very modest assistance have huge positive ramifications. Most of us aren't Achilles – but we can still be Patroclus. What does it mean to try to be an ethical person in a violent world?'[5]

If the impulse to give voices to the excluded or overlooked is strong in contemporary writing, the instinct to impose order on post-modern chaos is also emerging. That chaos may be literary, in the polyphonic, magic-realist collage of a novel such as Orhan Pamuk's *My Name is Red*, which is ordered by the most rigid of genre conventions, those of the crime thriller. But the chaos may also be real, as the writers of historical fictions increasingly invade the territory of journalism.

Ferro[6] noted the power of cinema in creating popular historical consciousness, but doing so with a politically pre-packaged, 'sterilised and unproblematical' reading of events. Cinema now is happy to be provocative, contrarian or partisan, but in doing so seems to have tangled with the consensual understanding of its audience. The 2013 Academy Award ceremony succeeded a campaigning period in which Ben Affleck made no strong claim to authenticity for his war-on-terror adventure and the eventual winner, *Argo*. *Zero Dark Thirty*, an account of the hunt for the terrorist leader Osama bin Laden, was marketed on the quality of its research and initially made the running, until the film's account was questioned by former intelligence officials.

The producer, Kathryn Bigelow, defended the film as 'kind of the first draft of history, or maybe the first rough cut of history' in a TV interview with Stephen Colbert, who concurred satirically by comparing the film to Mel Gibson's *Passion of Christ*. 'Americans don't read books. And this depiction of the torture, the investigation, the catching of Bin Laden, is going to be our record, just as surely as Jim Caviezel died for our sins.'[7]

Love and sex, fact and fiction

> *In the history of the West, infantile sexuality has sometimes been condoned and sometimes repressed; adolescent masturbation has sometimes been ignored and sometimes fanatically repressed; bisexual and homosexual instincts among men have usually been strongly condemned by the masses, but often tolerated by the elite; homosexual relations between women have usually been ignored; pre-marital sexual experiments have sometimes been tacitly tolerated and sometimes strictly forbidden; the double standard of sexual behaviour for men and women has usually, but not always, been deeply embedded in customary morality and in legal codes... The Freudian assumption that sex is an unchanging infrastructure, and that there has been no change in the strength of the libido over time has therefore no basis in reality, so deeply is it overlaid by cultural norms.*
> Lawrence Stone
> [Stone, Lawrence. *The Family, Sex and Marriage in England 1500–1800*. Weidenfeld & Nicholson, London, 1977. pp. 483–4]

Love is a problem. The writer who tries to tread a path between accurate history and engaging fiction is confronted by the fact that neither love nor sex meant the same to our ancestors as they do to us today. Worse, we have very little evidence to tell us how ordinary people felt, thought and acted about love, and what we do have – the poetry, the erotica, the court testimonies – was not created to provide a record, but to serve a purpose at the time. Finally, and worst of all, many authors have made considerable fortunes by ignoring these facts.

Love is the stuff of fiction, particularly popular fiction. But love has not always been the intense, intimate and sexual emotion we recognise today, nor was it always considered the best foundation for a marriage and family. History is not on the fiction writer's side. Affection and respect were nice work if you could get it in a marriage, but for most of history, love has been an anarchic challenge to the social order. Queen or goose-girl, king or ploughman, people were expected to direct their emotions for their long-term benefit and the good of society, whether by a diplomatic marriage or finding a healthy, loyal and hardworking partner.

Amor vincit omnia. We owe the saying to Virgil, but he and his contemporaries thought of love as a temporary madness, not as a glorious transcendent emotion. Ancient love stories seldom ended well. Rape, abduction, suicide, angry gods and years of warfare were the consequences, excellent for librettists, but a warning to average citizens not to indulge their affections.

Romantic love wasn't an ideal until the leisured elites of the late eighteenth century, when philosophers argued a reverence for nature, and grand emotions were suddenly admirable. The sociologist Anthony Giddens[8] has pointed out that the novel itself emerged at the same time as the concept of romantic love, and that their linguistic origins are intertwined, with the word 'romance' having double meaning – a love affair or a story.

It is ironic that the period of English history that is currently such a focus of fiction was in reality one of the least romantic. To modern readers, the attitudes to love and marriage expressed by men and women in Tudor England are depressingly pragmatic. The immense dynastic marriages of the time, such as that of the Earl of Shrewsbury and Bess of Hardwick, a three-wedding alliance which included four of the couple's adult children, seem cruel and incomprehensible to us.

Equally hard to understand is the story of Lady Catherine Grey, younger sister of Jane Grey, the 'nine days' queen', and, like her sister, a great-niece of King Henry VII. When Catherine was 20, and next in line to the throne after Queen Elizabeth I, she fell in love and married Edward Seymour, the Earl of Hertford. She did so in secret while negotiations for a diplomatic alliance for her were under way, thus very nearly conferring the throne of England on her husband.

Within months Catherine's young husband was sent abroad and his sister, the only witness to their marriage, died. Catherine lost the legal document that proved their marriage, and the priest who married them disappeared. She found herself pregnant, with a child who was, to all intents and purposes, illegitimate. The Queen suspected a plot and Catherine was imprisoned for the rest of her life – although Edward Seymour, when he returned to England, stood by her and they had a second son together. (Their first son, also named Edward, is in fact an ancestor of Queen Elizabeth II, through her mother.)

To modern readers, and to novelists including Alison Weir and Ella March Chase, this is a tragic story of true love. To an Elizabethan audience, this is a tragic story of an unbelievably silly and disloyal young couple. To many historians, mostly male, it has been proof that Queen Elizabeth was an embittered spinster consumed by sexual jealousy, rather than an astute monarch who did not want Edward Seymour to lead a rebellion against her.

The decline in the genre from the 1950s was accelerated by the popularity of novels such as *Forever Amber* by Kathleen Winsor, about a country girl who becomes a Restoration courtesan, and the extraordinary *Angélique* series by Anne Golon, about a French noblewoman at the time of Louis XIV. Both were, by the standards of the time, sexually explicit, and, in the puritanical post-war period, when all media depicted the life of a woman as no more interesting than a Doris Day movie, both were phenomenally successful. Helped by film versions, *Forever Amber* has sold 3 million copies, and the *Angélique* series of 13 novels in total has reached 150 million.

It is unfortunate for both authors that sex sold their books so well and obscured the scholarship evident in their work. And to the detriment of historical fiction for decades, the connection between sex and history was firmly established. The truth was rather different. Lawrence Stone's research into men's diaries of the Tudor period showed that a puritan ethic prevailed, and that the 'irresistible tidal force of sexual passion' of the Virginia gentleman William Boyd, for instance, never amounted to more than two orgasms a week, by all and any means. In the seventeenth century the famous 'compulsive womaniser' Pepys did little more than bribe or intimidate women of lower social class to let him grope them, and agonised over it afterwards. A rare female diarist, Anaïs Nin, left memoirs and erotica written almost three centuries later, from the 1920s onwards, which still seem almost naïve by the standards of later decades.

Nin's writing is particularly valuable, however, because she was a woman. The overwhelming majority of the records of sexual activity in past times was created and preserved by men. If we want to know what women's experience was, and how they felt and thought about it, we have very few documents to guide us. The poems of Veronica Franco, Venice's 'honest courtesan' of the sixteenth century, and the few surviving fragments of Sappho's works, while enduringly beautiful, are specific to their own social milieu and probably not indicative of the emotions of women in the wider population. Artistic conventions often mean that poems are maddeningly opaque as records, as in Madeleine de l'Aubespine's *Riddle*,[9] written in the late sixteenth century, in which the writer strains so hard for double entendre that she describes herself deriving ecstasy from manoeuvres more likely to induce mild boredom in most women.

There are obvious problems with taking any imaginative work as a historical record of sexual behaviour. Many of the works that have survived were created to arouse their audience, rather than to record everyday intimate life. The famous erotic wall paintings of Pompeii, for example, cover the walls of the buildings where they were found so comprehensively that most authorities have concluded that these were brothels, at which clients would have been paying for what was otherwise unavailable. In the twentieth century, Anaïs Nin's erotic stories, *The Delta of Venus*, were written for her lovers, as was one of the most famous erotic novels, *The Story of O*. Both record the fantasy life of bohemian, intellectual Paris in the mid-century, not the home life of a Midwestern married couple.

Like language, the love that a writer wants a historical character to feel must be a compromise between historical probability and contemporary expectations. Writers who've erred on the side of free-loving and passionate modern romance may find their scholarship overshadowed, but their readership increased.

Welcome to my storyworld: history in digital games

I blame Lara Croft. She's an archaeologist. Unlike many archaeologists of my acquaintance, she wears short shorts, accessorised with holsters for awesomely effective weaponry, and is in dire need of a decent sports bra. But the reason I blame her is that she's a multiplatform protagonist who has willingly abseiled out of her original video game into graphic novels, animated short films, mega-budget feature films (starring Angelina Jolie), and associated promotional merchandise including clothes, accessories, action figures, and model portrayals. She is also available (at an eye-watering price) for third-party promotion, including television and print advertisements, music-related appearances, and as a spokesmodel.

This, then, is the essence of a storyworld. To a novelist, it is simply the setting for the work. To a historical novelist, it is the whole fictional environment in which characters move. To those who see a novel as only the seed-corn for an immense harvest of artefacts, both cultural and material, it is the mysterious quality that allows a concept to translate into different media. This is what multiplatform means.

What Lara Croft demonstrated, however, is that in the storyworld arena there are as many people transfixed by history as there are tourists passing through the Uffizi gallery in a decade – in fact, probably more. Very early in the history of digital games it became clear that one of the most compelling qualities a game could have was a historical setting; and, as the art of games developed, the passion for authenticity in historical setting asserted itself anew.

The essence of a storyworld is that the media in which the story is told are not restricted. 'In the ideal form of transmedia storytelling, each medium does what it does best – so that a story might be introduced in a film, expanded through television, novels, and comics, and its world might be explored and experienced through game play. Each franchise entry needs to be self-contained enough to enable autonomous consumption. That is, you don't need to have seen the film to enjoy the game and vice-versa.'[10]

But in fact a storyworld is rarely introduced in a film – *Star Wars* being a notable exception. Films are expensive. By the time a storyworld has appeared in a film it will have proved itself in cheaper media. Storyworlds usually appear first in a novel, that wonderfully low-tech, low-risk format in which the essence of a narrative can be test-marketed without anyone losing too much money. Had *Harry Potter* bombed, Bloomsbury Publishing would have lost around GBP 2,000, about the price of an elderly town car preloved at least twice and with 100,000 miles on the clock.

The entire commercial side of the creative economy loves storyworlds, because they are products. A storyworld is a package of creative concepts that can be defined, copyrighted, invested with *droit moral*, licensed, exploited and sold. In the rights department, the only real difference between a storyworld and a novel is that text itself, and literary quality is not a key part of the product package – although literary quality may well be significant in establishing the platform for the original work, and from that platform the commercial development of the work begins.

The essence of a storyworld is little different from the setting of a work of fiction – a great work of fiction which works at a philosophical level. Oddly, although the concept has been developed in the entertainment industry, it is the moral, social and political dimensions of the storyworld that are crucial to its success. There must be a reason for the player to enter the gloomy crusader castle and a reason for the black knights to attack him. A storyworld defines the imperatives of the people in it, lays down the rules that make them do what they do.

Thus, Mike Jones, Screen Studies Lecturer at the Australian Film Televison and Radio School, writes: 'The notion of a Story-World has a further implication... [It] represents the Rules; the governing principles and parameters to which occupants of the Story-World (characters and events) will adhere...'.

'A perfect example might be seen in the production bible for the animated series of Batman (which you can download as a PDF). Here a set of rules about Batman's behaviour, what he will and won't do, what he does and doesn't do, are clearly laid out.'

'Batman does not work directly with the police. He's not a member of the force or a deputised agent. There's no Bat-signal or hotline, they can't contact him.'

'This entry sets out a clear relationship between the hero and the authorities and in doing so creates a focused dramatic paradigm for the whole series – Batman doesn't trust the police and the police don't trust Batman.'

A storyworld should offer more than one narrative path. This can be an awkward concept for a historian, for whom there is only one end to most stories and sometimes that end is extremely well known. As Robert Harris recalled, talking about his novel *Pompeii*, 'Everyone said, the problem you'll face is the book won't work because everyone knows what happens in the end – but of course, it's the remorseless inevitability of it, which the Greeks understood, which is far more gripping. The sinking of the Titanic is the obvious comparison – you're all waiting for it to happen.'[11]

So a more sophisticated approach to narrative is demanded. An overall story arc may define the plot of a novel, film or game, but there should be the potential to move to different resolutions with different characters. In a historical storyworld, the challenge is to create alternative or speculative history, not rest entirely on a historical premise.

Historical storyworlds were something that the transmedia multiplatform content creators did not foresee. In June 2000, a game called *Shogun: Total War* was released, developed by a British group, The Creative Assembly. The game is played on a map of Japan and set in the Warring States period from the fifteenth to the beginning of the seventeenth century. The player becomes the leader of a Japanese clan and tries to conquer the nation and become Shogun. Military strength, religion, espionage and diplomacy all influence the player's actions and players devise their strategy with reference to the ancient Chinese text, *The Art of War*. They can deploy samurai knights, ninja assassins, regiments of infantry, or cavalry groups galloping with red banners across green hillsides, in the shadow of mountains familiar from Hokusai prints.

Shogun was highly successful and the creators immediately realised that the historical setting for the game was a major factor in its appeal. The game then developed with a focus on historical authenticity – and the map was an essential feature. The Creative Assembly were advised by the distinguished historian Stephen Turnbull, an expert in Far Eastern military actions.

The Total War principle was soon extended into a franchise that embraced other ancient conflicts. *Rome: Total War* (often abbreviated to RTW) was released in 2004. The game is set during the late Roman Republic and early Roman Empire (270 BC–AD 14), and the players enact real-time tactical battles across Europe, North Africa and the Near East. Again, they are in control of the entire world in which their armies march, and have to conduct diplomacy, build roads and bridges and govern indigenous populations – using the time-tested tactics of taxes, bread and circuses. RTW is considered to be one the greatest strategy video games of all time. RTW players can re-fight historic actions such as the Battle of Lake Trasimeno or the Siege of Sparta or try the Alexander expansion, become Alexander the Great and take on the Persian army. Players probably wept when they found they had no new worlds to conquer, as RTW II went into development in 2012.

In 2003, another historical franchise appeared: *The Assassin's Creed*, the flagship product for the game development company Ubisoft. The game rests on the idea of a secret dynasty of assassins. A young bartender who has tried to escape his destiny as an Assassin is kidnapped by a multinational company and forced to use the Animus device to experience his ancestral memories. His captors rather predictably seek world domination through the Pieces of Eden, which the bartender has to find before they do, returning to the Third Crusade, Renaissance Italy and the American Revolution to do so.

An influential gaming blogger, Ben Newson, writing on the Sticktwiddlers site, looked forward to the release of *Assassin's Creed IV* in October 2013, and tried to analyse the game's appeal. Alongside the innovative movement potential and the 'stealthy killing components', he acknowledged:

'Another aspect that people love is the painstaking attention to detail and the historical accuracy whilst intricately interweaving an entirely fictional storyline of the order of Assassins and their centuries of battle against the Templars bent on world domination. Players are taken from the 12th century Middle East, through Renaissance Europe and eventually to civil war America, visiting strikingly accurate recreations of real world cities and towns.

Each location features an entire textbook of information about individual buildings and people that can be optionally read for even greater immersion. I've got to say I feel like I've learnt a hell of a lot about history that I would never have known otherwise and I think that a lot of other fans of the series would agree.'[12]

Within a decade, then, the new medium of gaming has discovered a love of history among its audience, and a craving for accuracy, authenticity and detail which suggests that the desire to experience history imaginatively is innate. In a totally modern medium, gamers exhibit the same passion for the past that enthralled their ancestors.

The land of stories: historical fiction for children

Life in the London suburbs is very quiet. The whole point of a suburb is that nothing should happen there. Terrible experiences, invasion, bombing or fleeing tanks on the streets only happen on television, or in the memories of people older than you. In a suburb, once the commuters leave, the school run is over and the postman has finished his round, it's nothing but birdsong and the hissing of the summer lawns. Except in the library. The library on our street was full of pirates, gladiators, wizards, brigands, Celtic horse-herders, Cossack cavalry and Cretan bull-dancers. And I could take them all home with me, in the books of Rosemary Sutcliff, Geoffrey Trease, T. H. White and Mary Renault.

The exoticism, the otherness, the escape offered by historical writing are irresistible to the creative child. Why put up with homework, a scratchy sweater and an annoying little sister when you could be speeding to St Petersburg in a troika through a blizzard to petition the Tsar, or saving your friends from being sacrificed to Poseidon? There seems to be an extra thrill, a heightened excitement about a story set in another time, even for readers who don't really understand when and where that other time was.

Perhaps the truth is that for most children the reality of imagination itself is more real than everyday life. The boundary isn't clear in any case; even the most timetabled child of a tiger mom spends time in that state between reverie and boredom that is the special privilege of the young. Time isn't a very defined concept to a child, either. Ten minutes or two hours are both too long, and 600 years means nothing at all to a person who has just passed their sixth birthday.

Nothing demonstrates the craving that children have for historical fantasy better than the extraordinary phenomenon of the *Harry Potter* series, which seized the imagination of children all over the world in a time when the publishing industry devoutly believed in the realism of Jacqueline Wilson or Jodi Picoult.

Some elements are clearly mythological – the entire concept of wizarding, Hagrid the half-giant and his dragons, centaurs again, the phoenix and the basilisk. Some are historical, even nostalgic, like the Hogwarts Express, straight from a railway museum, Hogwarts School – a gothic pile, Viollet-le-Duc on laudanum – and the concept of a boarding school adventure itself, last popular when Enid Blyton was alive. Other elements are completely modern, such as the anti-racist theme in the conflict between Lord Voldemort and Hermione, characters like Gilderoy Lockhart and Dolores Umbrage, and the personification of clinical depression in the Dementors.

This is not to say that children want their history only in fantasy form. As readers, as an audience, as cultural consumers, children are not always looking for an escape. Often they want the imaginative distance from which to consider their own world. Bruno Bettelheim demonstrated in *The Uses of Enchantment* (1976) that children use fairy stories to work through fears and anxieties, as well as real-life conflicts, in the same way that adults process experience in fiction.

Escapism starts to fail when it becomes nothing but an opiate. The anxieties of the young may be painted with a broad brush, so that a large-canvas conflict between good and evil, between Aslan and the White Witch, between Harry Potter and Voldemort, between King Arthur and Morgan le Fay, will engage them. But – particularly as they move towards their teens – children want to discriminate between real and pretend, and the real begins to fascinate in its own right.

 Children are capable, of course, of literary belief, when the story-maker's art is good enough to produce it.

> *That state of mind has been called 'willing suspension of disbelief'. But this does not seem to me a good description of what happens. What really happens is that the story-maker proves a successful "sub-creator". He makes a Secondary World which your mind can enter. Inside it, what he relates is "true": it accords with the laws of that world. You therefore believe it, while you are, as it were, inside. The moment disbelief arises, the spell is broken; the magic, or rather art, has failed.*
>
> J. R. R. Tolkien (1939)

This is the great paradox of historical fiction written for children. It may stretch to the most exotic fantasy and reference the most elaborate myths, but it must also be true. For the youngest age groups, the truth of emotions and experience is vital. Dragons are frightening. So are wolves and giants. And mothers get cross over the most ridiculous things, like selling a smelly old cow for some brilliant magic beans. These are things that everybody knows. As readers grow up, however, the truth seems more complicated and the search for it more worthy, attracting a proud army of nerds who begin to revel in the task of defining historical authenticity. The author who has Julius Caesar opening a window will be in big trouble with this tendency.

Perhaps twenty-first-century children have an exceptional challenge in separating fantasy from reality, because fantasies are so big, so loud and so relentlessly marketed. On a computer screen, as in a book, they come through the same medium as factual information. My daughter, as a teenager studying the history of the Second World War, asked me if the film *Life Is Beautiful* (1997), in which a man shields his son from the horror of a concentration camp by pretending their imprisonment is a game, was true. To me, it was obvious make-believe. To her, the illusion was deceptive. My students now understand that *Braveheart* (1995) is bad history, but at the time they first saw it, they weren't so sure. My colleagues use *Birdsong* (1993) by Sebastian Faulks to teach history students about the First World War.

A history lesson, of course, can be a Narnian wardrobe, a portal to a magical world, but at the time of writing, history is a subject that is increasingly crowded out of the good place it once occupied in the school curriculum. In America, debate has raged for more than a century about how and why history should be taught. In Britain, where the national curriculum is to be redesigned, the campaign group Better History found that one school in ten had replaced the study of history with lessons in general humanities or social science. Much less history is covered than a decade ago, and that is often divided into a set of unconnected study areas, leaving students without a sense of context or narrative.[13]

Perhaps this fragmentary contact with history in early education accounts in part for the historical trend in fantasy fiction for young adults and children. Like digital games, these novels are richly layered with historical detail, embedded in a historical setting, sometimes predicated on a historical event. They are also bursting with narrative and never dull.

The author tempted into this realm has a few points to consider:

- As Rudyard Kipling wrote, 'If history were taught in the form of stories, it would never be forgotten.' So look for the story in history. You need an engaging hero or heroine first, an excellent story second, and the historical setting third.

- Don't cheat on the reading research. Writing for children requires just as much understanding as writing for adults. There was a lifelong obsession with Norse mythology behind *The Lord of the Rings* and a degree in French and Classical Studies behind *Harry Potter*.

- Don't cheat on experiential research either. T.H. White, the author of *The Sword in the Stone*, advised the writer to do everything the characters do. 'Children are ten times more intelligent than grown-ups. They will know if you get it wrong, so you've got to do everything you write about – every bloody thing.....ride a horse, wear a suit of armour.'[14]

- Don't teach or preach. Your readers get enough of these experiences in their 'real' lives. This doesn't mean that you won't succeed if you have a moral purpose, only that you must put the story and the characters first. Most of C. S. Lewis's young readers, Neil Gaiman included, do not realise they are reading Christian parables until they are adults.

- Be very specific about the age of your intended readership and understand how they think – this is essential advice for all writers addressing children or young adults. A child's comprehension develops miraculously fast, and what an eight-year-old enjoys, a ten-year-old will find babyish.
- Bear in mind that children like a heroine or hero who is a couple of years older than they are.

Heroine addiction: women as protagonists in historical fiction

The headless woman is a visual cliché on the covers of historical novels.

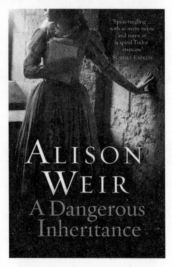

Above, the cover of *A Dangerous Inheritance*, Alison Weir's novel about Lady Catherine Grey – obviously a modern photograph, for which the art director did not feel it necessary to achieve a historically accurate costume or coiffure. And opposite, the cover of Philippa Gregory's novel *The Other Boleyn Girl*, again a contemporary photograph in which the frame bisects the model's averted head:

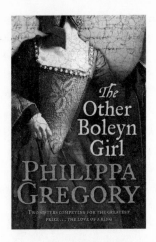

Matt Bates, Fiction Buyer for Britain's leading book retail chain WHS Travel, has remarked on the extraordinary compulsion shown by art directors in publishing to use a headless woman as a marketing motif.[15]

The figure is usually cropped so that neckline, *décolletage* or breasts are close to the title line. Here's a new edition of *Forever Amber*, where the title has been positioned to cover a wardrobe malfunction.

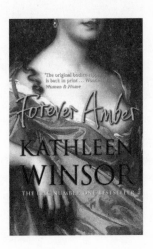

When it comes to book titles, a similar force seems to apply to the word 'Queen.' Choose a queen title on Amazon and the site will try to entice you with *The White Queen*, *The Red Queen*, *The Queen's Fool*, *The Queen's Vow*, *The Sister Queens*, *The Last Queen*, *Queen by Right*, *The Unfaithful Queen*, *The Queen's Pleasure*, *The Heretic Queen*, *Queen Defiant*, *The Other Queen* and dozens more. The word has been so over-used that Heather Lazare, senior editor at the Touchstone imprint of Simon & Schuster, observes 'We're running out of queens.'[16]

These are striking illustrations of the tensions that an author has to resolve when creating a female protagonist in a historical novel. Women, especially women not from a ruling class, are the largest group to have been marginalised, or even deleted from the record, in historical terms. So the first challenges will be not only a lack of records to research, but a consensual understanding that is thoughtlessly misogynistic. Royal blood has been no protection against the sexism of generations of historians and dramatists, who even today celebrate queens in European history as victims rather than rulers. Kleopatra and Boudicca are famous for their deaths rather than their lives; and Mary, Queen of Scots has been celebrated for her victimhood, while her incompetence was overlooked until Jenny Wormald published *Mary Queen of Scots: A Study in Failure* in 1991.[17]

If a female ruler was unquestionably successful, historians and writers alike have argued that she was in some way deficient as a woman, claiming that Elizabeth I's approach to her rule was founded on romantic disappointment, or holding up Queen Victoria as a bad mother to her 13 children.

Recently, historians have embarked on crusades to redress the balance. Dr Helen Castor, a Fellow of Sidney Sussex College, Cambridge, took issue with centuries of disparagement in *She Wolves: The Women Who Ruled England Before Elizabeth*, which became the foundation of a successful TV series. The publishing industry was not her ally, however, and the curse of the headless woman struck her book's cover, suggesting that there is something fictional about the very idea of women in power.

In many cases, a writer wishing to create a female historical character finds that as far as history is concerned, she does not exist. Philippa Gregory has described how her interest in Mary Boleyn was aroused by the sheer absence of evidence for her life. Even for a woman who was a figure of significance, the archives may be empty, or overlaid with later accounts that disparage her. The process of creating these false records may still be active.

Consider the descriptions of Hardwick Hall, the great architectural legacy of the woman who is still known to history as Bess of Hardwick, although her title at the time of building and of her death was Elizabeth, Countess of Shrewsbury. The house is frequently described as an ostentatious statement of wealth and power, an expression of its owner's materialism, arrogance and ambition. In fact, the Countess had it built after her last marriage had broken down under the strain of hosting the Queen of Scots, probably believing that, as part of the small farming estate on which she was born, it was the last piece of land in England that her husband would be able to appropriate.

Hardwick is certainly a 'prodigy house', meaning a very fashionable building for its time. But it is not large. It is a doll's house in comparison to the contemporary buildings owned by men, such as the nearby Burghley

House, and Longleat House, also by Robert Smythson, the builder-architect responsible for Hardwick. Many aspects of the decoration at Hardwick are almost primitive compared to the Italianate style of these vast mansions. The park at Longleat is 900 acres, the park at Hardwick only 300. Yet we learn from official sources that 'Hardwick is a conspicuous statement of the wealth and power of Bess of Hardwick.' The building is apparently such an expression of early modern fascist architecture that it was chosen as the model for Malfoy Manor in the *Harry Potter* films. I've heard visitors confidently describe it as a 'show-off house' or even a 'f*ck off house', in defiance of the record. Women of substance are still difficult to accept, it seems, while men of substance are unremarkable.

Our expectations of women changed radically in the twentieth century. For writers of the eighteenth and nineteenth century, women were archetypally helpless victims. The trope of the innocent young woman destroyed by exploitative men and a hypocritical society endured from *Clarissa, or, the History of a Young Lady*, the epistolary novel by Samuel Richardson published in 1748, to *Tess of the d'Urbervilles: A Pure Woman Faithfully Presented* by Thomas Hardy, published in 1891. Although Gustave Flaubert presents *Madame Bovary* (1856) as fatally intoxicated by romantic fantasies, she too is the helpless victim of a rich and powerful man.

With women writers, heroines were less often helpless, but still lived in a state of economic and social powerlessness. While *Jane Eyre* was able (within limits that seem pitiful to the modern reader) to assert herself against injustice, Catherine Earnshaw in *Wuthering Heights* can escape only through death. These narratives were created at a time when women were disenfranchised, had no legal status, and automatically ceded all wealth and possessions, including that achieved through their own labour, to their husbands upon marriage.

So it is hard to find unbiased records, to find any records at all in many cases, and hard to combat enduring portrayals of women as impotent victims. Many writers are concerned to re-imagine the events of the past with women as active protagonists, but encounter these forces as an undertow that is constantly dragging their imagination towards the stereotypes.

The protagonist in a narrative

Writing in 1927, E. M. Forster[18] defined the plot of a novel as 'a narrative of events, the emphasis falling on causality.' Since then, the influence of the cinema on all fiction, and of the work of Joseph Campbell on cinema, has become so dominant that readers and audiences crave three-act structure and search constantly to measure what they are reading against this dramatic template. The story, as Robert McKee observes, is the real star of every show.[19]

What makes a story? The action of the protagonist in response first to the inciting incident of the narrative, and subsequently against lesser and greater antagonists. A protagonist must be a do-er by the end of a story, if he or she is not active from the beginning. Even a protagonist who is trying to avoid action must be forced to take it – think about Hamlet, indecisive for four acts, but he has killed five people by the end of the play.

The need for the protagonist to drive the narrative is crucial in writing fiction. It is stronger than a simple expectation conditioned by contemporary plot structures. The ability to see yourself as the 'agent' of your own life story has been defined as an essential attribute of sanity by psychiatrists.[20] Whatever the reasons, a passive protagonist is a storykiller.

The agency of a heroine

Of course, you begin your novel with every intention of creating a feisty, active heroine, but what happens? This was the experience of Liesel Schwarz, author of *The Chronicles of Light & Shadow*, a steampunk trilogy in which the protagonist is Elle (Eleanor) Chance, an airship pilot.[21] Elle strides into *fin-de-siècle* Paris in fine style, but within a few pages is attacked by the agents of darkness, from whom a man has to save her. It just didn't seem feminine for her to fight.

In the early drafts of the first book, Elle came under attack again and again, and always allowed a man to rescue her. It seemed at first that it would be unfeminine for Elle to resist. An agent spotted the trend, so in Liesel's next draft, she gave Elle some heroic moves, but at the expense of the character's handsome husband, who had to become ineffectual in order to allow her to act. This in turn undermined the credibility of their relationship

– why was she attracted to this wimp? The shadow of Michael Douglas's character in *Romancing the Stone* fell on the scenario.

It required a conscious, sustained effort of imagination for the author to create the agency of her heroine and balance the male characters in the rest of the narrative so that she could be active without diminishing them. This particular period, the turn of the nineteenth century, saw the beginning of feminism, but was also a time in which middle-class women were admired for physical weakness and physically constrained in heavy dresses and tight corsets.

A protagonist needs something to strive towards, a goal or an ambition. There were political implications in Elle's role as a pilot which illustrate other challenges posed by female characters in historical fiction. Almost all professions were barred to women at this time. It was not until the 1920s that women could graduate from higher education institutions, while the right to equality in education and in employment had to wait another half-century. In 1929, 99 women pilots set up the first professional association, with Amelia Earhart as President. So for Elle to want to become a pilot in 1900 at all was immensely ambitious – in terms of historical accuracy.

It is interesting that this character was conceived as a pilot, a profession in which women are still significantly under-represented. Women today make up about 5 per cent of the 53,000 members of the Air Line Pilots Association. Liesel Schwarz is a writer with a killer instinct for an interesting proposition, and had chosen a field of endeavour for her heroine where extreme gender bias still obtains.

However, the expectations of twenty-first-century readers are that a woman's ambitons will at least be comparable to those of a man. Another aspect of the 'lack of agency' about which readers' early reports complained was that Elle was not aiming high enough. After all, she already was a pilot; and her stated ambition, to be hired for commercial flights, was a huge step for the real female aviator of the time, but a tame goal to a modern reader. Elle needed a larger ambition if she was to operate as the true protagonist of her own story.

Conclusion

A writer who wants to create a heroine in a work of historical fiction needs to consider that:

- historical records may be meagre and biased
- the consensual image of a prominent female figure will almost certainly be at odds with the historical record, and also with contemporary expectations of a woman
- powerful stereotypes will distort your imaginative process
- you will need to balance historical accuracy and current understanding of a woman's role and behaviour.

Notes

1. Ferro, Marc. *The Use and Abuse of History or How the Past is Taught to Children*, London, Routledge, 2003.
2. Southgate, Dr Beverley. Review of *The Use and Abuse of History, or, How the Past is Taught to our Children*, (review no. 441). Available at: http://www.history. ac.uk/reviews/review/441 [accessed 23 March, 2013].
3. Rothenstein, Mervyn: Toni Morrison, In Her Novel, Defends Women. August 26, 1987, Wednesday, Late City Final Edition Section C; Page 17, Column 1; Cultural Desk. Available at: http://www.nytimes.com/books/98/01/11/home/14013.html [accessed 27 January 2013].
4. Akbar, Arifa. Sarah Waters: Is There a Poltergeist Within Me. *The Independent*, 29 May 2009. Available at: http://www.independent.co.uk/arts-entertainment/ books/features/sarah-waters-is-there-a-poltergeist-within-me-1692335.html [accessed 27 January 2013].
5. Available at: http://www.madelinemiller.com/q-a-the-song-of-achilles/ [accessed 27 January 2013].
6. op cit.
7. Available at: http://www.colbertnation.com/the-colbert-report-videos/423116/ january-22-2013/kathryn-bigelow.
8. Giddens, Anthony. *The Transformation of Intimacy: Sexuality, Love, and Eroticism in Modern Societies*. Polity Press, Cambridge, 1992.
9. Quoted in Klosowksa, Anna, *Erotica and Women in Early Modern France: Madeleine de l'Aubespine's Queer Poems*, Journal of the History of Sexuality, Volume 17, Number 2, May 2008, pp. 190–215 I 10.1353/sex.0.0011.

10. Jenkins, Henry, Transmedia Storytelling, MIT Technology Review, http://www. technologyreview.com/biomedicine/13052/page3/, p. 3 [accessed 18 March 2013].

11. Hales, Shelley, and Paul, Joanna (eds), *Pompeii In the Public Imagination from its Rediscovery to Today*. 2011. Oxford University Press, New York..

12. Newson, Ben. *Why Do Gamers Love Assassin's Creed So Much?* Available at: http://sticktwiddlers.com/2013/03/07/why-do-gamers-love-assassins-creed-so-much/ [accessed 22 March 2013].

13. Available at: http://www.guardian.co.uk/education/2011/jan/12/history-lessons-dumbed-down-michael-gove [accessed 11 March 2013].

14. Available at: http://www.bbc.co.uk/archive/writers/12242.shtml [accessed 11 March 2013].

15. Matt Bates, Fiction Buyer, WHS Travel, speaking at the Historical Novel Society Conference, London, 2012.

16. Heather Lazare, also speaking at the Historical Novel Society Conference 2012.

17. Wormald, Jenny, *Mary Queen of Scots: A Study in Failure*, Collins & Brown Ltd, London, 1991.

18. Forster, E. M. *Aspects of the Novel* (1927) Penguin Classics, London, 2000.

19. McKee, Robert. *Story: Substance, Structure, Style and the Principles of Screenwriting,* Methuen Film, London, 1991.

20. Lysaker, P. H., Wickett, A. M., Wilke, N., Lysaker, J. T. 'Narrative incoherence in schizophrenia: the absent agent–protagonist and the collapse of internal dialogue'. *American Journal of Psychotherapy* 2003;57:153–66, *American Journal of Psychotherapy* 2003;57:153–66.

21. Schwarz, Liesel. *A Conspiracy of Alchemists.* Del Rey, London, 2013.

A short history of historical fiction

Gilgamesh to Rome

by Duncan Sprott

> **❝** The 'historical novel' was with us from the very
> beginning. **❞**
> Margaret Anne Doody, *The True History of the Novel*[1]

E. M. Forster defined the novel as 'any fictitious work over 50,000 words'.[2] For this 'prehistory' of the historical novel, the first thing to go out of the window is the prescription about length: the earliest works of literature survive only as fragments. However short, the scraps and off-cuts are no less 'novelistic' than the long; several of them are historical novels in miniature – micro-texts (and after all, a miniature painting is still a painting). We also ignore the requirement about prose. The most recent notable verse novel was Vikram Seth's *The Golden Gate* (1986). Nobody denounced it for not being a 'proper' novel. This was 'modern times', when you did what you liked and broke all the rules. 'Ancient times' was not much different. *Plus ça change...* And in the beginning historical fiction often manifests itself in the form of a long poem.

What about defining the *historical* novel? Most novels are, in some sense, historical novels. Walter Scott subtitled *Waverley* (1814) 'sixty years after': one or two generations before the present, has been used to categorise the historical novel ever since. Ours, in any case, is an age of genre-blur (but so was the first century BC). Some 'modern' histories read like novels, and may include passages of pure invention (but they always did – look at Herodotus and Thucydides); equally, some early historical novels were mistaken for history – such as the worthless fictions about Troy by Dictys of Crete and Dares of Phrygia.

Perhaps we can settle for 'a fiction in prose (or verse), set in the (distant) past'.

Or 'a fiction based on historical fact, using historical or invented characters, or both'.

Georg Lukács, in *The Historical Novel* (1962), held that historical fiction begins with *Waverley*, published in 1814. In *The Rise of the Novel* (1957), Ian Watt argued that the novel itself was not 'invented' until the eighteenth century, with Daniel Defoe, Samuel Richardson and Henry Fielding. All nonsense. The (historical) novel can be found in the Greek-speaking world as early as the 1st century BC.

It may be true to say that Scott *reinvented* the historical novel. Scott himself acknowledged one or two forerunners, but there are many more. It is time those forerunners were identified and rounded up. There is no room here for the complete history, but we can point out some landmarks.

The truth is that historical fiction is everywhere, even in antiquity.

Where, then, *does* historical fiction begin?

Beginnings

The *Epic of Gilgamesh* (c.2100/1500 BC), is a secular narrative poem from Sumer, what is now Southern Iraq. It was popular, meant to entertain,[3] and the earliest readable version, in cuneiform, dates from c.1200 BC, on 12 baked clay tablets from the ruins of King Assurbanipal's library in Babylon.[4] Young Gilgamesh, King of Uruk, a city of Mesopotamia, is two parts god and one part man, for his mother is a goddess, from whom he inherits beauty, strength and restlessness.[5] With the (tamed) wild man, Enkidu, Gilgamesh journeys to the Cedar Forest to slay Humbaba, a fearsome monster. When Enkidu dies, Gilgamesh rends his clothes and goes in quest of the secret of immortality. Utnapishtim, the Mesopotamian Noah, tells him of a plant growing on the sea-bed that brings immortality. Gilgamesh finds the plant but loses it at once: it's swallowed by a snake, which sheds its skin and is rejuvenated. Gilgamesh resigns himself to the inevitability of death, realising that the only true immortality is for work that endures, his own work of building the city walls of Uruk.[6]

Gilgamesh is a prototype of the quest, the wonderful journey undertaken to achieve impossible goals. It is also a love story, albeit that the protagonists are both male. Above all, it is the expression of the eternal solitude of man in a world where the odds are stacked against him, and of his search for individual expression and identity. *Gilgamesh* is also a study of profound psychological insights. Its hero is the first individual in literature. In following his journey through life we see the laying bare of a soul on a scale perhaps not approached in any other work until Shakespeare.[7] *The Epic of Gilgamesh* dramatises the central concern of the novel: a story about growing up, and accepting how things really are. *Gilgamesh* is short, and incomplete, but it's full of dialogue, it's a novel in verse[8] and it has its roots in history.

His life story took on the character of myth,[9] but a historical Gilgamesh did reign in Uruk, c.2,750 BC.[10] The 'Sumerian king-list' puts him in the first dynasty after the flood, reigning for a mythical 126 years.[11] He probably did lead an expedition to fetch timber from the northern cedar forests, home of uncanny powers: the historical motive for the expedition is the cities' need for timber.[12] *Gilgamesh* is the finest surviving epic poem from any period until Homer's *Iliad*, which it predates by 1,500 years. Even for the ancients, *Gilgamesh* was more about what it is to be a man than what it is to serve the gods.[13] Inasmuch as Gilgamesh was a historical character, his story looks something like historical fiction.

The epic happens to contain three of the 'Seven Basic Plots': the Journey, the Quest, and Slaying the Monster.[14] *Gilgamesh*, one might say, was the beginning of everything.

Ancient Egypt

The earliest examples of literary fiction in Egypt are four anonymous tales from the Twelfth Dynasty (c.1990–1800 BC), papyrus fragments of tales, each some 10–20 pages long.

Of the four the most highly regarded is *The Story of Sinuhe* from the twentieth-century BC[15] but set further back in time, reflecting a true historical situation: the death of Amenemhet I (c.1991–1962 BC) and the reign of Sesostris (Senwosret) I (c.1974–1929 BC).[16] At least one Egyptologist has felt that *Sinuhe* deserves to be called a novel.

The Middle Kingdom tale of *King Cheops and the Magician* was probably written in Dynasty 12 (1991–1786 BC) but relates events of the Old Kingdom and the foundation of Dynasty 5 (2494–2345 BC), some 500 years earlier.

The Tale of King Cheops' Court is a fragmentary cycle of five tales set in the 4th Dynasty, c.2600–2450 BC, some 700 years before its composition.[17] The fragments that remain comprise the most playful of the four Middle Kingdom tales. Pharaoh is bored. His sons try to entertain him with outrageous stories. At one point the waters of the lake part to retrieve a lost turquoise pendant. This is magic realism some 4,000 years ahead of its so-called invention.[18]

Fast forward to the Late Period and the story of *Setne Khamwas* (third century BC), which has been called 'schlocky stuff'[19] – it inspired the 1932 movie *The Mummy*. It's built around the historical Prince Khamwas, fourth son of Ramesses II. The real Khamwas was high priest of Memphis (his title, *setem* priest, turns into his name, Setne), a builder of temples and a famous sage. After his death, popular imagination made him a powerful magician with a passion for ancient books. Thus the motivations and motifs of the adventures which the Demotic tales spin around him.

Setne I is of Ptolemaic date, and written with care; *Setne II* is from the Roman period and full of mistakes. Khamwas desires to possess a book of magic written by Thoth, god of Wisdom, but this has been stolen by Naneferkaptah – the man had been buried with the book in his coffin, possession of the book having cost him his life. When Setne finds the tomb and steals the book, the two princes, one alive, *one dead*, both powerful magicians, engage in a battle of skills until Setne is defeated and hands the book back. The moral is not so 'schlocky': magic is a legitimate weapon for man, but the ultimate secrets of life and the world belong only to the gods.

The highlight of *Setne II* is Khamwas's trip to the netherworld, where he sees the blessed existence of the just, and the damned suffering everlasting punishment. These Egyptian motifs would end up in the parable of Dives and Lazarus in Luke's Gospel (16.19–31). The theme of a living person visiting the Underworld is, in fact, Greek recalling both Orpheus and Odysseus.[20] The *Tale of Petese* is the first full-length Egyptian novel, at 150–200 pages. Herodotus used parts of it, so it must be older than the fifth century BC. The narrative is carefully framed and structured, with recurring characters, and includes a metafictional account of its own making.[21] Egyptian fiction fizzles out when the Egyptian language is replaced by Coptic. The old writings are forgotten, and with them all of the above prototypes of the novel.[22]

Homer

Throughout antiquity Homer was treated as the literal truth. 'Modern' times changed all that. Homer went down in history as a myth-maker, peddling tales that could not possibly have been true. And yet the wheel turns.

At first Homer's works were passed down by word of mouth. Today we tend to find the idea of anybody memorising the whole of Homer unlikely, but history records that Cassander (d.297 BC) for one, could spout the entire *Iliad* and *Odyssey* by heart, as if this was a remarkable feat. (I suspect that the remarkable thing was that he was not a bard but a general.) The point is that Homeric epic could have been passed down almost *word for word* – even if, from time to time, singers did make changes and additions.

Contaminated though the tradition may be, it seems that Homer is 'truer' than anybody in recent times has believed possible. Around 1200 BC, the civilisation of the Bronze Age of the Eastern Mediterranean collapsed. Archaeology showed that Troy was destroyed, but without written sources, who destroyed it – and why – remained a mystery. While many Homerists were busy deconstructing the Trojan War, trying to deny that Homer ever existed, the orientalists brought the archives of the Hittite empire – found at Bogazköy, in central Turkey – into sharp focus and showed that many of Homer's details were substantially correct.[23]

Even if the political context in which Homer set the Greeks' attack on Troy is authentic for the thirteenth century BC, whoever would believe his nonsense about Helen of Troy running off with Paris (aka Alexandros)? Surely, no war was ever fought over a woman?

Hittite documents show that, c.1290–1272 BC, a King Alaksandu ruled at Wilusa (Ilios), i.e. Troy itself. His name is not Anatolian but Greek: 'Alexandros', meaning 'repeller of warriors'. But however did a Trojan king end up with a

Greek name? And why does Homer give Paris the same name? Alexandros' abduction of Helen from Sparta began to look like a dim recollection of an exogamous system of dynastic marriage. No Greek hero wanted his son to succeed him to the throne, because this always involved terrible things. Oedipus' sons, Eteocles and Polyneices, for example, killed each other over which of them would succeed him. The normal pattern of succession was different: the King held a contest for the hand of his daughter. Thus the sprinter Meleager won Atalanta. As in the best of fairytales, the winning suitor wins the girl *and the kingdom*. Thus a prince often ended up ruling a different land from his father. The system reflects historical reality, a system that, by Homer's time, had been forgotten.

So Troy was ruled by a Greek called Alexandros: he had obtained the throne by marrying a Trojan princess. Disputes probably did flare up between Greeks and Asiatics as to which successor should prevail. Wars probably were fought over women. From time to time civilisations must have clashed. Homer's supposedly fictitious Trojan War turns out to have its roots in historical events.[24] Homer's epics are classified as epic poetry, but in prose translation they look and read just like novels. T.E. Lawrence, among others, called the *Odyssey* the world's first novel. The *Iliad* is a story about the deep past, written down (probably) some 500 years after the Trojan War that it describes. The *Iliad* is not quite history; it still counts as epic, and as poetry; but it is also, in some sense, a historical fiction.

Herodotus

Fragments of earlier prose writers, such as Hecataeus of Abdera (fl. c.500 BC) do exist, but the oldest surviving complete work of prose in Western literature is Herodotus' *Histories*.

All ancient historians, most famously Thucydides, *made up* the speeches of their protagonists. Why? For the same reason all (or most) dialogue in antiquity was made up: nobody could remember what was said. In the heat of *living the life*, most of what occurs is forgotten. And in any case, made-up bits always meant a better story.

In a real sense, all history and most writtten discourse is fiction.[25] A history is still a *story*, and story is the same word as *historia*,[26] originally meaning *inquiry.* Herodotus' *Histories* was designed to investigate the reasons for the war between Greece and Persia.

Herodotus' inquiries are open-minded, appreciative of the cultures of Africa and Asia, full of chatty asides, digressions and strange legends. He helped the truth along, sometimes telling it how it must have been (rather than how it really was). Herodotus did *imagine*. The *Histories* were 'his version', and he wrote so that he could read aloud in public. He was a performer of his work, a prose *entertainer*.

What makes Herodotus the first serious historian is the combination of great scope and precise focus, his imaginative power as a storyteller and his rationalism, his concern with the truth. Herodotus is very carefully and elaborately planned. He knew that all the best stories *have* a plan. He knew it from Homer, whose epics both begin by plunging us in the middle of the story. He likes to tell a tale in a circle, winding his way back to where he began. This is oral storytelling technique.[27] If Herodotus was, famously, not only the Father of History but also the Father of Lies, what was disbelieved? His evidence, apparently, given as unqualified, direct statement, about remote times and places: the imaginary Persian speeches, or items from bazaar story tellers, of which the most elaborate is 'Rhampsinitus and the Thieves.'[28] Herodotus' successors were annoyed that such nonsense should be labelled as history.[29] Also his marvels, such as the phoenix, even though he takes care to say, 'I myself have not seen this bird, except in a picture.'[30]

Both Herodotus and Thucydides saw themselves as inheritors of the tradition of epic narrative, especially the *Iliad* and the commemoration of a great war. Like Homer, they invent significant speeches, and they select events. Herodotus is as much as an *alter ego* of Odysseus, intrepid traveller, spinner of tales, dispassionate observer and judge of all men. He both imitates and is the rival of Homer, imitating not external reality but a work of fiction.[31] His prefaces alone show that his work, far from being a mere mirror of history, is an immortal prose epic, embracing true and false, great and small, Greek and barbarian, the remote past and historical times. His work is vast in scope, yet has an ever-narrowing focus; its tone is objective, personal, dispassionate and involved, uncritical, vigorous, serious and entertaining.[32] He is a storyteller; he *tells stories*.

Herodotus sets out to trace a war, but what he gives us is a world.[33]

He is not so much the Father of History as the father of historical fiction.

Xenophon of Athens (c.430–352 BC)

After his successful conduct of the Retreat of the Ten Thousand, Xenophon joined the Spartans' conquest of the East, then lived in exile from Athens, near Olympia, where he wrote his *Anabasis*, and the *Cyropedia*, or *Education of Cyrus*, (c.360 BC), a fictionalised life of Cyrus the Great of Persia.

The *Cyropedia* is historical but not history; it contains Socratic dialogue but is not philosophy; it discusses education, ethics, politics, tactics, but isn't an essay; it's biographical but not quite a biography; it also includes the charming love story of Panthea and Abradates. *Cyropedia* is an actual, undisputed historical novel, the Western pioneer in the field,[34] a prototype of the Greek novel of later antiquity.[35]

Like other writers of historical fiction, Xenophon takes liberties with the facts of history.[36] The Persian constitution he describes is the Spartan one.[37] His Persians do un-Persian things, such as worshipping heroes; and marching into battle wearing garlands of flowers. Instead of Persian luxury there are the simple clothes and simple food of the austere Spartans. And Cyrus' teacher is Socrates in disguise.[38] Cyrus' invincible battle lines are the Spartan heavy brigade; his battle tactics are those of Xenophon, the consummate Greek general.[39]

The spirit of the *Cyropedia* is Greek: a picture of the East with a dash of local colour, but dominated by the civilisation in which Xenophon was raised and the ideals he had learned to cherish.[40] His hero is an idealistic composite portrait of Socrates, the Younger Cyrus, and... Xenophon himself. His true theme is not so much education as How to Rule and How to Be Ruled.

Love is not allowed to carry Cyrus (or Xenophon) away: his book is more like a business manual, in which Cyrus achieves an obsessive control,[41] showing how a single person could impose command over all other human beings.[42] As Cyrus says, 'To rule men might be a task neither impossible nor even difficult, if one should only go about it in an intelligent manner.'[43] Popular enough in its time (though maybe not in Athens), the *Cyropedia* is now famous only for dullness.

The Greek Alexander Romance

> **"** *All who wrote about Alexander preferred the marvellous to the true.* **"**
> Strabo

Like the *Cyropedia*, the *Greek Alexander Romance* is a biographical novel, or fictionalised biography, but lowbrow and fun, almost a *comic-book* version of the life of Alexander, which embroiders the facts, and has ended up full of ludicrous legends and outrageous fancies. Alexander is not the legitimate son of Philip of Macedon but the illegitimate son of Nectanebo, an Egyptian sorcerer, who tricks Olympias into thinking that she is having sex with the god Amun. Alexander grows up, kills the sorcerer, competes at the Olympic Games, then zooms off to conquer the world. He meets strange beasts and magicians, explores the sea in a diving bell, is flown up into the sky in a basket borne by eagles... He encounters Amazons and Centaurs, discovers the fountain of youth (*but fails to drink from it*), and fathers a daughter who turns into a mermaid... The *Alexander Romance* is notable mainly for its use of letters, in which Alexander writes home to Mama.[44]

Some scholars date the work soon after Alexander's death in 332 BC, but the earliest surviving manuscript is from the third century AD, some 600 years later, when its popularity coincides with huge interest in the lives of sages, holy men and wonderworkers, who inspired a whole new literature.

Despite the overlay of fantastic legend, there are chunks of genuine history embedded in the text, such as the founding of Alexandria.[45] And yet, even the historical bits are daft: characters who lived centuries apart get to meet each other; fictional characters mingle with real ones and set off on amazing adventures. Although the *Alexander Romance* was meant just to entertain, it tries to sound like real history.[46] In fact it stands in a long tradition of fabulous history, such as Herodotus' taller tales. What sets the *Alexander Romance* apart from mere wonder tales is having a historical figure as a hero.[47]

Alexander must have seemed tame compared with the genre of saints' lives that was all the rage in the third century AD; not nearly extravagant enough. To keep up with the Christian competition, the Alexander story was overlaid with the fantastic.[48] It's a long way from the sophisticated Greek novels that circulated in much the same period among the Alexandrian literati. In short, this is a kind of prototype of the trashy modern historical fiction that we all love to hate.

Excellent rubbish though it is, the *Alexander Romance* was the runaway bestseller of antiquity.

Apollonius of Rhodes

The *Argonautica* or *Voyage of the Argo* (c.250 BC), by Apollonius of Rhodes, is the only surviving epic from Hellenistic times, and is the missing link between Homer and Virgil. Apollonius' era was literary, looking back at tradition, eager to redraw the map of Greek achievement. But when the first two books of his epic appeared Apollonius received nothing but abuse. An epic? Pfff! What mattered was slim volumes. ('Big book, big crime', wrote Callimachus...).

Although *Argonautica* is the only full account of the Jason story we have, the Argonaut myth itself is ancient, preserving great deeds from the heroic past. In antiquity the myth was treated as historical, second only to the Trojan War. The 'age of heroes' was remote, but no less real than contemporary history.[49] Myth filled a need, satisfying people's aspirations and emotions.[50]

While Callimachus and co. had abandoned the forms of the golden age of poetry, Apollonius stuck to tradition, with Homer, using the style and subject matter of epic to write his tale of high romance and incredible adventure. He also made use of two non-epic devices: handling his characters with psychological insight; and writing from a personal viewpoint, putting himself in every scene as a critical observer. For the Alexandrian literati, this was Apollonius' worst crime: an author should NEVER be visible in his own work. Never mind that Apollonius had breathed new life into the old bones of epic. Nobody wanted to know. Apollonius went off to sulk in Rhodes, but carried on writing his poem.

Apollonius appeals to the muses for help at awkward moments. He blames them when he's going to tell a really tall story. He turns to his audience with naive asides to apologise for a digression that may have bored them. He pauses to make personal comments on his characters.

The divine ship *Argo* herself has a voice, and tells Jason that she wants to set sail.[51] In short, the *Argonautica* is *fun*. The tale of Argo was never fixed. Like Arthurian legend, it was anybody's playground:[52] Apollonius was free to embroider history and reinvent it how he liked; he romps through the story of Jason and the witch-maiden Medea. But Apollonius is also serious: famed for its deep understanding of human nature, *Argonautica* is a fine psychological study of love,[53] more like something out of a modern novel:

> *If we wish to appreciate what Apollonius has done, it is as a novelist that we must read him and analyze the characters he has created.*
> E.V. Rieu, in *The Voyage of Argo*[54]

Just so: as well as being an epic poem, *Argonautica* is an early chapter in the prehistory of the novel; the novel before the novel.[55]

Ancient Rome
Virgil (70—19 BC)

Virgil was already a star in his own lifetime, once – on a visit to Rome – having to hide in a friend's house when he was pursued by fans. Virgil would not have been a star without the *Aeneid*. Set in a remote past, 1100 years before Virgil's time and 400 years before the foundation of Rome, and making things up *ad libitum* about the past,[56] the *Aeneid* is a historical epic.

The first six books are an Odyssean narrative of wandering, an account of the Trojans' long quest for a new home after the destruction of Troy. In Book 7 they land in Latium, and Virgil devotes the rest of the *Aeneid* to the war they had to fight to establish themselves in Italy.

Although it's permeated with an intense awareness of the inter-penetration of past and present, the *Aeneid* is not history. Its events lie mostly beyond the frontiers of attestable fact, in ages dimly remembered in folk memory, and the truth comes via creative imagination. Virgil indulges in the creation and trans-mutation of history, the rise of Rome from obscurity to incontestable power.

Virgil's imperial epic of the birth and growth of Rome, and how it had been translated from out of the ashes of Troy by pious Aeneas, was all spun out of

Iliad Book Twenty, lines 307–8.[57] Spin is the operative word: Virgil *spins* the Roman takeover of power from Greece as the fated persistence of a plucky, defeated few, to create a story with a comfortable moral: 'Loser takes all'.

Virgil's Dido is an example of a woman experiencing the torments of love, a victim of erotic suffering, and Virgil's treatment of her is novelistic.[58] In fact, Virgil is not above shunting details from one historical character to another, deriving his picture of Priam, for example, from the historical death and mutilation of Pompey.[59] Far more than with Homer, the essence of Virgil lies not just in what is said but how it is said. His first two words, 'Arma virumque' famously allude to both the *Iliad* and the *Odyssey*, signalling right at the start that he's going to squash the themes of both Homeric epics into his single work.

The *Aeneid* gave the Romans a plausible account of their origins, the truth of which had long since been forgotten. Like Geoffrey of Monmouth 1,000 years later, Virgil concocted a fiction masquerading as history; a founding myth, wholly invented, designed to comfort an insecure nation regarding their uncertain past.

Lucan (AD 39–65)

Pharsalia is Lucan's sardonic anti-*Aeneid*,[60] a very long narrative poem about the battle of Pharsalus (48 BC) at which Pompey was defeated by Caesar.

Ever since Homer, epic had been the supreme form of poetic expression for the Greeks and Romans.[61] Lucan admired Homer, but he admired Virgil more, and chose a theme from Virgil's lifetime. He also used historical epic to establish his own domain, out of the great man's shadow.[62] Lucan, born some 87 years after Pharsalus, did not set out to write history any more than Virgil did, but he, too, must write about war.[63]

Pharsalia's subject is the first two years of the Civil War, from 49 to 47 BC, though Lucan presupposes knowledge of previous events, and sees the 20 years from 49 BC to the victory of Octavian as one long conflict.[64] His sources were Livy's (lost) books on the period and Caesar's *Civil War*, but where it suits his purpose, he freely manipulates the truth.

Lucan presents the Civil War as a tale of unspeakable horror and criminality leading to the destruction of the Roman Republic and the loss of liberty; as much as a 'world war'. As narrator, he often intrudes his own reactions, as in the shocked meditation on the death of Pompey. His goal is not realism. He abolishes the traditional epic divine machinery, replacing the gods of Homer and Virgil with the supernatural: wild dreams, dire prophecies and grim portents. Lucan is fascinated by death, often using gladiatorial imagery. A repeated image is suicide, symbol of Rome's self-destruction. If Lucan's style lacks the richness and colour of Virgil, his limited range of vocabulary is deliberate, reflecting his bleak subject matter. His monotonous metre is deliberate too, as befits the poetry of war.

Lucan himself fell from grace. In one of his lost writings, *On the Burning of the City*, he may have accused Nero of starting the famous conflagration himself.[65] Had Lucan stuck to historical fiction, instead of current affairs, he might have lived a bit longer. In AD 65, aged 25, implicated in the conspiracy of C. Calpurnius Piso, he was forced to commit suicide.

Plutarch (before AD 50–after AD 120)

Plutarch, author of *Parallel Lives*, is officially a biographer, but his works read more like fiction. His *Life of Alexander* is not a biography but a novel: it offers a psychological reading of its subject, as a driven man, with explanations of what caused him to be driven.[66] In his edition of Plutarch's *Life of Antony*, C.B.R. Pelling asks 'Is it true?' The answer is that Plutarch's way of reaching truth is not ours: he sacrifices precise historical truth to point a more interesting moral, or to *tell a better story*.[67]

> For it is not histories we are writing, but Lives. Nor is it always the most famous actions which reveal a man's good or bad qualities: a clearer insight into a man's character is often given by a small matter, a word or a jest, than by engagements where thousands die, or by the greatest pitched battles, or by the sieges of cities.
>
> Plutarch, *Life of Alexander*[68]

Plutarch doesn't want to be Thucydides, with a continuous history of events, which his readers could find elsewhere anyway. Like novelists, he's more interested in *character*. He hopes that his readers may be led by examples of virtue to be better men themselves. He has tried to improve himself, 'using history like a mirror'.[69] In the *Life of Antony*, Plutarch shows little interest in the history.[70] He has plenty of material, though it's not always the kind he wants. Sometimes the trouble is a gap, such as the gap of Antony's youth. But gaps could be filled. Plutarch reshapes whole episodes. He manipulates his source material, shifts stories to a different context, makes complex detail simple. To sharpen contrast, he exaggerates. Details, such as the course of a battle, he makes up. Plutarch manages to mention a non-existent range of hills (76.1–3) and invent a major river (48.6/49.2).[71] In history and rhetoric the good leader leads battle-charges himself, shows foresight, and daring: so does Antony. In New Comedy, the soldier is boastful, lecherous, extravagant and gullible: so is Antony. And Kleopatra behaves like the stock figure of the flatterer, adapting herself to her victim's tastes.

Not much of this will have appeared in Plutarch's sources.[72]

What did Plutarch think he was doing rewriting his source material like this? Would he have admitted that he was sacrificing the truth? Or would he have felt that he was *reconstructing* reality, arriving intuitively at a picture which simply *must* have been true? Probably a bit of both. For Plutarch, telling a story in the best way is the same as telling it with the most plausible detail: this is creative reconstruction.[73] Quite often, Plutarch was *improving on the truth*, and he knew it. At the same time, total fabrication of fictional detail is rare. He does not paper over gaps. When he does fabricate detail, he is *reconstructing*, not sacrificing, the truth; he can usually say 'it must have been true'.[74] Writing some 150 years after the event, with half the story he wanted to tell lost, or forgotten, the best Plutarch – or anybody else – could do was informed guesswork: creative reconstruction.

Beowulf to King Arthur

by Duncan Sprott

The Dark Ages

We are not meant to call them the Dark Ages any more, and they weren't 'dark' anyway. The idea began in the 1330s, with Petrarch, who saw the post-Roman era as 'dark' compared with the bright lights of classical antiquity. This is Europe after the collapse of the Roman Empire, the period of intellectual darkness between the extinguished 'light of Rome' and the bright sparks of the fourteenth-century Italian Renaissance.

Ahead lies the shining figure of King Arthur. But first, Beowulf.

Beowulf

Beowulf is the greatest among the warriors in the land of the Geats, i.e. what is now southern Sweden. He crosses the sea to the land of the Danes in order to rid their country of a man-eating monster called Grendel.[75] In a second contest he kills Grendel's mother and returns home in triumph. Eventually he rules as king for 50 years. When a dragon begins to terrorise the countryside, Beowulf slays it, but dies himself in the act. He enters the legends of his people as a warrior of high renown.[76]

Beowulf is not a historical account but a fanciful re-creation. The poet has armoured himself with words to perform a glorious linguistic deed to rival or outdo Beowulf's wrestling match with Grendel. The poem is a literary *performance* of the story, a display of the poet's wrestling match with words in which he emerges triumphant.[77]

Beowulf is usually pigeonholed as epic, heroic narrative, or folktale. Beowulf himself is usually seen as a fictional character who moves in a world of myth and legend.[78] While the historical period of *Beowulf* is the sixth century, the date of the poem is perhaps c.750 AD: the Beowulf poet is *looking back* in time, from the (Christian) present into the distant (and pagan) past, at places and legends that his ancestors knew before their migration to the island of the Britons. It's a historical poem, but it makes no attempt at literal historical fidelity.

The poem shows a sophisticated historical vision that avoids anachronism and even extends a sense of the past to its characters.[79] Although the poem was written in England, the events it descibes are set in Scandinavia, in a 'once upon a time' that is partly historical.[80] *Beowulf* is not an actual picture of historic Denmark or Geatland or Sweden around AD 500, but it creates the illusion of surveying a pagan past that reached into a dark antiquity of sorrow.[81] At the same time, the poet projects on to the distant past features of his own day, in order to provide continuity.[82]

Beowulf reverberates with ancestral legend, and with repeated reference to heirlooms, to the mighty works of forebears, long-dead smiths and giants, and to ancient treasure. Descriptions of past treasures, though – the dragon's hoard, for example – differ little from those of Beowulf and his companions, which would themselves have been archaic in the late tenth century when the poem was written down. For Anglo-Saxons, the past was, in a sense, the present.[83] The same thing is going on in *Beowulf* as in the *Aeneid* (which happens to have influenced the *Beowulf* poet).

Beowulf is the first native English epic. Set aside the fact that it's a poem, and an epic, and we can see that it is also, in some sense, a historical novel.[84]

Medieval Icelandic historical fiction

Icelandic literature develops in much the same way as that of Ireland. At first, oral tales circulate, from c.870, when the first Viking settlers arrived, down to 1000, when Iceland was converted to Christianity.

Icelandic fiction begins in the thirteenth to fourteenth century with old stories about life in pre-Christian Iceland in the form of 'sagas' (from *sagja*, to say, or tell), narratives based on family histories but arranged like tales. Some 100 sagas survive, including some dozen novellas, and half a dozen full-length books. The latter are the crowning achievement of the saga genre, and all are set in the past. They are not histories but imaginative works of art, created around a historical framework, using written records and genealogies, traditional oral stories, earlier sagas, and fragments of verses.

The sagas neither judge nor analyse their characters, nor suggest how the reader should view them. In unadorned minimalist prose the author just tells who a character's people were, what he did, who he married, how other people interacted with him, and, in the end, how he died. The tone is laconic and unemotional. There is little description, no philosophising, no milking of dramatic scenes and no special effects.

Most of the Icelandic sagas are datable to 1225–1325. *Volsunga Saga* (c.1200–70), is an example of *fornaldarsögur*, or legendary tales. There is no distinction here between the natural and the supernatural, legend and history. *Volsunga Saga* contains powerfully symbolic episodes that would be adapted by Richard Wagner for *The Ring of the Nibelung*, and by Tolkien for *The Lord of the Rings*.

Volsunga Saga is set in continental Europe, but deals with the Icelanders' oldest myths, and is the first of the multigenerational family sagas that would dominate medieval Icelandic fiction. Sigurd (Wagner's Siegfried), slays the gold-hoarding dragon Fafnir and rescues the Valkyrie Brunhild, a sleeping beauty enclosed in a wall of flame...[85] *Volsunga Saga* starts in myth but by the end looks like recorded history – the tumultuous fourth and fifth centuries in central Europe. Within the first two pages all the themes are set in motion: jealousy, inequality and violence. The first murder sets in train a curse that will last generations. *Volsunga Saga* is notable for no-nonsense women, e.g. Brynhild, who would rather fight in battle than run a household.

Egil's Saga (c.1230) is the earliest of the great family sagas. It was perhaps written by the historian Snorri Sturlason (1179–1241). Egil Skallagrimsson is not a hero: he is ugly, brutal, greedy, drunken – and, from the age of six, a murderer. But he also happens to be a poet. Nearly all his characters were real people. *Egil's Saga* is notable for wonderful details. Egil's grandfather is called Kveldulf (Night Wolf), meaning werewolf and shape-shifter. And for wonderful names, such as Grim Hairy-cheeks, Thorhalla Chatterbox and Ivar Horse-cock.[86]

Njal's Saga (c.1280), was written some 20 years after civil strife caused Iceland to lose its independence and come under Norwegian control. The author manages to comment obliquely on these events while telling a tale of similar civil strife 300 years earlier. The author is a Christian, though he seems to have mixed feelings about the new religion, filling his saga not with saints but with dreams, portents, prophecies, apparitions, ominous ravens, a witch-ride, visions of hell... *Njal's Saga* is striking above all for its relentless violence, murder after murder, all treated in the driest style.

No space left to consider the rest: *Laxdaela Saga*, *Erbyggja Saga*, *Grettir's Saga*, *Olaf Saga*, *Orkneyinga Saga*, *Hrafnkel's Saga*... Suffice to say that these are Europe's first historical novels, a bath of blood from start to finish, but all designed to *entertain*.

The Arthurian Legend

The Middle Ages – particularly the twelfth to fourteenth centuries – were seriously into history. The novels of antiquity that survived the Dark Ages tended to be historical, such as the *Alexander Romance*. It is easy to understand why Troy or Alexander should have the medieval reader hooked. It is *not* so easy to understand why Arthur exerted such a magnetic attention. Why should all Europe want to hear stories of Guinevere, Lancelot, Gawain, and the rest?[87] The simple answer is that Arthur was a rattling good yarn: the Arthur stories set the medieval imagination on fire.

The trouble with the search for the historical Arthur is that by the time of his first appearance in any document he had already vanished into the world of legend.[88] There are a few clues in the chronicle of Gildas (d.570), the first writer of history in Britain; also in the work of Nennius (fl.c.830), a mixture of legend and history, full of pride in the Celtic people of Britain. Nennius mentions a historical Arthur, as *dux bellorum*, or leader of battles. He also says that Arthur led the Britons against the Saxons in 12 battles, in one of which he zapped 960 men in a single attack.[89] In the Old Welsh poem, *The Gododdin*, Arthur is a byword for heroic achievement. The *Annales Cambriae* (c.950), or Welsh Annals, is the first document to pin Arthur down in exact time. The author owned an Irish chronicle which mentioned the battle of Badon, c.518 AD, in which 'Arthur carried the cross of our Lord Jesus Christ on his shoulders'. Also, c.527, 'The battle of Camlann in which Arthur and Medraut perished.'[90] But there's no further info. Even via the earliest sources we cannot reach a pre-mythical Arthur.[91]

All the same, by the twelfth century Arthur is a literary figure of international stature.[92] His rise can only be explained by a parallel but invisible Arthur of oral tradition, a folklore Arthur. What Nennius did was to establish the Arthur who has been regarded (since the collapse of belief in the later medieval pseudo-histories of Britain) as the 'real' one. Nennius is the point of departure in the quest for the 'real' King Arthur.[93] The whole trouble is that unknown quantities of material circulating about Arthur in the early Middle Ages have been *lost*.[94]

Geoffrey of Monmouth is largely to blame for what came afterwards. Anxious to glorify his native land, this twelfth-century British historian, a monk working at Oxford, concocted a book, the *Historia regum Britanniae* (The History of the Kings of Britain, c.1136), in which he magicked a fifth-century chieftain called Arthur into a national hero.[95] He describes King Arthur's battle with Lucius Tiberius, giving precise information about troop numbers and commanders. Just like Thucydides, he quotes the exact words of Arthur to his men. All made up. That battle *never took place*. And yet, as Geoffrey's story continues, 'history keeps peeping through the fiction.'[96]

Geoffrey drew on British traditions and perhaps on Old Welsh documents, now lost. He also drew on a fertile romantic imagination, virtually inventing the character of King Arthur single-handed. At first, people thought Geoffrey had told the truth, but as early as 1198 his veracity was condemned by the historian William of Newburgh.

Geoffrey had several good political reasons for writing, one of which was his desire to give 'a precedent for the dominions and ambitions of the Norman kings.'[97] Running through his book is a deep-felt and often bitter desire to denigrate the Romans and to restore the Britons to their proper place – at the forefront of history.[98] Using the techniques of historical fiction, he dived into territory where pukka history cannot go, for lack of evidence, and so liberated Arthur from history altogether.[99] Geoffrey purports to give an account of the historical Arthur: he conquers Gaul, bashes the Saxons, Picts, Scots and Irish. He conquers Europe, leading his armies as far as Rome. Moore calls it 'a fictitious work masquerading as nonfiction'.[100] We might call it historical fiction masquerading as history. Possibly Geoffrey made the whole thing up, including the story of being asked to translate an ancient manuscript by a friend. If so, it was a very old trick. Was Geoffrey an arch-hoaxer? Was he telling the truth? Nobody knows for sure.

Geoffrey mixed up bits of chronicles, Welsh legends, and personal fancies, and spun the story of Merlin, the boyhood of Arthur, his accession to the throne, his marriage to Guinevere, the order of knighthood, the lot... And at the end, 'Arthur was carried off to the Isle of Avalon, so that his wounds might be attended to', leaving open the question whether he was dead. What did the truth matter? As romanticised history, Geoffrey of Monmouth would be a marvellous source-book for the creative writing of others for all time.

After Geoffrey of Monmouth came Geoffrei Gaimar (fl. 1140), who translated the *History* into Anglo-Norman, and Wace (c.1100–after 1171) who distilled Geoffrey's *History* into an Anglo-Norman poem, the *Roman de Brut* (1155), but also added the first mention of a Round Table. Wace was quarried by La3amon (fl. late 12th century), whose verse history of England – *The Brut* – tells for the first time *in English* the story of Arthur (as well as those of Lear, Cymbeline and other famous names). Wace and La3amon, believing Geoffrey's account to be true, did not fiddle with the storyline. It needed a writer who felt no obligation to British history to change the face of Arthurian lit: Chrétien.[101] Geoffrey's *History* was now available in French and so Arthur took Europe by storm. German translations and adaptations followed, notably Wolfram von Eschenbach's *Parzival* (c.1205–25).

Most of the medieval works about Arthur are in verse. The finest are the romances of Chrétien de Troyes (1170–90), sophisticated versions of Perceval and the search for the Grail, in which Chrétien threw off the shackles of history for the freedom of fiction.[102]

The Arthurian myths, developed out of Celtic legend, had an endlessly recyclable cast: the noble but flawed leader (Arthur), his brave but unimaginative right-hand man (Gawain), the admirable but adulterous wife (Guinevere), the cunning adviser (Merlin), the romantic hero (Lancelot), the witch-woman (Morgan le Fay), the naive youth (Perceval), the rebellious son (Mordred), and so on.

It's a near-unstoppable flood of Arthuriana: Robert de Boron's *Book of the Grail* (c.1200), *Perlesvaus* (c.1202–4), *Lancelot of the Lake* (c.1215), *Lancelot-Grail* (c.1215–35), the 'Prose *Tristan*' (c.1250), 1,500 pages in Old French, *Perceforest* (c.1340), some 7,000 pages long...

The heyday of Middle English Arthurian romance was the reigns of Edward III (1322–77) and Richard II (1377–99). Definitely *not* fictional, Arthur belonged to the real world of history and modern politics. Edward I and III could still cite Arthur's conquests to support their claims to overlordship of Scotland (historical fiction has its uses...), and both of them liked to play at being Arthur: in 1344, Edward III set up his own Round Table at Winchester. From this period the literary highlight is *Sir Gawain and the Green Knight* (c.1375–1400), the acknowledged masterpiece of English

Arthurian romance.[103] The Arthurian world might have disappeared for good had not Sir Thomas Malory (c.1400–71) organised all the legends into one masterwork.[104] Malory's hefty tome, published by William Caxton as *Le Morte d'Arthur* (1485), would be read by English readers ever after.

Belief in the 'real' Arthur was fading. The first hammer blow was landed by the Italian-born historian Polydore Vergil, in his *Anglica Historia* (c.1512),[105] who dismissed the Arthur stories as rubbish.

No new treatment of Arthur appeared after Malory. The Renaissance had arrived, and the revival of Classical learning rendered the medieval nonsense about Arthur unfashionable. Aeneas was a more credible nation-builder. The Tudors kept their distance from the king who was advised by a wizard. The Catholic Arthur and the Grail didn't quite belong in a Protestant kingdom. The Puritans found the sex and violence of Arthurian romance most unsavoury. Arthur would not be *rexque futurus* until Walter Scott put him in *The Lady of the Lake* (1810).

The King and the legend, as Chrétien realised 700 years earlier, are, and can be, whatever we want them to be. As every historical novelist knows, there is always more than one truth about history.

Notes

1. Margaret Anne Doody, *The True History of the Novel*, London, 1997, p. 27.
2. E. M. Forster, *Aspects of the Novel* (1927), Penguin, 1976, p. 17.
3. N. K. Sandars (ed.), *The Epic of Gilgamesh*, Penguin, 1960, p. 13.
4. Michael Rice, *The Power of the Bull*, Routledge, New York, 1998, p. 95.
5. Sandars, op. cit., p. 21.
6. Steven Moore, *The Novel: An Alternative History*, Continuum, London, 2010, p. 54.
7. Rice, op. cit., 95.
8. Moore, op. cit., 53.
9. Rice, op. cit., 94.
10. Andrew George, *The Epic of Gilgamesh*, Penguin Classics, 1999, p. xxxi.
11. Sandars, op. cit., p. 21.
12. Sandars, op. cit., p. 15.
13. George, op. cit., p. xxxiii.
14. Christopher Booker, *The Seven Basic Plots*, Continuum, London, 2004, pp. 598–601.

15. Moore, op. cit., p. 40f.
16. Miriam Lichtheim (ed.), *Ancient Egyptian Literature, I: The Old and Middle Kingdoms*, University of California Press, 1973, pp. 211, 222–3.
17. Lichtheim, op. cit., I, pp. 216–7.
18. Moore, op. cit., p. 43.
19. Moore, op. cit., p. 49.
20. Lichtheim, op. cit., III, pp. 125ff.
21. See *The Petese Stories* II: *The Carlsberg Papyri 6*, ed. Kim Ryholt, Copenhagen: Museum Tusculanum, 2006.
22. Moore, op. cit., p. 49.
23. Richard Janko, 'Go away and rule', review of Joachim Latacz et al., *Troy and Homer* (2004), *Times Literary Supplement*, 15 April 2005.
24. Janko, op. cit.
25. Doody, op. cit., p. 16.
26. Doody, op. cit., p. 21.
27. Peter Levi, *The Pelican History of Greek Literature*, Pelican, 1985, pp. 272–3.
28. *Herodotus* II.121.
29. A.R. Burn, *Herodotus: The Histories*, Penguin, 1988, p. 29.
30. Herodotus II.73.
31. J. L. Moles in Gill and Wiseman (eds), *Lies and Fiction in the Classical World*, Exeter University Press, Exeter, 1993, pp. 96–7.
32. Moles in Gill and Wiseman, p. 98.
33. Levi, op. cit., p. 285.
34. Walter Miller (ed.), *Xenophon: Cyropaedia*, Loeb Classical Library, Harvard University Press, 1983, vol. 1, p. viii.
35. J.R. Morgan and Richard Stoneman, *Greek Fiction: The Greek Novel in Context*, Routledge, London and New York, 1994, p. 16.
36. Miller, op. cit., p. viii.
37. Miller, op. cit., pp. viii-ix.
38. Miller, op. cit., p. ix.
39. Miller, op. cit., p. ix.
40. Miller, op. cit., p. xi.
41. Doody, op. cit., p. 30.
42. Morgan and Stoneman, op. cit., p. 23.
43. Miller, op. cit., 1. p. 5.
44. Moore, op. cit., p. 79.
45. Richard Stoneman (trans.), *The Greek Alexander Romance*, Penguin Classics, 1991, p. 10.

46. Stoneman, op. cit., p. 11.
47. Stoneman, op. cit., p. 18.
48. Stoneman, op. cit., p. 21.
49. Peter Green, in Paul Cartledge, Peter Garnsey, and Erich Gruen (eds), *Hellenistic Constructs*, University of California Press, 1997, p. 39.
50. Green, op. cit., p. 45.
51. E.V. Rieu (trans.), *The Voyage of Argo*, Penguin, 1959, p. 14.
52. Rieu, op. cit., p. 29.
53. Rieu op. cit., p. 15.
54. Rieu, op. cit., p.15.
55. Morgan and Stoneman, op. cit., p. 15.
56. Douglas Little, *Lucan: Pharsalia*, University of Otago Press, Dunedin, New Zealand, 1989, pp. 5–6.
57. Eric Griffiths, *Times Literary Supplement*, 15 September 2006.
58. Doody, op. cit., p. 27.
59. Raphael Lyne, 'Textures of influence' *Times Literary Supplement*, 7 August 1998.
60. Richard Jenkins, *Times Literary Supplement*, 9 February 2007.
61. Little, op. cit., p. 5.
62. Little, op. cit., p. 7.
63. Little, op. cit., p. 18.
64. Little, op. cit., p. 8n. 12.
65. Little, op. cit., p. 64.
66. Doody, op. cit., p. 31.
67. C. B. R. Pelling, *Plutarch: Life of Antony*, Cambridge University Press, Cambridge, 1988, p. vii.
68. Pelling, op. cit., p. 11.
69. Pelling, op. cit., p. 11.
70. Pelling, op. cit., p. 12.
71. Pelling, op. cit., p. 35.
72. Pelling, op. cit., p. 35.
73. Pelling, op. cit., p. 36.
74. Pelling, op. cit., p. 36.
75. Seamus Heaney (trans.), and Daniel Donoghue (ed.), *Beowulf: A Verse Translation*, Norton, New York and London, 2002, p. xxiii.
76. Heaney and Donoghue, op. cit., p. xxiv.
77. Moore, op. cit., p. 11.
78. Heaney and Donoghue, op. cit., p. x.

79. Heaney and Donoghue, op. cit., p. xi.
80. Heaney and Donoghue, op. cit., p. xxiii.
81. Heaney and Donoghue, op. cit., p. 124.
82. Heaney and Donoghue, op. cit., p. 180.
83. Heaney and Donoghue, op. cit., p. 213.
84. Roberta Frank, in Heaney and Donoghue, op. cit., p. 179.
85. Moore, op. cit., p. 147.
86. Moore, op. cit., p. 151n. 27.
87. Doody, op. cit., p. 182.
88. Elizabeth Archibald and Ad Putter (eds), *The Cambridge Companion to the Arthurian Legend*, Cambridge University Press, Cambridge, 2009, p. 3.
89. Archibald and Putter, op. cit., p. 3.
90. Archibald and Putter, op. cit., p. 26.
91. Archibald and Putter, op. cit., p. 4.
92. Archibald and Putter, op. cit., p. 26.
93. Ronald Hutton in Archibald and Putter, op. cit., p. 27.
94. Archibald and Putter, op. cit., p. 29.
95. Moore, op. cit., p. 198.
96. Lewis Thorpe (ed.), Geoffrey of Monmouth, *History of the Kings of* Britain, Penguin, 1978, pp. 18–19.
97. Thorpe, op. cit., p. 10.
98. Thorpe, op. cit., p. 10.
99. Archibald and Putter, op. cit., p. 42.
100. Moore, op. cit., p. 32.
101. Archibald and Putter, op. cit., p. 43.
102. Archibald and Putter, op. cit., p. 5.
103. Archibald and Putter, op. cit., p. 5, 75.
104. Archibald and Putter, op. cit., p. 5.
105. Archibald and Putter, op. cit., p. 6–7.

Le Morte d'Arthur to *The Castle of Otranto*

by Celia Brayfield

When William Caxton imported a printing press to England in 1476 his first book was a history of Troy. Another early success for him was Thomas Malory's *Le Morte d'Arthur*, a poetic interpretation of French romance tales and English legends, which was so popular that it was reprinted five times over the next 150 years. From the very beginning of the publishing industry, the roots of historical fiction and of historical fact were entwined.

From the Renaissance onwards, an educated people studied the great historians of antiquity and could invoke ancient history as a rationale for both argument and action. They wrote poems and masques in which historical figures, mythological beings and characters of pure imagination all appeared together, and staged popular plays which, like Shakespeare's history plays, dramatised the recent past to confirm the foundations of the present, whether by delivering a gory lesson in the evils of intolerance or by emphasising the legitimacy of the Tudor dynasty.

The printers found they could sell books by historians with a gift for colourful writing, such as Polydore Vergil, an Italian historian who was commissioned by Henry VII to write a history of England. His admirers praised his 'singular invention, good judgement, and good reading', suggesting that skilful invention was part of the historian's duty.

Printers in England began to guess the public taste and commission historians on popular themes, knowing that they could sell their books – Holinshed's *Chronicles*, re-published in 1587 and a substantial source for Shakespeare's history plays, was conceived by the printer Reginald Wolfe, who hired Holinshed and several other writers to create the work his market wanted.

The readers of these works were the highly educated elite and the rising middle-class, of whom the males at least were literate. The majority of the European population could not read, but consumed history through plays. The attitude towards historical accuracy in audiences and readers alike was coloured by the sense that facts were arguable. Historians might compete in their scholarship, but the audience in general also seemed to enjoy history for its affirmative narratives and entertainment value. Knowing, perhaps, how confused a battlefield was or how easily forgotten the exact words of a diplomatic exchange, they seldom censured writers for inaccuracy, even if they were fully aware that the account was at least partly invented.

Sir Philip Sidney, in his famous *Defence of Poesy*, defined the symbiosis of history and imagination:

> *And even the historiographers, although their lips sound of things done and verity be written in their foreheads, have been glad to borrow both fashion and perchance weight of the poets. So Herodotus entitled his History by the name of the nine muses, and both he... and all the rest that followed him either stale or usurped of poetry their passionate describing of passions, the many particularities of battles which no man could affirm, or, if that be denied me, long orations put in the mouths of great kings and captains, which it is certain they never pronounced.*

Europe in this era was torn apart along great axes of social division, and its people turned equally to allegedly factual accounts, such as Foxe's *Book of Martyres,* and imaginative reconstructions, such as Christopher Marlowe's play *The Massacre at Paris,* for historical evidence to resolve their conflicts of faith or allegiance. In England, successive monarchs continued the Tudor dynasty, but opposition to their rule, and the disputed right of each king or queen to the throne, were based on historical justification. The Tudor heritage was reaffirmed in England throughout the sixteenth century and eventually produced one of the greatest plays and most questionable interpretations of history ever staged, Shakespeare's *Richard III.*

Shakespeare's Richard is a psychopathic mass murderer embittered by his deformity. History's Richard was a 'good lord' to his people, an admired and courageous military commander and, since the discovery and authentication of his remains by the University of Leicester in 2013, a slightly built man with a lateral scoliosis of his lower spine.

The actor, writer and director Steven Berkoff, commenting on the discovery of Richard's remains, has suggested that Shakespeare's gift to humankind was far greater than mere accuracy, and in doing so he identified one of the highest functions of historical fiction. 'What Shakespeare gave us was some of the most definitive insights into the nature of evil. For Shakespeare, what makes great drama is a villain but he also created villains because that was the nature of monarchy ....kingship wasn't a very pleasant thing – we had many psychopathic monarchs. And much of English history would be unknown but for Shakespeare.'[1]

In the Renaissance audience, a fascination with history ran alongside a passion for romances. This era of social mobility, materialism and religious conflict sustained a nostalgia for an idealised age of nobility and altruism, for Camelot, the lost kingdom of chivalry inhabited by King Arthur and his knights. This concept, currently the inspiration for the long-running TV series *Merlin*, has had an extraordinary resonance not only with the elite but also with mass audiences. In Elizabethan London the blend of nationalism and nostalgia gave rise to the tradition of the 'Queen's Day', a celebration of the accession of Queen Elizabeth I, for which the entire court would dress in fantasy costumes as medieval knights and ladies.

The romances also spoke to the growing sense of European identity, defined in terms of race and faith. One of the most popular, *Le Roman de Fierabras le Géant*, concerns a mythical Moorish prince from Spain and shares characters and events with the legends of the French Holy Roman Emperor, Charlemagne. The Reconquista, the defeat of the Moors that was completed with the fall of Granada in 1492, is still celebrated in folk traditions such as the Basque Mascarades and the English Morris dance. In *Le Morte d'Arthur* the Crusades are an offstage presence, while the collection brings together many of the foundation myths of England, in which pagan enemies come from mainland Europe.

The yearning for a romanticised age of chivalry became self-conscious after the publication of the celebrated ironic romance by Miguel Cervantes that appeared in Spain in 1605, with the English translation following in 1620: *El Ingenioso Hidalgo Don Quixote de la Mancha.* (It is worth noting that the contemporary meaning of word 'ingenious' was closer to 'imaginative' than its modern sense.) The book seized the attention of the age, but although it satirised the passion for romance, it did not dim it in the slightest.

Don Quixote is a 50-year-old country gentleman so addicted to reading romances that he has become delusional. He sets out on a mission to open a new age of chivalry, seeing his bony old horse as a noble steed, a local farm girl as a damsel in distress and, famously, a group of windmills as enemy knights. His servant, Sancho Panza, and his family, burn his books and brick up his library in an attempt to stop him. Finally, at the end of the second book, the Don regains his sanity, blames his reading and makes a will disinheriting his niece if she marries a man who reads romances.

This epic and affectionate satire was wildly popular and the work was translated and published all over Europe within a few years. It is said that Cervantes 'smiled Spanish chivalry away', although most commentators attribute the end of that era to the brutal materialism of the conquistadors. The work gave a voice to all who questioned romance-reading, but did nothing to stop the genre from evolving and capturing mass imagination for the next two centuries. For all these readers, then as now, it is the otherness of the past that appealed. History is an exotic setting for high passions, noble motives and great deeds, an escape from the grubby mundaneness of the present. Spanish romances, such as the *Amadis di Gaula* novels in particular, featured the bloody conquest of far-off magical lands, the imagined landscape of the conquistadors.

The gothic romances of the late eighteenth century added the thrill of terror, vicariously enjoyed at the domestic fireside. The past was a fantasy place of extreme evil, where rape, murder, kidnapping and forced marriage were commonplace and supernatural events took place in brooding landscapes dominated by mysterious castles. *The Castle of Otranto*, by Horace Walpole, published in 1764, was the first significant novel in this genre, which, by the end of the century, was dominated by *The Monk*, by the 19-year-old Matthew Gregory Lewis, and a series of novels by Ann Radcliffe, of which *The Mysteries of Udolpho* is the best known, perhaps because the heroine of Jane Austen's first novel, *Northanger Abbey,* is obsessed with it.

The novel itself was held in contempt by many as a consequence of the popularity of gothic romance, yet individual authors were admired by literary figures such as Coleridge and cited as influences by Sir Walter Scott. One of the greatest champions of the genre was William Godwin, philosopher and husband of Mary Wollstonecraft, who considered that 'The writer of romance is to be considered as the writer of real history......The historian is confided to individual incident and individual man, and must hang upon that his invention or conjectures as he can. The writer collects his materials from all sources, experience, report, and the records of human affairs; then generalises them; and finally selects, from those instances which is best qualified to portray, and which he judges most calculated to impress the hearer and improve the faculties of his reader.'

It was a group homage to the genre made by Byron, Shelley and their friends that encouraged Godwin's daughter Mary Shelley to write *Frankenstein* in 1818, a work that decisively moved the horror genre into contemporary territory.

The victimised heroine was an essential feature of the gothic romance. It has been argued that the gothic romance created 'a fantasy space in which [the author] can centralise a female consciousness and explore female fears and desires'. But it is hard not to see in these heroines the precursor of Alfred Hitchcock's screaming blondes, the archetypal women in jeopardy.

Enjoyment of the gothic romance was at its peak at a time when The Terror, the ritualised mass murder of the French Revolution, and the American Revolutionary War were raw memories. In *The Historical Novel* Georg Lukács argues that a general consciousness of historicity – of the present as a product of the past – evolved at this time, and from this shared experience of trauma the historical novel as we recognise it today appeared.

Waverley to Middlemarch
by Celia Brayfield

In Edinburgh, the marble face of Sir Walter Scott looks out over the city from its monument with as much gravitas as the famous statue of Abraham Lincoln that gazes down on Washington. The statue honours a writer whose historical novels created the nations of the nineteenth century in spirit, while political forces shaped them on the ground.

Waverley (1814), like the almost 30 other novels which followed it, is dense and discursive to the modern reader; but to the audiences of the nineteenth century these were dazzlingly realistic recreations of Scottish national mythology that clearly spoke to people worldwide.

Scott imagined history as the context to the present, not an escape from it. He wrenched the past out of the hands of the romance writers and connected it to the present. Writing in the infancy of capitalism, as industrialisation engulfed people and landscape, Scott animated subversive folk heroes, the Highland Rob Roy and his English precursor, Robin Hood. He was less concerned with the makers of history, the 'great lives' of generals, statesmen or monarchs, than with ordinary individuals struggling to live by their own beliefs in turbulent times. In addition, his novels share with those of Dickens a population of plain citizens as vivid secondary characters and walk-on parts who, because they are viewed with respect and often affection, can be articulate without seeming inauthentic.

'The writer must be faithful to the manners of the times,' Scott insisted, and was at pains to make the reader feel the full experience of a forced march over heather-covered hills or of life in a crusader's tent. Female experience was outside his scope, and his women are at best allowed short episodes of assertion before they relapse into nubile, passive and self-sacrificing creatures. His men, however, are all action, duelling, jousting and leading their peers in revolt. This balance undoubtedly reclaimed historical fiction from the low status it had acquired as a consequence of popularity with women readers, and helped to move the genre away from fantasy romance and back into the literary mainstream.

The ability of history to present a new nation with the elements of its own identity was central to the global influence of Scott's novels. The American Civil War (1861–5), the Risorgimento in Italy, the reunification of Germany in 1871 and Russia's long road to reclaim its Slavonic and Asian heritage all left millions of people with a sense of not knowing quite who they were. Culturally deracinated, they set about retelling their own histories as a way of affirming new identities. Every artistic medium fed this hunger for nationality; and the novels of this period were read alongside, and sometimes inspired, plays, operas, symphonies and painting on the same themes.

Waverley fathered a series of books that were to be overwhelmingly popular for half a century. Thus the title of 'the American Scott' was soon awarded to James Fenimore Cooper, whose novels evoked the New York State backwoods in which he had grown up. The hardy, courageous frontiersmen of his best known novel, *The Last of the Mohicans* (1826), seized the public imagination; while his Native American characters, noble, tragic and sometimes vengeful, inhabited an almost mythical heartland of forests and rivers. Cooper's vision was not only of a more innocent past, however, but of the America of his day becoming a cruel, materialistic industrial state; and this critical view eventually lost him public sympathy,

At the same time in Russia, a young poet, already under house arrest because of his dissident views, began a novel based on the life story of his great-grandfather. Pushkin family tradition held that Abram Petrovich Hannibal was an African prince who was captured by slavers, and sold in Constantinople to a Russian nobleman who gave him to the Tsar Peter the Great. The great Tsar treated Hannibal as a favoured ward and took him to Paris – where the novel begins – to be educated as an engineer.

Many writers begin with the determination to bring their own family history to life, but for Alexander Pushkin the story of his African great-grandfather offered him a character whose uprooting and loss of heritage could stand for the brutal deracination of the country itself.

Pushkin's novel *Peter the Great's Blackamoor* was published unfinished after his death in 1837. His interest seemed to have shifted from his personal heritage to Peter the Great himself: he had abandoned this early work and moved on to two fully realised novels, *The Captain's Daughter* and *The Bronze Horseman*, both set in Peter's reign, and both attempting to investigate the character of the man who reinvented his country.

Scott's influence touched almost every novelist of the age, each selecting the epoch and the characters that were best suited to dramatise their argument. The century saw the birth of the novel as a mass medium and – although their readers were still a tiny proportion of the population as a whole – writers could at last earn a living from sales, rather than depending on a wealthy patron, and could connect more directly with an audience. In France, Victor Hugo was one of many tempted to put aside poetry and, under extreme pressure from a hungry publisher, completed *Notre-Dame de Paris*, known in English as *The Hunchback of Notre Dame*, in 1831.

Hugo, conceiving the novel as 'epic theatre', went much further than Scott in depicting the full range of society, from king to beggar, and in focusing on the fate of the most marginalised of outcasts, the gypsy Esmeralda and Quasimodo the hunchback. Like his fellow-countrymen Honoré de Balzac, Stendhal and Gustave Flaubert, Hugo was deeply affected by the day-to-day tragedies of a time when starvation was common, prostitution rife and men such as his hero Jean Valjean went to prison for stealing food. He set aside his next novel to pursue a political career that ended in his exile, so that *Les Misérables* (1862) was almost 20 years in production. His intention was to look back on France's years of turmoil and revolt; but the book, he said, was 'meant for everyone. It addresses England as well as Spain, Italy as well as France, Germany as well as Ireland, the republics that harbour slaves as well as empires that have serfs....Humankind's wounds, those huge sores that litter the world, do not stop at the blue and red lines drawn on maps.'

The novel itself reached a zenith in this period; but another revolution, in print technology, dramatically widened the audience by adding newspaper readers to the small circle of book-buyers and library subscribers. The new newspapers, sold directly on the streets, were immediately locked in circulation wars, in which a novelist with a strong narrative gift, able to keep readers buying week after week, was a decisive weapon. Thus in Paris in 1844 *Le Siècle* (*The Century*) dropped the grim realism of Balzac and ran with adventure, romance and *The Three Musketeers* by another young statesman of African descent, Alexandre Dumas.

The d'Artagnan trilogy was based on the memoirs of a Gascon gentleman and captain of the musketeers whose birthplace was the tiny village of Lupiac. The musketeers, Athos, Porthos and Aramis, are also loosely based on seventeenth-century noblemen from the southwestern province of Le Béarn, a sleepy, remote province far from Paris. The opening passage of *The Three Musketeers*, in which d'Artagnan rides into the capital as a penniless country boy on a ridiculous yellow horse, establishes him firmly as a hero in the *Waverley* mould: an outsider, an innocent, rich only in courage and integrity.

Dumas found the great figures of history irresistible, and few pages pass in any of his novels without the appearance of a king, queen or cardinal; but his sympathies are always with the underdogs, the men of the people and the unlucky princess Marguerite, forced by her mother into a doomed political marriage with another Southerner, Henri of Navarre.

When he travelled around Europe in the 1860s, Count Leo Tolstoy was a young Russian aristocrat with some fame as a society writer and some experience as an officer in the Crimean War. He met Victor Hugo, read *Les Misérables* as a newly-completed manuscript; and realised that the political ideas still forming in his mind could inform his literary work. His novel *War and Peace* (1869) was begun with the intention of exploring the causes of the Decembrist Revolt of 1825, whose aged leaders had recently been pardoned and released from exile in Siberia.

Tolstoy is often described as a writer at war with himself, in whose work political and artistic imperatives compete. Russia was a country in which unimaginable extremes of poverty and wealth existed in increasing conflict. Although serfdom was abolished in 1861, the vast majority of the population remained landless, disenfranchised, uneducated and dependent on the landowning aristocracy for their existence. One of many reforming landowners, Tolstoy created the central character of Pierre, the illegitimate son of a count who unexpectedly inherits his father's immense wealth, to give voice to his own egalitarian principles and set him in an immense canvas peopled with characters from the whole spectrum of political belief, from dissolute, nihilistic hedonism to altruistic martyrdom.

Marian Evans, known to history by her pen name of George Eliot, began her masterpiece, *Middlemarch*, in the year *War and Peace* appeared, taking as her subject the comparatively miniature world of an English provincial town, yet creating one of the most admired English novels. Here is idealism in action, with all the principal characters struggling to make the world a better place, hampered by their own innocence as much as by the corrupt, venal, sexist or captivatingly foolish people around them. And yet they win through and Dorothea Brooke finally escapes the beyond-the-grave control of the husband she misguidedly took at his own estimation.

By the final decades of the nineteenth century the historical novel had taken the nostalgic instinct that lies at the root of our desire to relive the past and made it a vehicle for reform and revolution. The greatest works of this age can justly claim to have shaped nations. And many are still with us, in a global afterlife of film adaptations, plays, musicals and marketing schemes, continuing their authors' work of awakening conscience and compassion.

Tess of the d'Urbervilles to Wolf Hall

Change is accelerating, and so we have the sense of history speeding up, collapsing, imploding, condensing. The lives of our grandparents were so different from ours that we marvel that they endured them, and the difference divides us. Yet for the first 5,000 years of recorded history, very little changed.

When does history begin? Antique thinking begins when a mother and daughter can't relate their lives. A generation gap, defined as the time period in which things have changed so much that those at the beginning and end of the span have entirely different experiences and beliefs, used to be 50 years, then 30 and now, 15. So history – where does history start?

History doesn't need to tell us what happened any more. The record is not a precious and barely decipherable manuscript which only the highly-trained few can consult. The record is on TV every night, where archives of recordings can re-run for us the great events of the world as well as the minutiae of daily life. The camera, as much as the acceleration of change, has transformed our conception of history and with it the form and function of historical fiction.

Partly, of course, because all the arts of the image have had an impact both on literature and on our understanding of life. Technology has also trans-formed publishing in the twentieth century, bringing first the paperback book in the corner shop library, the magazines and newspapers printed and sold as fast as they could be read, and then the books in shops on every high street, the books in supermarkets. Publishing has become a global industry, with annual awards for marketing and publicity as well as for writing itself. Books are written to order, marketed like washing powder, acquired in line with editorial policy objectives, imported, exported and published as downloads to a device the size of a postcard. Perhaps the twentieth century was the golden age of the publishing industry, because disintermediation has now set authors free to find their readers and sell them books without the expertise of some charming fellow in a bow-tie and his assistant, Bridget Jones.

There are many omissions in this section, because the candidates for inclusion are so many. I have chosen to focus on the works that have had a profound influence on their audiences as they tried to process traumatic events of the time, the books that, if they did not change the world, made it easier to understand how the world had changed.

Traditional literary criticism would mark the end of the historical novel as a literary form with Virginia Woolf's *Orlando* in 1928, pass over the hijacking by market forces that rendered the genre a pariah state inhabited by bodice-rippers, pop-militaria and clogs-and-shawls sagas mid-century, and note with some surprise that, since Rose Tremain's *Restoration* (1989) demonstrated that formal experimentation is still possible in a novel set in the past, these books can attract critical acclaim.

If historical fiction is considered by theme, it is possible to see the flow of ideas in the vast output of the twentieth and twenty-first centuries, and understand what role historical fiction plays in our lives. The themes I have chosen are War, New Women, and Seeing with Fresh Eyes.

War

The two world wars consumed the developed world between 1914 and 1918 and again between 1939 and 1945, a period in which whole populations faced death every day. Millions died, in military actions, in bombing raids and in the systematic genocide of the Holocaust. Millions more were brutalised, traumatised and displaced, if not in the wars themselves then in the civil conflicts that followed. The physical scars endured for decades and the media images seem eternal, there every night on dedicated TV channels.

The response of the writers caught in these conflicts was immediate, in journalism and memoir, and rapid in fiction too. The generation gap shrank to 10 or 15 years almost at once. *All Quiet on the Western Front* by a war veteran, Erich Maria Remarque, appeared as a serial in a German newspaper in 1928 and as a book a year later, selling 2.5 million copies in the next eighteen months. The narrator is an ordinary soldier, a boy who runs from his school classroom to enlist and becomes so brutalised that he loses even the ability to comfort his mother on her death bed. Despite the mass appeal of the novel's bleak indictment of war, it was a book that the Nazis burned another short generation later.

At the same time in Russia, where revolution took the country out of the global conflict, Mikhail Aleksandrovich Sholokhov began a book intended as a prequel to a novel about the impact of the revolution on a Cossack village. *The Quiet Don* first appeared as a serial from 1928 to 1940. This panoramic novel set in a peasant community sees events through the eyes of plain citizens; at one point the author implied that the founding fathers of the Cossack village were serfs who had fled their owners. The novels, usually treated as a trilogy, show the community torn apart in the struggle between revolutionary and Tsarist forces and the Communists, traumatised by their harsh existence, yet heroic in their survival, loyalty and courage. While the combat scenes are unsparing, they contrast with the lyrical evocation of the landscape. *The Quiet Don* proved to be a key work in the creation of a national identity for Russia and was officially praised in the Stalinist era, although Sholokhov was awarded the Nobel Prize in 1966, confirming his international reputation. Acclaim may not be good for literature. When I read these books as a teenager in my suburban London library, I was enthralled by them. My Russian friends, made to read them at school, were bored senseless.

The dissident Russian writer Alexander Solzhenitsyn attacked these books. His own novel of Russia during World War I, *August 1914* (1971) sets aside the experience of soldiers or farmers and focuses on the Battle of Tannenberg in August 1914 through the eyes of a Colonel reporting back to the Grand Duke in command of the army.

The novel blends fiction and historiography, using contemporary documents in the text. Colonel Vorotyntsev is sent to investigate the state of the Imperial Russian Army, which is invading eastern Germany under the command of General Samsonov. The chaotic state of the force, which mirrors the state of the Tsarist regime, leads to a terrible defeat after the four-day battle, and the suicide of their commander. Only 10,000 Russian soldiers, out of 150,000, survived Tannenberg. After he was expelled from Russia Solzhenitsyn revised the novel, adding passages about the role of the secret police in the tragedy. He intended it to begin a cycle of historical novels about his country.

The response of writers to the Second World War seems distorted by the huge output of propaganda literature that continued for more than a decade after the conflict ended. The prevailing impulses were to sanitise and glamorise the war; the action-adventure stories that emphasized heroism and comradeship are too numerous to mention, with *The Cruel Sea* (1951) by Nicholas Montserrat, *The Guns of Navarone* (1957) by Alistair MacLean or *The Bridge on the River Kwai* (1952) by Pierre Boulle, typical of immensely popular novels focused on major events in the War. One of the most astonishing traductions of an author's purpose in literature is the adaptation of the bitter, realistic short stories of James

A. Michener, *Tales of the South Pacific* (1947), which were awarded a Pulitzer Prize, into *South Pacific* (1949) the lavish, romantic musical.

For the first time in history both officers and soldiers were literate and wrote accounts of their experiences that were published for mass audiences rather than kept with family records or military archives. Realism, literary intention and challenging subject matter allowed novels to stand out and, in due time, challenge the victors' versions of wartime history. *The Naked And The Dead* (1948) established Norman Mailer's reputation when it was first published and, in its portrayal of the fatal internecine hatreds in an American army unit during the Philippines campaign, challenged the sanctioned heroic narratives. Another debut novel, *King Rat* (1962) by James Clavell, spared readers nothing of the degradation of the lives of Japanese prisoners-of-war in Singapore, creating a world in which traditional social mores were inverted and portraying the ruthless chief survivor as a natural capitalist.

The pacifism of the post-war generation finally found expression in two darkly ironic, self-conscious and experimental novels, Joseph Heller's *Catch-22* (1961) a huge, fragmented satire on self-defeating military bureaucracy, the creator of the double-bind in which American pilots stationed in Italy found themselves; and in Kurt Vonnegut's *Slaughterhouse Five* (1969) which blends science fiction and history and takes its name from an underground abattoir where the hero, Billy Pilgrim, and his German guards, survive the fire-bombing of Dresden. It's notable that these novels appeared during the Vietnam War (1955–75) and, although rooted in the history of World War II in Europe, attacked the cruelty and futility of combat in both actions and at a time when the TV news was nightly bringing the developed world images of dead and wounded American soldiers and Vietnamese children immolated in napalm attacks. The ideological arena in which these novels addressed their readers was not wholly that of their historical setting.

A taste for military history began to find expression in popular historical sub-genres, the *Hornblower* (1937 onwards) novels of C. S. Forester, concerning a young midshipman in Nelson's navy who rises to become Admiral of the Fleet by the end of the series, and the *Sharpe* (1988 onwards) novels of Bernard Cornwell, whose hero joins the army as a London street kid and, during the Napoleonic Wars, becomes an officer in spite of his rebellious nature. These series are notable for their meticulous accuracy in uniforms, weaponry, ships and tactics, and the keen appreciation of these details by their fans. In the parallel historical satire, the *Flashman* (1969 onwards) series of George MacDonald Fraser, history, humour and cynicism combine to suggest that a hero may be nothing but a scoundrel in the right place at the right time.

Gradually, interest in the wars from a non-military perspective found a voice. The two trilogies known together as *Fortunes of War* by Olivia Manning appeared in 1960 and portrayed the conflict through the experiences of a young English couple posted to Romania. Fleeing Nazi invasion, they become refugees and escape through the Middle East to Egypt in the early days of World War II. Terror and deprivation strain their relationship in what Anthony Burgess praised as 'the finest fictional record of the war produced by a British writer.'

Even with the eternal memory of film, the natural watershed in understanding, the span beyond which living memories are few, after grandparents have died, taking with them the living record of their lives, was reflected in novels about the war. So after 35 years, the human legacy of the Holocaust was addressed in the poetic complexity of *The White Hotel* (1981) by D. M. Thomas and *The Reader* (1995) by Bernhard Schlink.

For some writers the history of the world wars offered what Louisa Young calls a setting for 'proper drama,' in which love can be juxtaposed with death, where tragedy has stature. Sebastian Faulks was the first author to annexe the battlefield as a counterpoint in a love story, in *Birdsong* (1993), and *Charlotte Gray* (1999). In *Atonement* (2001), Ian McEwan weights the guilt of his central character, who falsely accuses her sister's lover of rape, with the separate deaths of the couple during World War II. Robert Harris's debut novel was a spectacular exercise in alternative history, a thriller, *Fatherland* (1992), set in the totalitarian Nazi state of Germany of the 1960s after that country had won the war and in part inspired by Albert Speer's architectural plans for a new Berlin. He followed it with *Enigma* (1995) which turned a spotlight on the mis-matched team of intellectuals and the women clerks who worked alongside them as code-breakers at the British intelligence unit at Bletchley Park. Fiction for children also used war as a setting, notably Michael Morpurgo's *War Horse* (1982) which revitalised the theme of a child and animal companion, finding a way to portray the horrors of World War I through the love of a boy for a horse bought by the British army.

The big questions posed by twentieth century history remained, however often it was used as a backdrop to an intimate narrative. How did people survive, how can a species survive when the world is consumed in self-annihilating madness? This question elicited the most powerful novels of the later decades. Pat Barker's *Regeneration* (1991) trilogy considers World War I from the viewpoint of the doctor in charge of a hospital for shell-shocked British officers and one of his patients, the poet Siegfried Sassoon. Almost all the characters in the novels are based on real people, but Barker has said that she chose this war, 'because it's come to stand in for other wars ... (because) of the idealism of young people in August 1914 in Germany and in England ... (who) really felt this was the start of a better world. And the disillusionment, the horror and the pain followed that. I think because of that it's come to stand for the pain of all wars.' She also identified the post-modern impulse to write an untold history, 'The trilogy is trying to tell something about the parts of war that don't get into the official accounts,' and identified the experience of women as a major aspect of the conflict that was poorly recorded in fact and stereotypically recreated in fiction.

Love is the regenerative force in *The English Patient* (1992) by Michael Ondaatje, set in a ruined building in Italy in the last days of World War II, where a Canadian nurse cares tenderly for a patient dying slowly of terrible burns, so badly injured he cannot at first remember his own identity. Described by Anthony Minghella, who wrote and directed the film adaptation, as 'fragmented, mosaic-like' it proceeds through flashbacks and memories, investigating the nature of memory and of history itself – the patient's most treasured possession is an edition of Herodotus, used as a scrap book. Ondaatje's purpose was partly to respond to the British war movies he remembered from living in England in the 1950s, creating a picture of the war that was neither British nor action-packed, yet heroic in the actions of individual characters.

New women

Historical fiction has always played a special role in the lives of women who found themselves suddenly cut off from their social and cultural roots by change. The sense of ordinary lives struggling in the turbulence brought about by the industrialisation, by war, by revolution and by nationalism, begins with the novels of Thomas Hardy in the late nineteenth century, and particularly with *Tess of the d'Urbervilles* (1891), set in a period of poverty known in Europe as the Long Depression that had ended 20 years earlier.

Ironically, a work appreciated now for its depiction of the English rural idyll, of harvest suppers, trusty shepherds and rosy milk-maids, is an unremitting tragedy of female oppression and was considered obscene and offensive in its time. Hardy gave the book a challenging subtitle, *A Pure Woman Faithfully Presented*, and portrays Tess as an intelligent girl of good morals who is effectively prostituted by her father, raped by her employer and then abandoned by her fiancé for her supposed immorality. It was to be the first of many books by men which challenged the inequity of women's social position.

In *Orlando* (1928) Virginia Woolf challenged the most primary assumptions about gender with an immortal narrator who, as a young man, has a love affair with Queen Elizabeth I, and who undertakes a diplomatic mission 60 years later to Constantinople, where she wakes as a woman. A novel that revels in its historical settings, *Orlando* exemplifies the anarchic, anti-realistic and self-conscious modernist spirit, merely touching base with iconic figures before bolting back to the present.

Just over a decade later a young American writer finished a novel generated by that near-universal impulse to capture the experience of her grandparents' generation before the opportunity passed. As a child of the American South, born and raised in Atlanta, with several confederate officers among her grandparents, Margaret Mitchell grew up listening to stories of the Civil War, and hearing the warning of her suffragist mother that the women of that generation had seen all their lives 'swept away'. In this sense, Scarlett O'Hara, the heroine of *Gone with the Wind* (1936), stands for every woman in this period for whom all the certainties of life were destroyed.

The novel was awarded the Pulitzer Prize in 1937 and, with over 30 million copies sold, is one of the most successful in publishing history. The author, who was killed by a drunk driver in 1949, did not live to hear the accusations of racism later made against the book. A lifelong liberal who lived in an acutely racist time and place, she had endowed scholarships[2] at the all-black Morehouse College, alma mater of Dr Martin Luther King; but Scarlett O'Hara's world is undoubtedly limited because she is a woman, and lives in a milieu in which well-born women are considered incapable of dealing with reality. Just as the fall of Atlanta happens offstage, so the brutal reality of mass slave ownership is hidden from her. The book consciously depicts Scarlett raging against the enforced passivity of her gender and at the same time defeated by her enforced ignorance and the bad judgement it fosters.

By the time *Gone with the Wind* was published the historical romance genre, to which many other significant novels were consigned, had been established by Georgette Heyer, whose first Regency novel, *Regency Buck*, was published in 1935. Intended as a homage to Jane Austen, it establishes the enduring motif of a rebellious young woman and the older man appointed her guardian. The characters are modern in their attitudes, more like the feisty gals and grumpy guys from Hollywood workplace comedies of the 1940s, but the settings are historic and often elaborately described, a feature that was itself immensely appealing to Heyer's fans. As A. S. Byatt observed, her awareness of the historical milieu, 'both of the minute details of the social pursuits of her leisured classes and of the emotional structure behind the fiction it produced – is her greatest asset'.[3]

It seems ironic that, at the same time as women won equality in one field of life after another, the sales of romantic fiction, and of historical romances, increased. Historical romances revisited the abject condition of women before the suffrage movement at the turn of the twentieth century, and typically concerned a female protagonist in a situation of total oppression, an orphan, a minor, living in poverty or sexually exploited. In her influential study of the romance genre, *Reading the Romance*[4] Janice Radway notes that all romance novels reach a happy ending after the struggle of the heroine, who often has little power in a patriarchal society. 'By picturing the heroine in relative positions of weakness, romances are not necessarily endorsing her situation, but examining an all-too-common state of affairs in order to display possible strategies for coping with it.'

Historical settings therefore enlarged the issues in women's lives. From sales figures, which for successful authors in this genre and period typically run to over 100 million, it is clear that women all over the developed world shared a powerful need to have their concerns externalised in these narratives..

There is an element of *samizdat* in women's popular fiction, in that it is a medium in which the woman-centred worldview can be shared in secret. Historical novels also permitted fictional characters to have experiences that were not considered appropriate for twentieth-century women until after the advent of reliable contraception around 1960 and the sexual revolution that followed it.

A country girl in Restoration England or the France of Louis XIV could credibly have a wide range of sexual experiences that would have been taboo for a modern heroine. She might indulge a healthy libido, like the heroines of *Forever Amber* (1944) and *Angélique, Marquise of the Angels* (1957) – whose author Anne Golon was forced to share the writing credit with her husband (as Serge and Anne, or even Sergeanne Golon) by Paris literary agents, who decided that readers would be much more comfortable if they thought that the book had been written by a man, as it would 'make it appear more serious.'[5]

The Parisian agents were morally wrong but culturally correct, as by the 1950s the taint of historical romance was enough to overpower the achievements of any woman author setting a novel in the past, whatever her intentions. Dorothy Dunnett's *King Hereafter* (1982) dramatises her argument for identifying the eleventh-century Earl Thorfinn of Orkney as the model for Macbeth, but her books had sentimental landscape covers and were shelved in the romance ghetto.

Some authors chose to relegate themselves. I suspect that I, and many other women novelists, have the marketing savvy of Eleanor Alice Burford Hibbert to thank for the most irritating recurrent question we have to answer: 'Do you write under your own name?' Eleanor wrote under half a dozen pseudonyms, most notably as Jean Plaidy, under whose name appeared a series of 77 popular novels which fictionalised the lives of female historical figures, including Lucrezia Borgia, Catherine de Medici, Anne Boleyn and Mary, Queen of Scots.

Catherine Cookson, the most successful British author of all time before J. K. Rowling, turned to her own life for inspiration. The daughter of an unwed, alcoholic mother in the declining industrial region of north-east England, she left school at 13 and went into domestic service. She prospered through her own enterprise, married, and began writing to cure her depression after a series of miscarriages. *Kate Hannigan*, the first of over 100 books, was published in 1950. With their focus on rags-to-riches trajectories of working-class women at the turn of the century, they inspired so many imitators that a sub-genre known in publishing as clogs-and-shawls was born and endured for a good three decades.

By 1986, when my own first novel appeared, historical fiction was an impossibility outside these degraded genres, and I had to create parallel modern narratives in order to be allowed an excursion to Singapore in 1940 or St Petersburg in 1913. Even then, my publishers advised me to cut 'all this war stuff.'

The certainty remained that history had so far been written by men, and in this process many women had been misrepresented and many more simply silenced, overlooked or deleted. In *Alias Grace* (1996) Margaret Atwood explored her instinct that the story of a sixteen-year-old housemaid, Grace Marks, convicted of murder in 1863, was not one story but many, and all shaped by the misogyny of the time. Tracy Chevalier, with a poster of Vermeer's portrait on her wall since her student days, saw the strange mix of excitement, apprehension and daring in the subject's expression, and determined to imagine the life of the un-named *Girl With a Pearl Earring* (1999). Sarah Dunant vividly portrayed Renaissance Italy through the lives of ordinary women – including nuns and courtesans – in a series of novels that began with *The Birth of Venus* (2003).

Philippa Gregory was the first popular writer of the late twentieth century to re-establish historical fiction about women in the process of rethinking and inclusion which had already preoccupied literary novelists. She exposed the society of eighteenth-century Bristol, whose prosperity rested on slavery, in *A Respectable Trade* (1992), in which the central love affair is between an aristocratic woman and one of her husband's slaves; since then she has written a series of novels about Tudor women, many retracing the steps of

Jean Plaidy. *The Other Boleyn Girl* (2001) is notable for the sheer detective work and imaginative verve needed to recreate the life of Mary Boleyn.

In his study *The Historical Novel*,[6] Jerome de Groot devotes a whole section to Mary's better-known sister, Anne Boleyn, as an extraordinary literary phenomenon. A woman whose love affair changed the course of history, the mother of Queen Elizabeth I, and a woman killed by her husband simply because his feelings for her had changed, has come to symbolise wronged womanhood like no other figure from the past. The publishing industry and the educational establishment focus on these few years of English history in a thoughtless process of familiarisation. Novels set in this period speak to a consensual understanding created by its abundant cultural references, thereby adding to those references, while far more significant events from other periods are overlooked. For a writer, especially a writer who wants to respond to the challenges of being a woman, there is an uncomfortable sense that archetype is working against you and that the industry is more willing to back the archetype than innovation.

Seeing with fresh eyes

'Does illustrating in a new way signify a new way of seeing?' asks Orhan Pamuk in his remarkable novel *My Name is Red* (2001), which evokes the world of a miniaturist painter in sixteenth-century Istanbul, consumed with the tension between the Islamic tradition of calligraphic illustration and the realist painting of Europe. The novel is also a crime thriller, a love story, a postmodernist fable and vast magic-realist collage. Pamuk, who was awarded the Nobel Prize in Literature in 2006, insists that 'the East-West question was somewhere in the background',[7] and that his primary purpose was to meditate on the question of style. The multiplicity of the novel itself, however, argues that it has not one purpose but many, and that, for a writer addressing the past, literary ambition and political intent are inseparable.

In writing *Things Fall Apart* (1958), Chinua Achebe described his intention to create a picture of the Igbo people of Nigeria before their culture was destroyed and their human achievements reconceived and devalued. Set in the late nineteenth century, and focusing on Okonkwo, a village leader and wrestling champion, the novel also extends understanding to the colonial officials and the missionaries invading Nigeria, and draws on African traditions of mythology and storytelling.

To rewrite the winner's view of history is to reclaim the histories effaced by colonialism, extending the imagination to recreate the excluded figures missing from historical records and establishing a transnational perspective of the past. Many of the most eminent writers of our times have married these impulses to experiments in form and style that in themselves address the nature of history and prompt the reader to look carefully at the border between memory and reality, and even to question whether such a division truly exists. *Midnight's Children* (1981) by Salman Rushdie, awarded the Booker of Bookers in 1993, also uses magic realism to evoke post-imperial India through a vast panorama of people and events linked by the life story of its narrator, Saleem Sinai, as he relates it to his bride-to-be.

Rushdie intended to show 'the provisional nature of all truths and certainties', and began with the belief that 'Reality is built on our prejudices, misconceptions and ignorance as well as our perceptiveness and knowledge.'[8] In this search for something that will serve as truth, the motif of the detective, often the scholarly investigator, appears and reappears frequently in twentieth-century historical novels. In *The Name of the Rose* (1980), for example, Umberto Eco placed his investigator in a fourteenth-century monastery in France, where a serial killer operates in the scriptorium. The investigation is almost fruitless and the genre conventions are used to question the nature of knowledge itself.

In *The French Lieutenant's Woman* (1969), John Fowles undermines history by challenging the concept of evolution as an orderly, sequential process and proposing different endings to the story of a an amateur palaeontologist and his lover. Gabriel García Márquez created a community in the process of relinquishing its history in *One Hundred Years of Solitude* (1978), which locates the epic history of a family in a South American town where 'the voracity of oblivion' is slowly destroying memories of the past.

A.S. Byatt's *Possession* (1990) concerns two pairs of lovers, two modern academics and the two Victorian poets who are the object of their research, using diaries, letters and the characters' poetry as textual devices to explore the question of artistic legacy. The theme of the title extends from the human relationships through the collection of texts and research material, to the sense in which biographers 'own' their subjects.

In some writers the need to challenge a dominant reading of history in fiction is paramount. The power of fiction to achieve recognition of great wrongs can be seen in the reception of *Beloved* (1987) by Toni Morrison, dedicated to the '60 million and more', the number of Africans who died as slaves, and focusing on a young woman who kills her own child before escaping a slave plantation. The memory will not be lost, nor is the future possible until it is contained.

The history to be challenged is sometimes created by historical fiction itself, a response not to a deficient archive or a long-overlooked record but to the process of overlaying memory with literature. Hari Kunzru, discussing *The Impressionists* (2002), said that the novel was 'largely a game I was playing with orientalism, with a Merchant Ivory view of India, and with the history of the British novel....The book is anti-Kim, but also plays around with *A Passage to India, Heart of Darkness, Hindoo Holiday* and others.'

A similar impulse has led novelists to examine gender and sexuality in a historical context, evoking unwitnessed lives and refracting past societies through the lens of contemporary gender awareness. Jeanette Winterson, in *The Passion* (1987), called her protagonist Villanelle, the name of an intricate poetic form, self-consciously suggesting her imaginary nature. Sarah Waters' novels, notably her debut, *Tipping The Velvet* (1998), explored an imagined lesbian sub-culture in Victorian London and rested on her PhD thesis on gay themes in historical fiction. Allan Hollinghurst in *The Line of Beauty* (2004) dissected the tensions of class, race and sexual orientation in Thatcherite Britain.

Have we arrived at a point at which historical fiction has destroyed history itself? Memory is false, reality illusory, records misleading, incomplete, politically tainted or entirely missing. *Did* winners write history, or is history a place where there are no winners and the act of recording events is in itself suspect – outside the infinite galaxies of records generated in new media?

Notes
1. Berkoff, Steven, speaking on BBC Radio 4, *PM*, 4 February 2013.

2. PBS American Masters documentary *Margaret Mitchell: American Rebel* screened 2 April 2012.

3. Byatt, A. S. '*Georgette Heyer Is a Better Novelist Than You Think*', in Fahnestock-Thomas, Mary, Georgette Heyer: A Critical Retrospective, Saraland, AL: Prinnyworld Press. 1969, US.

4. Radway, Janice. 1984. *Reading the Romance: Women, Patriarchy, and Popular Literature*. USA. University of North Carolina Press.

5. Available at: http://www.worldofangelique.com/anneor.htm [accessed 18 March 2013.].

6. de Groot, Jerome. (2010) *The Historical Novel*, Abingdon and New York, Routledge.

7. Pamuk, Orhan. (2007) *Other Colours*. London. Faber & Faber.

8. Quoted in de Groot, op cit.

Part 2:
Tips and tales

Guest contributions

Margaret Atwood

Margaret Atwood has received numerous awards and honorary degrees. She is the author of more than 50 volumes, of poetry, children's literature, fiction, and non-fiction and is perhaps best known for her novels, which include *Alias Grace* (1996)

We live in a period in which memory of all kinds, including the sort of larger memory we call history, is being called into question. For history as for the individual, forgetting can be just as convenient as remembering, and remembering what was once forgotten can be distinctly uncomfortable. As a rule, we tend to remember the awful things done to us and to forget the awful things we did. The Blitz is still remembered; the fire-bombing of Dresden – well, not so much, or not by us. To challenge an accepted version of history – what we've decided it's proper to remember – by dredging up things that society has decided are better forgotten, can cause cries of anguish and outrage, as the makers of a recent documentary about the Second World War could testify. Remembrance Day, like Mother's Day, is a highly ritualised occasion; for instance, we are not allowed, on Mother's Day, to commemorate bad mothers, or even to acknowledge that such persons exist would be considered – on that date – to be in shoddy taste.

Here is the conundrum, for history and individual memory alike, and therefore for fiction also: How do we know we know what we think we know? And if we find that, after all, we don't know what it is that we once thought we knew, how do we know we are who we think we are, or thought we were yesterday, or thought we were – for instance – a hundred years ago? These are the questions one asks onself, at my age, whenever one says, Whatever happened to old what's-his-name? They are also the questions that arise in any contemplation of what used to be called 'character'; they are thus central to the conception of the novel. For the novel concerns itself, above all, with time. Any plot is a this followed by a that; there must be change in a novel, a change can only take place over time, and this change can only have significance if either the character in the book, or, at the very least, the reader, can remember what came before. As Henry James's biographer Leon Edel has said, if there is a clock in it, you know it's a novel.

Thus there can be no history, and no novel either, without memory of some sort; but when it comes right down to it, how reliable is memory itself – our individual memory, or our collective memory as a society? Once, memory was a given. You could lose it and you could recover it, but the thing lost and then recovered was as solid and all-of-a-piece, was as much a thing, as a gold coin....If the seventeenth century revolved around faith – that is, what you believed – and the eighteenth around knowledge – that is, what you could prove – the nineteenth could be said to have revolved around memory. You can't have Tennyson's 'Tears, idle tears....Oh death in life, the days that used to be,' unless you can remember those days that used to be and are no more. Without memory, and the belief that it can be recovered whole, like treasure fished out of a swamp, Proust's famous madeleine is reduced to a casual snack. The nineteenth-century novel would be unimaginable without a belief in the integrity of memory, for what is the self without a more or less continuous memory of itself, and what is the novel without the self? Or so they would have argued back then.

As for the twentieth century, at least in Europe, it has been on the whole more interested in forgetting – forgetting as an organic process, and sometimes a willed act.[1]

Ian Beck

Ian Beck studied illustration and graphic design at Brighton College of Art and became one of Britain's most acclaimed illustrators. His work included the triple gatefold album cover of *Goodbye Yellow Brick Road* for Sir Elton John, and Philip Pullman's *His Dark Materials* trilogy. His first novel for children, *The Secret History of Tom Trueheart, Boy Adventurer* was published in 2006. Two sequels followed, *Tom Trueheart and The Land of Dark Stories*, and *Tom Trueheart and The Land of Myths and Legends*, as well as three other novels.

WRITING IN THE LAND OF STORIES

For my first book, *The Secret History of Tom Trueheart, Boy Adventurer*, I pictured the characters and settings of the story very clearly. I saw it being set in a kind of Grimm's fairy tale central European world. A world of dense dark forests, castles, woodcutters' huts and palaces, a world part constructed from the cinema and from illustrations in old books. The scenery was all courtesy of our collective folk imaginations.

It was also set in its own historic period, a kind of agrarian early nineteenth century. The only research I did of any kind was to read fairy tales for the form and structure and then to imagine the rest and make it all up. The advantage of writing in the Land of Stories lies in its very nonexistence. We are all free to picture and invent it for ourselves. We know the kind of farm carts, hovels, inns and weapons that these pasteboard figures used and inhabited. I had only to animate these elements and throw them all together with a believable young and doubting hero to make a new story out of old, like the lamps in Aladdin.

I have so far written three novels about my character Tom Trueheart. I began with the intention of just writing one. Tom was to be the youngest (12) in a family of seven boys. All of his strapping brothers would be called Jack or at least variations on the name Jack. They live with their fierce and protective mother in a little house in a forest. Their father, also named Jack, went missing on a quest when Tom was a baby. It is the Trueheart family's job to carry out Fairy Tales at the behest of the Story Bureau in the Land of Stories. The Bureau devise a scenario up to a point and then a Trueheart is sent out to find out how the story plays and crucially ends. A story deviser, one Brother Ormestone, goes rogue and attempts to hijack the stories for himself. Only Tom remains free to rescue his brothers and finish the stories.

For me, coming at longer fiction for the first time from writing and illustrating picture books, it was a steep learning curve. I had the advantage of an encouraging agent and a good editor who were both crucial in the initial development of the story. I learned pretty quickly to trust their judgement. I had finished the first draft of the book, (there would be two more drafts), ending with a climactic scene where the hero is reduced to the size of a thumb (Tom Thumb) before confronting the villain.

My editor said that this was not the end but the beginning of another book which would become book two. I had no plans for a book two until she suggested that. You cannot have two books, no more than you can have two wishes, and so a third book was also discussed and eventually written and published. The missing father from book one provided an unplanned but welcome overarching theme/quest to be followed through all three books. *Tom Trueheart* has gone on to be published in over 20 languages.

Madison Smartt Bell

Madison Smartt Bell is the author of 12 novels and story collections. *All Souls' Rising* was a finalist for the 1995 National Book Award and the 1996 PEN/Faulkner Award and winner of the 1996 Anisfield-Wolf award for the best book of the year dealing with matters of race. Together with *Master of the Crossroads* (2000) and *The Stone That The Builder Refused* (2004), it forms a trilogy of the Haitian Revolution. *Toussaint L'Ouverture: A Biography*, appeared in 2007. *Devil's Dream* (2009) is based on the career of confederate Cavalry General Nathan Bedford Forrest. His latest novel is *The Color of Night*. Madison Smartt Bell was one of Granta's 1996 Best of Young American Novelists. He is professor of English at Goucher College, Towson, Maryland.

NOTE ON WRITING HISTORICAL FICTION

'When we speak about the past', wrote William Maxwell, 'we lie with every breath we draw'. Or something like that. I don't remember, not exactly. And that's the problem.

Maxwell's life and mine overlap; he was roughly the age of my grand-parents. I am a Southerner and Maxwell was not, but in some of his work he seemed to share the Southern interest in the past, embracing guilt and pride together, nostalgia and obsession. For the Southerner (of my generation and those immediately before) the past is lodestone to the moral compass. History is for losers, we know; those who win conflicts are free to forget them. Those of us with the historical sense can remove ourselves from present adversity and credit ourselves with a deeper consciousness than those who live for the future can own.

As a young fiction writer I was interested in exploring facets of the present unfamiliar to me. I grew up on a Tennessee farm; my first handful of novels had urban settings, a little London and a lot of New York. Then came a moment when to find something new I had to look backward. Southern history had been well worked over by two generations of writers before me. Any subject can be made new, with sufficient energy and talent, but fresh ground (fresh to me at least) seemed more attractive. Practically no white people in the United States knew anything about the Haitian Revolution in the early 1980s when I first stumbled on it (while looking, of course, for something else). For black Americans it was a different story, but then I didn't know that either at the time.

You can't tell absolute or complete truth even when writing about your own time. The best you can do is record your own perceptions and the limited bits of stuff that you know. Memory, as Maxwell said, is a notorious trickster anyway. The reason this issue matters in fiction, where in theory you can make up whatever you want, is that in the act of writing you have to convince yourself, at least, that your tale has reasonable verisimilitude, if it can't have real veracity. And you want to convince your audience of that too.

At one pole of historical fiction is sheer fantasy – which puts people like us in period costumes and can take considerable liberties with recorded historical 'fact'. At the other pole there is an effort to write accurately about the past and the people who inhabited it. Difficulties: not only are situation and setting unknown at the start (especially at the level of mundane detail – What did these people have for breakfast? How did they fasten their clothes?), but also, those long ago people had sensibilities very different from our own.

It can't be done perfectly, but a conscientious effort can be made. The question becomes, who do you want to persuade and convince? I might have limited my ambition to the American audience, which would know very little about my subject beforehand. In the end I wanted to try to convince Haitians too, and they tend to know their own history rather well. I reached for the latter group and brought in a few.

In this effort I was aided by two coincident phenomena: I have always had a mystical attitude toward inspiration, and in Haiti people never really die; they just become invisible. Spirits of those who've left their bodies are still nearby, available as guides. You can't tell the whole truth about what they thought and did when they walked the earth. But you can try to keep faith with them. I hope that I have.

Ronan Bennett

Ronan Bennett is the author *of Havoc, in Its Third Year*, set in Yorkshire in the 1620s; *The Catastrophist*, set in the Belgian Congo in 1959–60; and *Zugzwang*, set in St Petersburg in 1914. He also writes for film and television.

I have written three historical novels and a number of films and television dramas with historical settings. I have enjoyed cohabiting with my characters in their vanished worlds, imagining the different material cultures, and the *mentalités*. And the languages: that of seventeenth-century England in particular, poetic, tender and robust.

Yet for all this enjoyment I still can never escape feeling that I need to justify what I do. To someone of my generation (b.1956), my nationality (Irish, Belfast), and politics (anti-capitalist), writing fiction can seem like little more than a parlour game, a pleasant diversion from the here and now and all the problems, some of them truly apocalyptic, that we have been busy creating for ourselves over the centuries. And of all the parlour games we play, historical fiction has to be among the most trivial. Historical fiction does not even pretend to be concerned with the state we're in.

William Styron once said that he often felt like delivering his readers an edifying sermon. The trouble, he noted wistfully, is that readers aren't interested in sermons. Who can blame them? When we open a book, we want story, character, and beauty in the language. We want to be intrigued, moved, surprised, even shocked. Insight is good ... but a lecture? That's for the polemicists.

I have the Styron problem. I cannot write without wanting to draw the attention of whoever might care to pick up the book to something I believe they should be thinking about. It's the only way I can justify to myself what I do. It has led me to set stories in the past in order to discuss the present.

When William Cavendish, 1st Duke of Newcastle, was entrusted with the education of Prince Charles, the future Charles II, he advised his pupil: 'What you read, I would have it history that so you might compare the dead with the living; for the same humours is now as was then, there is no alteration but in names'. Newcastle nailed it: 'there is no alteration but in names!' Everything that is happening now has happened before. Religious fundamentalism? Try Germany in the Peasants' War, Florence under Savonarola, England under the early Stuarts. Banking collapse? Try the Fuggers or the Riccardi. If you're interested in what happens when one culture decides its civilisation *must* be adopted by Kipling's 'lesser breeds without the law', there are any number of examples from which to choose: among the more obvious are the wars of Elizabeth and Cromwell in Ireland, and US government campaigns against Native American tribes. The outcomes for the lesser breeds are generally not happy, and are rarely what the zealous civilisers of men and nations set out to achieve.

The idea that there are 'lessons from history' has an old-fashioned, teleo-logical ring which tends to make modern academic historians wince. They are happier telling us what happened and why than – perish the thought – suggesting contemporary resonance. But if you believe as Newcastle did, as I do, that history repeats itself, is it ridiculous to try to learn from what has gone before? Is it absurd to shout jeremiads, that we've been here before and it doesn't end well? Or encouragements when we find a path success-fully trodden before?

Sermons are boring. We twiddle our thumbs. Stories have real power. The best fiction prompts self-interrogation. Historical fiction can bring us up with a jolt, like an eerie *déjà vu*. This is what I tell myself. I hope it's true.

Vanora Bennett

As a journalist, Vanora Bennett became a foreign correspondent and a conflict reporter and worked in Cambodia, Angola, Mozambique and Chechnya. Her fascination with the cultural and religious differences between Russians and the many peoples once ruled by Moscow grew into books on the Chechen war and the illegal caviar trade. She is the author of five historical novels, of which the latest is *Midnight in St Petersburg*.

ON RESEARCH

Researching a historical novel is fascinating. In some ways, it's the best bit. You go into the library with your glimmering of an idea. You order lots of books. You browse. Eventually, Eureka! You open some unpromising-looking volume, and suddenly you're gripped, because what you're finding out about what actually happened is way more exciting than anything you could have imagined. It's the romance of reality.

As you can probably tell, I spend months in libraries. Sometimes that all-important research period has completely changed what I eventually write. When I wanted to do a book about Chaucer, for instance, I got my basic idea from the brick-sized Riverside edition of his work. There I found to my great joy that, in the middle of his highly respectable life, Chaucer was caught up in a medieval version of a tabloid sting.

He was accused by a girl with a wonderfully made-up-sounding name, Cecily Champagne, of rape, or possibly abduction – the Latin word for both is 'raptus'. Cecily, it appeared, was the stepdaughter of the recently dead King Edward III's highly unpopular mistress, Alice Perrers. I went into the library thinking I would be writing a story about Cecily blackmailing Chaucer, with her wicked stepmother's help. But the more I read the more fascinated I got by Alice – a wonderful character, far too entrepreneurial, and the cause of the credit crunch of the fourteenth century, but also earthy, humorous and perhaps the real-life basis for the Wife of Bath. In the end, Alice ran away with me. The book I wrote was all about her. Poor Cecily never got a look-in.

That's the upside of thorough research. Of course there's a downside. It's horribly easy to get so carried away by facts that you forget that a historical fiction is really your character's personal story. As an author, you have to carry your history lightly – figure out your characters' trajectory and weave a few contemporary events into that, without letting the people in your story be crushed by your knowledge of too many other things about the period.

And, oh, how hard I find that. My first drafts are always popping with extraneous facts. It's my great failing. And what a lot of time it wastes, because my second drafts are all about getting rid of the overload. In my latest book, set in the Russian Revolution, the peasant mystic Rasputin has a bit part. I got so fascinated I spent months reading about and writing him. And then I cut almost everything. I had to. It was superfluous to the story I was telling. It still slightly hurts to remember. But the lesson I learned was a good one. Don't forget to read. Use the facts you learn to build a solid stage for your characters. But don't forget to stop, either. Facts are just tools. The people you're writing about need space to move about, breathe and live. Your story's about them.

Tracy Chevalier

Tracy Chevalier grew up in Washington DC and studied Creative Writing at the University of East Anglia. Her novel *Girl With a Pearl Earring* was inspired by Vermeer's painting of the same name and, when filmed, won three Academy Award nominations. Her latest historical novel is *The Last Runaway*, about an English Quaker who moves to rural Ohio and gets involved in the Underground Railroad.

When have I done enough research to start writing an historical novel?

When have I read all the studies relevant to my subject; sought out diaries, notebooks, letters, ephemera; visited locations and soaked up their atmosphere; talked to experts and taken classes; read books and newspapers and magazines contemporary to the period; found information on the Internet from passionate lovers of the subject; looked at paintings, drawings, etchings from the period; visited museums; watched people weave, or quilt, or make hats, or paint.

The short answer? Never. There are still books about Vermeer on my bookshelves that I feel I should read – yet I wrote *Girl with a Pearl Earring* in 1998! In fact, as I look over my books I spot one or two for each novel I've written that I really should have read, and probably never will – though I keep them, just in case. They are my dirty little secret.

There are always more sources that might help me. I could seek out that expert who can explain all about the best straw to use when making a bonnet, or how to take apart a Victorian grave, or how to milk a cow or make cheese. I could read more attentively, take more notes, review those notes more often. It is never enough.

In general my research for a book takes place in four stages:

- the specific subject I've been inspired by: a Vermeer painting, the fossil hunter Mary Anning, the Underground Railroad in pre-Civil War America

- the general feel of the place and time: seventeenth-century Holland, fifteenth-century Paris, eighteenth-century London, Ohio in 1850

- the very specific details that arise from plot demands: How do you make a hat? What flowers are blooming in Ohio in September 1850? What do you see when you walk from Soho to Bedlam in 1793 London?

- the hands-on stuff, where I do what my characters do: make a quilt, find a fossil, weave on a medieval-style loom.

The reality is that there is never enough time, or space in my brain, to do absolutely thorough research. There is the efficient use of time to consider, for one thing. Annie Proulx once gave an account of going to see a knife maker while researching her novel *That Old Ace in the Hole*. She drove eight hours to see him – twice – and got really interested in knives. The result? Two sentences in the book. I could not do that: I don't have Annie's strength of character.

Instead I am always hoping for the perfect research day where I get exactly what I need in a condensed amount of time. It happens rarely: most of the time I get bogged down in the wrong book, or look through an archive and am uninspired. But just occasionally I have a charmed day, and think, 'This is what it's all about.'

Research only takes me so far, however. It is wonderful, the best part of the process of writing a book, I think. And yet, it never quite reaches the mark. After a while, when I've read a lot of books, taken a lot of notes, been places and talked to people and gotten my hands dirty with quilts or fossils or cemeteries, I find I am still searching for something – that imprecise something. The thing moving out of the corner of my eye. The paragraph I read over and over and don't quite understand. The bibliography listing primary sources I just can't get to. The article in an obscure journal I manage to track down and discover doesn't tell me anything. I look and read and sew and breathe in pig shit, yet the itch is not scratched. 'If only I could find just the right book to fill this gap,' I think. 'The article that explains exactly what I need to know.'

When that thought grows loud enough to overwhelm what I'm researching, I know it is time to set aside my notes and start writing. For the book that will explain exactly what I want to know? That is the book I must write.

Lindsay Clarke

Lindsay Clarke is the author of seven novels, including *The Chymical Wedding*, which won the Whitbread Prize for Fiction, *The War at Troy* and *The Return from Troy*.

Whatever the genre in which a fiction writer is working, imagination is the name of the game. Yet, if my own experience is any guide, the imagination works in mysterious ways, and I have found that to be particularly the case when I try my hand at writing about the past.

A case in point is *The Chymical Wedding*, a novel set in a single location but in two time-frames, 1980 and 1848, with a structure reflecting the strange behaviour of quantum particles when two events occurring at different times so influence each other that they appear to happen simultaneously. I've been pleased by responses to the novel which congratulate me on its well-realised texture of Victorian life, but they also leave me feeling slightly fraudulent.

Why should that be so? After all, I had done some research, reading George Eliot's *Amos Barton* for details of life in a provincial parish, and a couple of texts about social change in Victorian England, while picking up several useful details elsewhere. But the most exhilarating times in writing the book, and the most profitable, came not from imitating the past through research but when I felt to be channelling it.

I know that's a disreputable word in this sceptical age, but it's what seemed to happen after I despaired of my ability to do justice to a historical period with which I don't have much sympathy, loosened my immediate control over the writing, and decided simply to let things come. Soon, as all the strongest moments in the Victorian tale unfolded that way, I began to feel more like a pipeline than an engineer. I remember coming out of my study after such mediumistic hours at my desk and saying to my wife, 'I don't know where this stuff is coming from but I hope it keeps coming.'

A similar experience opened the way into writing my Troy books, which were supposed to be a short retelling of the myths but expanded into two long novels as the material revealed itself. So I now prefer to think of what happened as the active power of the imagination, equipped by relevant research, but more deeply informed by the rich resources of the unconscious, where I had probably been working on those books for a considerable time. That, along with whatever other sources of imaginative energy may be available so long as we don't jam the frequencies through which they can reach us.

Another analogy might be with the work of a method actor so completely identified with the part, and so open to whatever presents itself there, that the performance moves through into otherwise unattainable depths of authenticity. (The ancient Greeks would have said that the actor was 'possessed by the god'). The point is that research may furnish you with as much detail as a medieval tapestry, but your book will leap into life only through the mysterious power of a receptive and fully activated imagination. Trust it above all else.

Elizabeth Cook

Elizabeth Cook is a poet, fiction writer and scholar. She is the author of *Achilles* (Methuen and Picador USA), a fiction that also has a performance

life, and is the editor of *John Keats: the Major Works* (Oxford). She wrote
the libretto for Francis Grier's oratorio *The Passion of Jesus of Nazareth*,
jointly commissioned by VocalEssence in Minneapolis and the BBC. The
title poem of her collection, *Bowl* (Worple Press) was a Poem on the
Underground. She is currently working on a novel, *Lux*, set in the reign
of King David and in sixteenth-century England.

NO *NOW* OR *THEN*: IMAGINING THE PAST

Keats is reported to have said 'there is no *now* or *then* for the Holy Ghost'[2]
Any writer who is drawn to imagining the past will recognise the truth of
that. What we imagine, we imagine *now*; experience cannot take place at
any other moment.

I am fascinated and moved by the knowledge that, as human creatures,
we have the same physiological structures and processes as every other
human creature, including those greatly separate from us in time and
space. This is always the place where I start. When I wrote the libretto for
Francis Grier's *The Passion of Jesus of Nazareth*, the recognition of a shared
physicality enabled me to write about Jesus in the Garden of Gethsemane,
drawing his cloak more closely around his shoulders to keep out the cold
of the night (we know from the Gospels that there was a brazier nearby).
It would also be where I would start if I were to set a piece of writing in
prehistory: what is almost inexpressibly touching about works of prehistoric
art such as the 21,000-year-or-so-old bison from Zarysk in the Osetr Valley
in Russia is that it was fashioned by mortal creatures like ourselves and so
clearly represents another recognisable mortal creature. I am correspondingly
troubled by the way in which certain places where great suffering took place
in a distant past can become themed tourist attractions, the real human
suffering of – for example – torture victims in the Middle Ages, reduced to
an 'experience' advertised in Gothic script. One of the virtues of imagination
is that it can extend our capacity for compassion – for other creatures, in
other places and other times. Jeremy Bentham famously said that the great
question regarding our treatment of animals was not 'Can they reason?' but
'Can they suffer?' The reasoning and thinking of past peoples may at times

seem as unlike ours as that of non-human creatures, but the capacity that these peoples had for suffering is the same.

The fact of a shared physicality – with its attendant vulnerabilities and limitations – allowed me to tell the story of Achilles – a story which concludes with the poet John Keats reflecting on the fact of a common anatomy. In the course of writing *Achilles* I spent some time on Pelion, the part of the Greek mainland where Achilles grew up. I wanted to experience the way the light fell on the sea, the scents and sounds in the air, the mix of deciduous and coniferous trees on Mount Pelion (though I expect the mix has changed in 3,000 years). But I also wrote some of it on Shetland – as sea-centred a place as Greece but in other ways very unlike.

From the fulcrum of a shared physicality it is possible to grow into sensing what is different: a different sense of self and other, different reference points. I have a personal rule of *decorum* which prevents me from putting anything into a metaphor which would not have been available at the period in question. For example, '[Achilles] has hooked great Hector's body *like a plough* to the back of his chariot'. It is a stealthy way of building up a world picture.[3]

I considered the possibility of writing *Achilles* in the first person but realised that to do so would suggest an anachronistic degree of self-consciousness in a man whose identity is created by his actions. Voice and lexicon are important. Deliberate anachronism can be witty but nothing can be more jarring than, as so often occurs in filmed costume dramas, an accidentally anachronistic idiom – such as a supposedly nineteenth-century woman saying 'It is *so* not my style'! Of course one cannot write in the exact language or idiom of a very distant or foreign period and still remain comprehensible, but it is important to find a way in which to honour the otherness of that distant world. A sense of strangeness should be present. Walter Benjamin described the act of successful translation as one in which the host language is stretched and changed to accommodate what has not been said in it before. *Translation* simply means a carrying over: what is transported from a distant time and place should not be completely at home in our present but make us see our present and its past in a new and sharper way.

Anne Doughty

Anne Doughty grew up in Armagh and has written 12 novels, all set in Ireland. Nine of them form *The Hamiltons Sequence: The Story of an Ulster Family* from 1860 to 1966.

WINDOWS ON THE PAST

I had no idea that I was writing 'historical fiction' when I first set out to tell a story, but when I began my first novel, *Stranger in the Place*, in the 1970s, using my experiences in a remote area of Co. Clare where I had chosen to do fieldwork for my undergraduate thesis, the world of 1960 which I was re-creating was already part of history. Something similar happened with *A Few Late Roses*. Set in 1968 and not published till 1997, the first turbulence of The Troubles was already documented in the history books. Only in *Summer of the Hawthorn* where the story moved between the twentieth century and the fifth century could I perhaps have guessed that 'historical fiction' was to be my chosen genre.

It was only after my return to Ireland in 1998 and the rapid appearance of a sequence covering a period of over a hundred years in the life of one particular family that I began to ask what had led me in this direction.

To begin with, I probably have to confess to curiosity. Even as a small child I always wanted to understand why things were the way they were. I can remember at some early age standing in the churchyard near my grandfather's forge staring at a tombstone and asking why a child only three years old should have died. Only old people died. What had happened? No one could tell me. Nor could anyone tell me who had lived in the tumbled ruins of cottages I studied so minutely on Sunday afternoon walks.

I should have guessed then. I had always wanted to write, but I had always insisted that my own life was too ordinary, too unadventurous, to provide the material of fiction. It was when I returned to Ireland and began a novel using some autobiographical material from the 1940s that things fell into place and I saw exactly what had to happen.

I could not understand my own life and times if I did not go back and reconstruct the life of my grandparents and great-grandparents. We are the product of our history, as individuals, as communities. As a geographer I had made a close study of people in relation to place; now I had to bring in other dimensions, people in relation to events, social, economic and political.

That was when the tombstones and the ruined houses came back into mind. What I wanted to write was the story of those forgotten people, not those whose names were in the history books, but those who had laboured on the land, or in the mills, those who had emigrated, or returned, who had been involved in events not of their own making, who had lived and loved and faced up to whatever life threw at them, often with a courage that would never be recognised.

From my return in 1998 I had not only the inspiration of the land and its people to encourage me, but the extraordinary resources of the Internet where I could now reconstruct in detail the 'tables and chairs' of everyday life at any point in time, along with the thoughts and feelings my characters might have about a world I could now explore as concretely and in as much detail as I could walk the lanes and fields of my chosen locations.

Sarah Dunant

After writing eight modern thrillers, Sarah Dunant's love of history was rekindled on an extended visit to Florence. *The Birth of Venus* was the first of a series of historical explorations of what it was like to be a woman within the Italian Renaissance. Her most recent book, *Blood and Beauty*, reimagines the Borgia dynasty. Sarah Dunant is a founding patron of the Orange Prize and a teaching fellow at Oxford Brookes University.

DROWNING IN ORDER TO SWIM

At best, historical novelists are time travellers, creating worlds that no longer exist and peopling them with living, breathing characters that both remind us of ourselves and yet are subtly – sometimes dramatically – different.

How do we do it? By time travelling ourselves. Only since the past is tricky to access by conventional transport we have to use other means. Research: a boring word for a wondrous thing, a ticket into that country from which no actual traveller has ever returned: the dead.

I have spent literally years of my life researching, sitting in libraries accompanied with notebooks and a variety of coloured pens, half student and half detective. I start simply: what happened at the time I am interested in? Who did what to whom, when, why and how? (Actually it is never that simple – that is the first wonder). Then, gradually, the questions change. This world I am creating, what did it look, sound, smell and taste like? Its inhabitants – men and women – how did they think, what did they read, what did they wear, what did they believe, what did they eat, what made them ill, what made them well, what were they ashamed of and how did they interact with each other? Science, religion, architecture, education, economics, culture, medicine, superstition, I read it about it all. A footnote in one book takes me to another where the bibliography is a treasure trove. It is not all easy. But these days history is so rich that even the driest works have sparks to kindle fire. Stories, voices, prayers, poetry, court records, inventories, diaries, shopping lists – new history has extended our definition of what is worth studying so that now, if you have the patience to look, almost all of human life is there.

Yes, there are times when it is too much. When I get muddled, lost, when so many facts feel like quicksand sucking me under. But that is part of the job. Eventually this past becomes as insistent as the present, so that even when I not working I am thinking, talking, dreaming it so that soon fragments of characters and conflicts have begun to suggest themselves.

This is not to say the novel writes itself (who ever came up with that dumb idea?) But oh, does it help. And there is another method to this madness. If you know the period – truly, deeply, madly know it – then it will lead you to the surprises that all good novels need to work.

One example. I was a quarter way through *The Birth of Venus* when it occurred to me that one of my characters might be gay. I knew a little – but not enough – about gay culture in the Renaissance. So I plunged back into the library. A single book – a published PhD thesis that had filleted the records of the night police in Florence in the fifteenth century revealed a whole sub-culture of sin, subversion and punishment with deadly political overtones. Not only did I have my character, I also had the most fabulous plot device home grown from history as it had happened.

Research. There is nothing like it.

Michel Faber

Michel Faber is the author of three short-story collections including *The Fahrenheit Twins*, and five novels, including *Under The Skin*, *The Fire Gospel* and *The Crimson Petal and the White*, set in the 1870s. He lives in the Scottish highlands with his wife and cats and thousands of CDs, LPs and cassettes of unpopular music.

I think there are two kinds of historical novelist. The kind who wants to write a novel set in a particular past era because everything was more thrilling and romantic back then. And the kind who wants to write a novel exploring a specific clutch of themes and human conflicts, and who realises that a particular era, which happens to be in the past, is right for this story.

If you want to write a historical novel, I recommend that you decide which of those two kinds you are. If you're the kind that grooves on the Middle Ages or the Victorian period, do your research and then do your best to entertain the fans of that niche. There is no shame in being an entertainer, as long as you're a good one. Wise editors will advise you to use your research like an iceberg: only a small part of it should show, but it should inspire confidence that a vast amount of knowledge is below the surface. All wannabe historical novelists have heard that advice and most of them are convinced they've followed it, but they're often deluded because when it comes down to it, they just can't bear not to show off all the info they've gathered. Try harder. Don't mention the things that people living in that era wouldn't bother to mention. A character who's worried sick about her children or who's hot for sex is not going to admire the ambient architecture or reflect upon Napoleon's invasion of Russia, even if it's 1812. Don't drop names like Michelangelo, Queen Victoria, Copernicus, etc. They are unlikely to be relevant to your characters' existence. Do you think about Gerhard Richter, Queen Elizabeth II or Stephen Hawking in your own day-to-day life? I doubt it.

If you're the other kind of novelist, the kind who just wants to write a great novel regardless of what era it's set in, you don't have to worry as much about over-employment of research. You'll be so preoccupied with characterisation and getting to the heart of human complexity that you're unlikely to get distracted by crinolines or flintlock pistols. You will use whatever historical details help you to illuminate your characters' souls and ignore the rest. When I wrote *The Crimson Petal and the White* – my only 'historical' novel – I needed to work through certain obsessions with harmful parenting, the war of the sexes, the tension between idealism and cynicism, power and disempowerment. It occurred to me that England in the 1870s was a superb context for those concerns. Instead of being a visit to a Victorian theme park, *The Crimson Petal* took real people back in time. It wasn't the first instalment of a franchise, it was a one-off experience.

Whether your aim is to write a one-off or start a franchise, don't foist mediocrity onto the marketplace. There are too many third-rate genre books and too many dull literary novels. We need the trees.

Margaret George

Margaret George is the author of six epic biographical novels, set in the ancient world and Tudor England. They are: *The Autobiography of Henry VIII* (1986), *Mary Queen of Scotland and the Isles* (1992), *The Memoirs of Cleopatra* (1997), *Mary Called Magdalene* (2002), *Helen of Troy* (2006), and *Elizabeth I* (2011). All of these have been New York Times bestsellers. *The Memoirs of Cleopatra* was made into a 1999 Emmy-nominated ABC-TV miniseries. Her books have been translated into 20 languages.

MUSINGS ON THE HISTORICAL NOVEL AND ITS JOURNEYS

When I was a young reader, historical novels weren't sequestered in a niche category, but were read by the general public. Some were more literary than others – Marguerite Yourcenar, Gore Vidal, Mary Renault – but there were many other popular writers, like James Michener, James Clavell and Irving Stone, whose works introduced large numbers of people to wide-ranging subjects: the history of Hawaii, shoguns of Japan, the life of Van Gogh. These were 'pure' historical novels. College textbooks would recommend them as a way of fleshing out the dry facts.

But somewhere along the line, historical novels began evolving, interbreeding, as it were, with other genres. First came the 'women's historical romances' of the 1970s, aka 'bodice-rippers.' After that, a serious writer had to clarify, upon introduction, 'I write historical novels – no, not THAT kind!'

Other cross-breeding offspring were the historical thriller (Dan Brown), the historical mystery (*Brother Cadfael*), and the historical fantasy/time travel (*Outlander* series). A popular new trend now is the dual storyline, in which there is a link of some sort between a character who lived long ago and a modern person (*Possession*). All these hybrids are keeping the historical novel genre alive and well.

But it also has bred confusion. The term 'historical novel' covers a wide spectrum, ranging from the meticulous, fact-perfect sort on one end, to the 'it's fiction – it needn't really have happened that way' on the other.

A perennial subject for debate at writing conferences and interviews is: how much history, how much fiction in our chosen field? Mere accuracy does not ensure that something comes alive, but too much imagination renders it meaningless. Perhaps the truth lies in the old adage 'Something can be accurate but not true; or it can be true but not accurate.' The challenge of the historical novel is to somehow be both true and accurate. But better to be true, if one must choose one over the other.

My own work is anchored firmly at the fact-based pole, because I see what I write – biographical novels – as having an obligation to my subjects to render them as truthfully as possible. I feel that someday I must account to them for any willful distortions. I project myself into their mindset and think how angry I'd be if someone twisted my life around 500 years from now. When I write, my audience is my characters. But, I acknowledge that being such a stickler can certainly shackle creativity. Shakespeare didn't mind changing a few things, and Hotspur hasn't suffered. Even Richard III is more famous than he would have been without Shakespeare.

I feel as if I've actually had the privilege of spending time in the company of Henry VIII, Mary, Queen of Scots, Cleopatra, Mary Magdalene, Helen of Troy and Elizabeth I as I have recreated their lives in fictional drama. Whether they feel the same way is another question!

Philippa Gregory

Philippa Gregory was an established historian and writer when she discovered her interest in the Tudor period and wrote the novel *The Other Boleyn Girl*, which was made into a television drama and a feature film. Now, six novels later, she is looking at the royal dynasty that preceded the Tudors: the Plantagenets, a family of complex rivalries, loves and hatreds.

After years of defending my position as a professional historian who chooses to write fiction I am experiencing something of a revelation. I apologise that it's rather obvious; but it speaks to me – Historical fiction – the definition is in the title. It is historical and it is fiction. It's both.

Obviously this puzzles some people and clearly irritates the irritable, but it has become essential to me that my work should have the form, shape, language and pace of a good novel, and equally be rooted on the accuracy, complexity and thoughtfulness of good history.

In addition, as a feminist and a Marxist my work is always going to be about the unequal distribution of power, and the role of women. This has led me to some half-hidden stories. I was researching for a novel that was going to be about Tudor piracy when I found a document which named a ship: The Mary Boleyn. I checked on 'Mary Boleyn' and found the woman whose story would be the basis of one of my most successful novels: *The Other Boleyn Girl*.

Researching her history was the first essential half of the work. Writing a novel is the second, equally important part. As a woman she was rarely mentioned, not even her birth was recorded. As a discarded mistress she was sometimes described with contempt. To find the history of a woman like her I have to read through a document, sometimes piecing small events together to get a timeline, often turning descriptions on their head – understanding that male contempt often tells me more about the man than the woman he is describing. Thus Henry VIII's eternally-quoted description of Anne of Cleves as being slack-breasted and noisome, tells me a lot about the ill, impotent husband with a festering open wound on his leg. There was a fat smelly person in the royal marital bed, but probably not Anne. To write a historical novel about a woman like her requires me to search for the emotional truth behind the historical facts.

The descriptions of medieval women come from medieval chroniclers. These were, without exception, all men, most of them churchmen in a celibate and misogynistic church which taught that all evil in the world came from the fall of Eve. These descriptions informed all later historians, especially those enthusiastic medievalists, the Victorians, who also had a strong view of the morally weak nature of women. I have to read these caricatures and read through them: to create a new portrait of the woman.

In my more recent work on the Plantagenets I have the greatest challenge: I am arguing with Shakespeare. But he is too good a dramatist to really believe the biased story that his pro-Tudor prejudice forces him to tell. Shakespeare, working for Elizabeth I and her heir James I, had to justify the Tudor usurpation of the Plantagenet throne. He had to blacken the reputation of Richard III. The hunch-backed monster captures a widow who resists him so little that he himself cannot believe it.

'Was ever woman in this humour woo'd? Was ever woman in this humour won?'

I think this is a great give-away line. Shakespeare himself knew that his Lady Anne was passive beyond belief. My Lady Anne, drawing on many of the same historical documents that were available to Shakespeare, is a heroine, choosing her own husband to play in the realpolitik of the royal court, imprisoning her own mother, getting herself to the throne of England, fully aware of the better claims of her nephews in the Tower of London.

But she cannot be a modern character. She fears witchcraft, she sees her first husband die in battle when she is just 15, she consents to the imprisoning of her mother, she dies of TB. She has to be the heroine of a modern novel, but one based on a historical character. The facts have to be accurate, and the fiction has to have the form, shape, language and pace of a good novel.

Katharine McMahon

Katharine McMahon has published eight novels. Her theme has always been to draw powerful women out of the shadows of history. Her

latest, *Season of Light*, was set during the French Revolution. Other novels include *The Crimson Rooms*, about a pioneering woman lawyer, and the bestselling *The Rose of Sebastopol*, which was set during the Crimean War and was shortlisted for the Best Read Award at the Galaxy British Book Awards. *The Alchemist's Daughter* dealt with the clash between ancient and modern science and *Confinement* juxtaposed a modern schoolteacher with her Victorian counterpart. Katharine has worked as an advisory fellow with the Royal Literary Fund and has wide experience of teaching and mentoring, including a Guardian masterclass on historical fiction. www.katharinemcmahon.com

THE HISTORICAL SPARK

There's a particular feeling I have come to recognise; a tingling behind my breastbone when I stumble on something that might be the start of a novel. It is electric, and I presume to do with wires in my emotional and intellectual memory connecting with other elements such as insatiable curiosity and a fear of being left out. I remember two early examples of this frisson. The first is a childhood experience of theatre, when I was taken to see an amateur production of Gilbert and Sullivan at my primary school. Though I have no memory of the show, what I do remember, most vividly, are the grey curtains at the side of the stage between which the performers mysteriously disappeared. Where were they going? I wanted to know. What was happening in that hidden backstage place to which I had no access?

Memory number two is somewhat more literary – a trip to Haworth to view the Bronte parsonage. In those days the house was shabbier and the sisters hovered, a breath away, as I viewed the faded couch upon which Emily had rested her dying head, and one of Charlotte's diminutive frocks. The house allowed me the merest tantalising glimpse into the world of those astonishing girls; the rest I had to imagine.

This is the connective tingle I am seeking to ignite when I write – and read – historical fiction; an imaginative arc which binds me to the past and lets me in. Behind the two experiences I've just described are themes I've explored again and again. What was it like to be one of those historical women we glimpse but cannot fully see – a nurse who travelled out to the Crimea with Nightingale, the daughter of an eighteenth-century alchemist, an English woman who has a Wordsworthian obsession with the Revolution taking place in France, a woman forging a career in the law in 1924? Of course these are not stories, they are ideas. The brew that makes a novel is a potent one consisting of this first spark, the historical context, my own emotional preoccupations, and the story I end up telling.

The trick, I think, is to allow the story to grow from the elements that inspired it. So, for instance, what ignited the spark when I researched Florence Nightingale? Cumbersome gowns, single-minded determination, a bloody and ill-thought out war, rivalry between women, loss and disease, and unrequited love. The story I eventually tell is of a woman who disappears behind enemy lines, and her timid cousin who goes looking for her. Thus, there is a symbiotic relationship between the story and the context. And it's no good being rigid. If I'm truly engaged with my research, I have to be receptive to extraordinary discoveries and interventions. My characters, in their relationship with events – battles, politics, discoveries, arguments, love affairs – will develop a dynamic of their own and they have to be allowed a free rein.

So my recipe for great fiction is to be attentive to the spark, tireless in research, tune in to the emotional connection with my material and thus allow characters to uncover for themselves the mysteries and untold stories of their created and historical worlds.

Valerio Massimo Manfredi

Valerio Massimo Manfredi is an archaeologist, screenwriter and TV host for cultural programmes. He has taught in prestigious universities in Italy and abroad. He has published 15 novels. His 1998 trilogy on Alexander the Great (*Child of a Dream, The Sands of Ammon, The Ends of the Earth*) was published in 39 languages in 75 countries and was bought by Universal Pictures. *The Last Legion* (2002), was made into a major film starring Colin Firth and Ben Kingsley.

STORYTELLING: THEORY AND PRACTICE

All novels are historical because history is everything and everywhere and when we speak of 'historical fiction' we are just accepting a category created by the market in order to classify literary expression (bad or good doesn't make any difference) into genres that are quite captious and questionable. In fact, considering everything that is outside of a generation's memory 'historical' is questionable but quite practical for the publishing business because a book becomes a product with its label, easier to sell and advertise. To give an example: If I set a film in the seventies – even though it is in my generation's memory – it would be a film that would need historical costumes and sets: objects, clothing, autos, TVs, billboards: everything would have to be reconstructed exactly, just as if I had set it in the age of Mark Antony and Cleopatra.

This considered, we must remember that the first examples of historical fiction in our literary tradition were the poems of Homer, the very pillars of Western textuality. The *Odyssey*, in particular, is so incredibly complex, inventive and creative that we can find in it the most modern narrative instruments and panoplias: flashbacks, *coups de théâtre*, suspense, mystery and horror, sex (to pique the reader's attention), extreme realism in scenes of violence, even science fiction! The hero is represented at the start in total impotence and humiliation, having lost his ships and all his companions, even stripped of his clothing, in order to create tension and empathy for him in the reader and make this reader intensely desire to see the protagonist finally make it back home and revenge his family, his honour, his love. Not much else has ever been invented in all these years of story telling.

So, given this challenging model, how can today's so-called historical fiction live up to its past? Exactly and only by being the best piece of literature possible. The art of narrating is as ancient as the human being and was invented to satisfy a deep human need for emotions and adventures as strong and deep as the need for truth, memory and identity which is at the base of history writing. The original storytelling evolved into many other forms of communication through the centuries: epics, prose, theatre, opera, up to the cinema and television of today, but the meaning and the aim remain the same: to communicate emotions and, through emotions, to transmit ethical, existential, religious messages and the like.

We can have different kinds of 'historical fiction'. The most common consists of just setting a story or an adventure in ancient times, a story that might be totally or partially invented. Or, we could have a story that is substantially a narrative translation of a historical event reported by the ancient sources. In the first case, not only the style but also part of the plot is original, while in the second case we can have lots of writers who might be good in style and rhythm of narration but not so much in imagination. Some writers also can try to 'modernise' or reinvent an ancient story in a modern style to make it more reader-friendly, but this is a very delicate operation. Recycling the past is something that was already done in antiquity for many different purposes, from political propaganda to legitimising a dynasty through genealogy, but in modern times it is very easy to fall into anachronistic expressions and concepts which will sound more hilarious than epic or dramatic.

Some rules should always be respected in any case: the accepted historical vulgata cannot be changed and the historical background should be impeccable. This 'background' should include not only objects such as buildings, ornaments, food, clothes, artwork, weapons but also religion, philosophy, ideology, political organisation and even terminology. To give an example: writing something such as 'The pharaoh felt nervous when he woke up that morning' would be nonsense because at the time of the pharaohs nobody knew that a nervous system existed. Or even saying: 'he waited a few seconds ...' because the concept of 'seconds' implies the existence of a watch. Such humoristic expressions nevertheless can be found frequently in many examples of so-called historical fiction.

All these sorts of details are, of course, essential to make the story credible but hardly the most important. A novel could be impeccable in its setting but very modest in literary quality, suffer from a lack of imagination, scarce originality or flatness in conveying emotions, counting merely on the fascination of the classic exoticism of other times and other places. Finally, in historical fiction, as in any other kind of literary expression, what really matters is something that can't be reached only by study and research: talent.

Hilary Mantel

Hilary Mantel CBE won the 2009 Booker Prize for *Wolf Hall*, the first of a trilogy of novels about Henry VIII's minister, Thomas Cromwell, and the court of Henry VIII. The sequel, *Bring Up the Bodies*, was awarded the 2012 Booker Prize and she is currently at work on the final book in the series. In 1974 she began her first historical novel, published in 1992 as *A Place of Greater Safety*, which follows the French Revolution through the lives of Georges Danton, Camille Desmoulins and Maximilien Robespierre.

Those of us who write about the far past, beyond living memory and beyond the reach of recording instruments, have to find a way to give history a human voice. We don't want to misrepresent our ancestors, but we don't want to make the reader impatient. Too much period flavour, and you slow up the story. 'Nay, damsel, be not afeared', may be authentic, but will make your reader giggle. If you give way to an outbreak of 'prithee' and 'perchance', then perchance your reader will hurl the book across the room.

Recently I've been writing about the early Tudor period. We simply don't know how people conversed in that era. Our written sources are mostly official. The letters that are preserved tend to have been kept because they deal with political, legal or financial matters. The tone of private life is largely lost. We may have a record of the public utterances of kings. But we can only imagine how servants talked between themselves, or how the mass of illiterate men and women communicated.

Also, words have changed their meaning since the Tudor era. If I used them now as they were used then, I would confuse the reader. The verb 'let' for example, now means 'permit'; to the Tudors it meant 'forbid.' What we call a clever man, they called a 'witty' man. The challenge goes beyond single words. You need to catch the tone of your chosen age, and to do that you must read as widely as you can in contemporary sources. On the record at least, our ancestors were more formal, more respectful than we are. Nowadays, allowing for educational level, language is egalitarian. In the past, princesses and stable boys did not sound the same.

You must broker a compromise between then and now, and choose a plain style that you can adapt to your different characters: not just to their ages and personalities and intelligence level, but to their place in life. I use modern English, but shift it sideways a little, so that there are some unusual words, some Tudor rhythms, a suggestion of otherness. If the words of real people have come down to us, I try to work them in among my inventions so that you can't see the join. I check the first usage of my vocabulary, but sometimes I let words from 20 years later sneak under the wire; the first written usage may not reflect the first spoken usage.

It can be a distraction to concentrate on individual words. What is vital is to understand the world view of your characters, and reflect it in their speech. They mustn't express ideas they couldn't have had, and feelings they wouldn't have had. They did not draw metaphors from a scientific world view but from a religious one. They weren't democrats. They weren't feminists. The past doesn't respect the sensitivities of the present. The reader should be braced by the shock of the old; or why write about the past at all?[4]

Alan Massie

Allan Massie is one of the UK's most highly regarded literary and historical novelists. His novels include *The Caesars* (1983), *Augustus* (1986), *Tiberius* (1991), *Caesar* (1993), *King David* (1995), *Antony* (1997), *Nero's Heirs* (1999), *Arthur the King* (2003), *Caligula* (2004) and *Charlemagne and Roland* (2007). His latest books are *Life & Letters*, a collection of his Spectator columns, and *Dark Summer in Bordeaux*, part of a crime series set during the Second World War. He lives in the Scottish Borders.

Everyone knows L. P. Hartley's line: 'The past is a foreign country: they do things differently there.' He was no more than half right, if even that, you may say. They fell in love in the past. They lied and cheated and betrayed in the past. They fought and went to war. They struggled for power. They suffered. They displayed courage and kindness. They were born, lived and died.

This is one way of saying that writing a novel set in the past is not essentially different from writing one set in the present.

Yes, the past is another country, but one in important respects like our own. We can't visit it physically as we can visit the USA or Australia, but we can visit it in our imagination. We recognise there are differences, but then there are differences between life in the United Kingdom and life in Africa or China. Some writers move to and fro geographically; others back in time. Writing any novel is a voyage of exploration for the writer, and, one hopes, for the reader too.

A novel is a novel is a novel. I've written more than 20 of them, some set in the here and now, some in the still recent past – the mid-twentieth century – one in the Middle Ages, half a dozen in late-Republican and early Imperial Rome, three in a largely imaginary Dark Ages. I called these three Romances, rather than novels, because of the freedom from historical fact I allowed myself.

Essentially however, the writer's problems are the same, whatever the period or setting. You have a situation to be developed and a story to be told. You have characters to inhabit, dramatic conflicts to devise. Historical events may determine your structure, but need not constrain you. You choose a period because it interests you, just as you might set a contemporary fiction in Paraguay because that country interests you.

It is hard to avoid the word 'genre' and yet one would like to. In writing about Roman emperors, for instance, I was interested in trying to examine the effect that possessing great power may have on the character. This isn't a remote question. When Ford Madox Ford in *The Fifth Queen* trilogy and Hilary Mantel in her novels about Thomas Cromwell bring Henry VIII's court to life, they are writing about the naked and treacherous politics of power. Ancient Rome, Tudor England, Stalin's Kremlin; they do things much the same in all of them.

Ian Mortimer

Ian Mortimer is a qualified archivist and a historical novelist (as James Forrester) as well as a historian. His specialism is developing innovative approaches to writing about the past. He is best known as the author of the *Time Traveller's Guides* – books about life in medieval and Elizabethan times as if you could actually go there.

THE RELATIONSHIP BETWEEN HISTORICAL FICTION AND HISTORY

It's a story I've told before but it's worth repeating. My brother – who works for the London Fire Brigade – was leafing through one of my books. A colleague asked him what he was reading and, on being told, announced that he too was a historian. 'Oh, really?' said my brother, 'What's your specialist period?' 'The Peninsular War?' replied his colleague. 'I've read every single one of the *Sharpe* novels.'

I like this little exchange because it indicates that the relationship between historical fiction and history is not a single point of interchange but a very wide spectrum. At one end, there is the idea that historical novelists impart historical knowledge. At the other, there is a conviction that the two are completely separate, as if by writing fiction, novelists forego any claim to historical verisimilitude. Clearly, some historical novels are less historical than others. But that is not saying much when both historical fiction and history are on independent sliding scales in relation to the actual past.

For the public, the relativeness of history is a difficult concept to grasp. People have a much stricter view of whether something is 'historical' or not if it is a non-fiction title. Anything deviating from the academic consensus is often portrayed as simply 'bad' history. However, much historical writing is just like fiction in that it can be (and usually is) only partially and tangentially related to past events, and our understanding of these is always filtered through the modern eye. History is not just a series of facts that have to be arranged in the right order. There are dozens of contrasting interpretations of the conflict between Richard II and Henry IV, for example. You could write that story from the point of view of every single person then at court – and no one point of view would be truer than another. As E.H. Carr famously pointed out over 50 years ago, if the past is an unchanging mountain that is not to say it does not appear to change – when we look at it from different angles.

Alternatively, consider an old beam in the living room of a 400-year-old cottage. People know that beam represents much more than a structural support. It speaks of a different age, or lastingness. When academic historians talk about 'the past, which has gone', they tend to forget that, for many of us, the past is all around us. It can no more be treated as 'gone' than it can be pretended that a listed building is brand new. Moreover, to describe that beam being laid in place might be impossible in the strict academic sense. But an intelligent, fictional narrative – based on historical and practical experience – can fill the gap. That fictional account, even if conjectural, will be far closer to the truth of the event than an academically correct statement that 'there is insufficient evidence to comment'.

For me, as both a historical novelist and a historian, the questions of 'what historical fiction is' and 'what history is' come together in that beam. This is because what is 'historical' – be it fact or fiction – is not primarily about the past. It is about us and our awareness of time. If you are interested in the human race, in people, this is essential. How can you understand what society can endure without reference to an event such as the Black Death or slavery? How can you appreciate the cruelty of mankind without reference to the Romans, the Crusades, the Holocaust or Stalin's purges? You have to have a historical view of mankind to understand what we are, in all our dark secrets as well as our pride and splendour.

Kate Mosse

Kate Mosse is a novelist, playwright, non-fiction and short-story writer. Her books include the No. 1 international bestselling Languedoc Trilogy – *Labyrinth, Sepulchre* and *Citadel* – as well as *The Winter Ghosts*, set after the Great War. Her first collection of short stories – *The Mistletoe Bride & Other Ghostly Tales* – comes out in October 2013. The Co-Founder and Honorary Director of the prestigious Women's Prize for Fiction, she was awarded an OBE in 2013.

THE PLEASURES AND PITFALLS OF TIME-SLIP FICTION

I write historical time-slip adventure novels, though there is no such category on the bookshelves, virtual or solid. With pure historical fiction, the most important requirement is to be able to conjure up an authentic vision of the period about which one is writing – language, food, customs, clothes, place. The reader must believe themselves there. Adventure stories, although sometimes historical, are just as likely to be set in the present day – *King Solomon's Mines*, a 'lost-world' adventure novel – was almost contemporary when it was published in 1885. Adventure fiction must have excitement and momentum. There are certain traditions that are common to all the great adventure novels: a hero (mine are women rather than men), the character who carries the story and who we trust will survive any number of risks to triumph in the end. There must be jeopardy and danger; a clear sense of right and wrong; often a quest at the heart of things. As with historical fiction, there will be a strong sense of places, a multi-layered and textured fictional world, so vivid the reader will imagine themselves there.When you add time slip to the mix, the best pleasures and pitfalls of historical fiction and contemporary adventure combine.

So what is a time slip? Usually, there will be two periods of time brought to life on the page – although of course there can be more. Sometimes, one will be historic and one contemporary – this is what I did in the first two novels of my Languedoc Trilogy – although both can be historic. Often, the dual storylines evolve hand in hand, with the present-day characters discovering an intriguing past that emerges from documents or dreams. In *Labyrinth*, my contemporary hero, Alice Tanner, finds herself linked to my medieval hero, Alaïs, by virtue of being in the same place – Carcassonne. In 2005, she finds objects that had belonged to – had been held by – Alaïs in 1209.

In *Sepulchre*, the time slip is between 1891–96 and 2008. The historical characters – neighbours of Claude Achille Debussy as it happens – are trapped in their *fin-de-siècle* era of steam trains and syphilis, penury for many, prosperity for some. My modern hero Meredith is intelligent, strong-willed, attractive and adrift. Again, it is the spirit of place that connects them and brings them together, as well as a piece of music and a deck of Tarot cards.

In *Citadel*, the third in the Languedoc Trilogy, there is no echo or parallel set of characters and the adventure elements of the plot are stronger than the time slip. The novel is set in fourth-century Gaul and in Carcassonne during the Occupation of 1942–4. Sandrine, the leader of a women's resistance unit, has no connection with the fourth-century monk who is carrying a precious religious text to safety, but again they inhabit the same physical space, though separated by more than a thousand years. Here, the time slip is both place, of course, but also emotion – the parallels in the emotional lives of the characters who lived in the two different time periods, both eras of great instability, of invasion and occupation and collaboration.

The key element in time slip is that both periods of history happen live on the page before the readers' eyes. Many historical novels have flash-backs – as does much contemporary fiction – but this is not a trick of time slip. Time slip novels are an invitation for the reader to choose the epoch and the characters with whom they most identify, in whom they are most interested. Because, in truth, we all inhabit a time slip. As we go about our daily business, we are accompanied by the thoughts and feelings, the hopes and memories of our pasts. They shape how we behave and think and feel. History is a part of who we are – personal history and the greater forces that have shaped us.

The challenges of writing historical time-slip fiction (adventure or otherwise) are obvious: for example, will there be too many characters for the reader to care enough about any of them? Will one period of history be more engaging, more exciting on the page than the other? Will the reader get frustrated by getting settled into one story line, one set of characters, only to find themselves whisked away just as things are getting inter-esting? Will the author succeed in bringing the two storylines together in a climax that is satisfying and coherent? Will one historical period outshine the other?

For me, though, the pleasures far outweigh the pitfalls. All the challenges listed above are great opportunities. If you pull these things off, then it is the most satisfying and exhilarating kind of writing to engage with. I can inhabit the past, discover it, enjoy it, but also reflect upon it from the present. With two casts of characters and parallel storylines, nothing is dull. There is a sense of the big sweep of the epic – if you like, opera rather than *lieder*.

In a way, time slip fiction is simply a matter of art imitating life. As a novelist writing in the early years of the twenty-first-century, my sense of 'how things used to be', the reality of the history against which I set my adventures, is obviously shaped by now – by how things are and by who I am. The past casts a long shadow and the hindsight of being able to reflect upon the past, even as you are putting that past on the page, allows for romance and celebration. And when you add this to adventure and history – battles, heroes and villains, emotions of love and sacrifice and honour, lost worlds and hidden civilisations – there is no more rewarding fiction to try to write.

Charles Palliser

Charles Palliser has published four works of fiction including the historical novels *The Quincunx* (1989) and *The Unburied* (1999). His new novel, *Rustication,* is set in the 1860s and is published by W. W. Norton in 2013. Before becoming a full-time writer in 1990, he taught literature and creative writing in universities in the UK and the USA.

BEYOND QUAINTNESS

Can the historical novel be more than an opportunity for the writer to exploit the quaintness and colour of a past period? Is it inherently escapist or can it offer insights into both the earlier period and our own in a way that nothing else can?

The novel of the past 200 years has played a crucial role in defining the 'self' – the concept of a consciousness directing our lives by making choices involving emotional, moral and political judgements. That 'self' has, of course, evolved over the period – not least because of the impact of Freud. To read Jane Austen, George Eliot, Henry James, Virginia Woolf and Saul Bellow is to study the history of consciousness, conscience, sexuality, etc. A modern novelist can therefore achieve a very intriguing effect by creating what looks like a novel of, say, the Victorian period (in that it represents that world as we think we know it and uses the conventions and the language of that age to do so) and then disconcerting the reader by showing things that an author of that time would not have depicted and being explicit about matters which were off-limits.

Sarah Waters has done that to superb effect in *Affinity* and *Fingersmith* which take their heroines into prisons and madhouses and depict lesbian relationships. I attempted the same in my first novel, *The Quincunx,* in which the hero discovers his mother working as a prostitute, finds himself consigned to a madhouse and later earns his living as a scavenger in the sewers under London.

The modern novelist is thereby showing us parts of the picture which readers of the time knew were there but did not expect to be shown. But because the writer has chosen the 'strait-jacket' of Victorian conventions, something even more illuminating emerges: an exploration of the ways in which the 'self' of someone born in the early nineteenth century is not like ours. So although my hero sees and experiences social injustice and gross abuses of human rights, he does not have our reaction. With his ingrained assumptions about class and gender, he accepts as inevitable situations that seem intolerable to us. (Just as our descendants will, probably, be horrified by our complacency about the imbalance between rich and poor nations.) And the irony is not necessarily working against my hero. He has stronger concepts of loyalty, duty, and community than our age. And he holds a notion of human nature which it would be patronising to call 'innocent' and fairer to see as unreductive. He doesn't know, for example, what Freud has made us all assume about close mother–son relationships.

By pretending to write as a contemporary of Dickens, the modern novelist can throw into relief the unspoken assumptions of that period, but, more importantly, tease the reader into seeing that the 'truths' that our own age accepts are similarly the product of changing conventions.

Orhan Pamuk

Orhan Pamuk was awarded the Nobel Prize in Literature in 2006. His novels include *The White Castle, The Black Book, Snow* and *The Museum of Innocence*. *My Name Is Red* was awarded Prix du Meilleur Livre Étranger in 2002, the Premio Grinzane Cavour in 2002 and the International IMPAC Dublin Literary Award in 2003. Pamuk is Robert Yik-Fong Tam Professor in the Humanities at Columbia University, where he teaches comparative literature and writing. A prominent campaigner for human rights, he jointly proposed The European Writers' Parliament with José Saramago. He lives in Istanbul.

The real hero of *My Name is Red* is the storyteller: Every night he goes to a coffeehouse to stand next to a picture and tell a story. The saddest part of the book is his sorry end. I know how this storyteller feels – the constant pressure. Don't write this, don't write that; if you're going to write that then put it this way; your mother will be angry, your father will be angry, the state will be angry, the publishers will be angry, the newspaper will be angry, everyone will be angry, they'll cluck their tongues and wag their fingers; whatever you do, they interfere. You might say, 'So help me God,' but at the same time you'll think, I am going to write this in such a way that it will make everyone angry, but it will be so beautiful that they'll bow their heads. In a cobbled-together demi-democracy like ours, in this society so riddled with prohibitions, writing novels puts me in a position not altogether different from my traditional storyteller's; and whatever the explicitly political prohibitions might be, a writer will also find himself hemmed in by taboos, family relations, religious injunctions, the state, and much else. In this sense, writing historical fiction speaks of a desire to put on a disguise.

One of my main preoccupations in *My Name is Red* was the question of style. Style, as I understand it today, is a post-Renaissance concept embraced by Western art historians in the nineteenth century, and it is what distinguishes each artist from all others. But to dramatise the singularity of a particular artist's style is to encourage a cult of personality. Persian artists and miniaturists of the fifteenth and sixteenth centuries are not known for their individual styles but for the reigning shah, the workshop, the city in which they worked.

The central issue of *My Name is Red* is not the East–West question; it is the arduous work of the miniaturist: the artist's suffering and his complete dedication to his work. This is a book about art, life, marriage and happiness. The East-West question is lurking somewhere in the background...

If you ask me, *My Name is Red*, at its deepest level is about the fear of being forgotten, the fear of being lost. For 250 years, under the influence of the Persians, from the time of Tamburlaine to the end of the seventeenth century – after which Western influence changed things – the Ottomans painted, for better or worse. The miniaturists challenged the Islamic prohibition against representation from the sides and the corners. Because they did their small paintings to illustrate books printed for sultans, shahs, potentates, princes and pashas, no one questioned this. No one saw them. They stayed inside books. The shahs were the greatest admirers of such work... Afterward, this fine art was cruelly lost and forgotten – such is the merciless power of history – supplanted by Western post-Renaissance ways of painting and seeing, especially in portraiture. This was simply because Western ways of seeing and painting were more attractive. My book is about the sorrow and tragedy of this loss, this erasure. It is about the sorrow and pain of lost history.[5]

Edward Rutherfurd

Edward Rutherfurd was born in England, in the cathedral city of Salisbury. Educated locally, and at the universities of Cambridge, and Stanford, California, he worked in political research, bookselling and publishing. After numerous attempts to write books and plays, he finally abandoned his career in the book trade in 1983, and returned to his childhood home to write *Sarum*, a historical novel with a ten-thousand year story, set in the area around the ancient monument of Stonehenge and Salisbury. Four years later, when the book was published, it became an instant international bestseller, remaining 23 weeks on *The New York Times* Bestseller List. Since then he has written five more bestsellers and his books have been translated into 20 languages.

NOVELS AND PROPAGANDA

Writing has the power to disseminate ideas. Those of us who write novels, or make movies, may have the ability to reach a large, and often worldwide audience. We've been given a wonderful gift. But it's a dangerous gift, as well.

Novels aren't dangerous, you might say: They're only stories; nobody takes them too seriously. And that may be true.

But that's just the problem. If I read a newspaper article, or listen to the radio, I know that the account may be biased. But when I read a novel, I'm just enjoying the story. I may be critical if it makes some outrageous claim, but generally my guard is down. And that's where the propaganda may be lurking.

It's not just the information we novelists provide – when a battle happened, or a queen was killed, and why. It's who we choose as heroes and villains, the attitudes expressed by our characters, the assumptions that underlie our telling of the story – all these seep out, in subtle ways, into the mind of the reader. We may be helping to create or fortify prejudices.

An example often cited is the anti-semitism to be found in the otherwise enjoyable works of John Buchan (*The Thirty-Nine Steps*). While it may seem unfair to single out Buchan in a period when a degree of anti-semitism was endemic in most of Europe's upper classes, the criticism is that, precisely because he was such a popular novelist, Buchan contributed to the acceptability of the anti-semitic idea.

And what is so terrible is how long these ideas can last. Take the example of a popular tract, this time, rather than a novel – but a tract that was pure fiction. In 1641, there was a revolt in the province of Ulster, in Ireland. For reasons that were complex, numerous Catholics rose against the Protestants in the Ulster plantations. The Protestants retaliated. The fighting was bloody and, between the two sides, perhaps 5,000 people died. Yet not long afterwards, a pamphlet appeared in England which, making no mention of the Protestant killing of Catholics, alleged that the Irish Catholics had risen and murdered over 300,000 innocent Protestant men, women and children. (This would have been greater than the total Protestant population of Ulster). Not only was this tract believed – Cromwell's men imagined they were avenging this stupendous crime – but it became part of popular myth. Two centuries later, in Victorian times, it was still being quoted in the British Parliament as an example of why the Irish were not fit to govern themselves.

The writers of novels and the makers of movies, therefore, need to beware. If we misrepresent the historical record, we may be contributing more than we ourselves imagine to the way that our readers consciously or subconsciously think about the world. If, in a movie, we say that the English burned a congregation of American colonists alive in their church – which never happened – then we are making propaganda. If I were to write that at the start of the Second World War, the French collapsed and failed to fight against the Germans, I should equally be making propaganda – the French fought bravely and took huge casualties. If, conversely, I wrote a romantic story about how the whole of French society was secretly in the Resistance under German occupation, and that the deportation of Jews from France was a purely Nazi affair, then, sadly, I should also be misleading my readers.

There's still room for endless invention – that's what storytelling is all about. But we writers had better be careful. We may not wish it, but we can't avoid the uncomfortable fact: Every historical novel, potentially, is propaganda.

Manda Scott

Manda (MC) Scott was a veterinary surgeon until she took to writing full-time at the turn of the millennium. She began with contemporary thrillers and then moved back in time. Her historical novels include the bestselling *Boudica: Dreaming* series and the *ROME* quartet of first-century spy thrillers. She has been shortlisted for the Orange Prize and the Edgar Awards and her novels have been translated into 19 languages. She is founder and current Chair of the Historical Writers' Association.

WRITING HISTORY, WRITING FOR NOW

> *The past is a foreign country: they do things differently there.*
> L. P. Hartley

Indeed. Not only is the past a foreign country, but it is one we can only possibly view through the lens of our own experience.

In writing the *Boudica* series, I read several academic papers deconstructing the meaning of a particular piece of jewelry. It was, respectively, a necklace, a bracelet or a brooch. It was shaped in concave fashion to act as a receptacle for makeup, and was therefore worn solely by women of a pro-Roman bent; or it was shaped thus for the grinding of woad and was therefore worn solely by anti-Roman men; it was phallic; it was vulval; it was meaninglessly decorative.

It was, in short, whatever best fitted the authors' prejudices.

Similar reading of a doctoral thesis on the midden remains of the Eceni revealed that, while our ancestors might have thrown away items adorned with the feathers of swans and geese (white birds of sky and water), or crows and ravens (black birds that feast on the dead), there was never a single recorded instance of anything decorated with magpie feathers – a bird of carrion which is clad in both black and white. We can infer from this what we like about life and death and taboo, but the underlying fact is as secure as the ash layer in the foundations of Colchester: there were no magpies (nor were there otters); there was a fire.

We were, in fact, an outstandingly creative culture, those of us who lived on this land in the late, pre-Roman, Iron Age: our goldwork was unmatched by anyone anywhere in the world for at least another 800 years. And, if the Roman records are even vaguely correct, we were producing more grain in the South-East of England in the time before the Roman invasion than at any subsequent time up until the end of the First World War, when agriculture ceased to be a massively labour intensive occupation and became instead the steady transformation of oil into food.

We could argue – and I do – that a culture which can spare so many man-, woman- and child-hours to tend the fields, train the horses, work the gold, silver, iron, is not a culture in which every able-bodied individual is training for war and running raids on the nearby tribes.

Thus the image of hide-wearing barbarians constantly at war which was so carefully fostered by Rome, may be less than accurate. We can't prove it, though, and I freely admit that my own inner prejudice wants us to have been more equal, more creative, more shamanic than Rome. I particularly want the women to have been warriors, and just because Julius Caesar tells us they were, doesn't mean they weren't. Just this once, he might have been telling the truth.

And if he was, then the construction of a historical fiction becomes more than simply a story of dead white men (or women) and the battles they fought. It becomes a tale of who we were before the modern profit motive took over, before we lived in nuclear families where the ownership of a woman was passed by law from her father to her husband on her marriage out of the family home, before our gods taught us that we had dominion over all the earth.

Before all of that, we were other. And so a history becomes a lens through which we see who we were, in order to build a vision of who we might become. Because why else would we write history?

Adam Thorpe

Adam Thorpe is the author of ten novels – including *Ulverton, Nineteen Twenty-One, The Rules of Perspective* and *Hodd* – two short-story collections and six poetry volumes. *Ulverton* is a Vintage Classic; *Hodd* was shortlisted for the inaugural Walter Scott Prize for Historical Fiction. His translation of Flaubert's *Madame Bovary* appeared in 2011, and of Zola's *Thérèse Raquin* in 2013.

I have never felt comfortable with the term 'historical fiction'. Several of my novels have been set in the past, both recent and far-off, but the past is not history. History recalls a miniscule number of lives, things, objects, experiences: what has happened to all those peasants, or shopkeepers, or jugglers, or wig-makers? Silence. Fiction makes up for this. Where history gives up for lack of evidence, imagination begins.

My first novel, *Ulverton*, was the account of 12 generations of a village in the guise of 'real' documents, starting in the seventeenth century. Loss and distortion were its main themes: the flickery, elusive nature of survival. The chapters (except for the first) are written in the language of their time, including dialect or scraps of barely literate letters. I had read plenty of obscure documents as part of my research, and there were moments when I felt as if I had actually lived their period in another life. This was, I realised, due to the language. I wasn't reading about, I was reading in.

The strongest period scent came when I went to the Public Record Office and unrolled the original 1830 depositions of the rural 'Captain Swing' rioters, protesting against machines and starvation wages. The lawyer's clerk had scribbled down what the farm labourers were saying, and traces of their speech, their real voices, were left like bits of straw in the scrawled roughs, before being tidied up for the neat versions that would condemn many of the accused to exile in Van Diemen's Land.

I once bought a set of nineteenth-century perfume salesman's unopened sample cards in a flea-market; I went home and sniffed the nineteenth century – heady, rose-scented, different – like an addict. The act of reading obscure bits of non-contemporary English was similarly potent. It happened again when I decided to write a novel about an 'authentically' brutal Robin Hood. I'd always had a soft spot for the Middle Ages. My research demolished various received ideas: woodland was patchy, people's teeth (unmined by sugar) were not that bad, it felt crowded, roads were busy, no one went out at night, the liver was the seat of love, tiny demons came out of your mouth when you were whipped because they felt pain, too.

Received ideas are not good history, and they make for bad fiction, which should be going beyond history into the present tense of the past, the immediacy of how that past felt to those who were its flesh and blood, whose sole reality was that particular time. I was losing my personal idea of the Middle Ages and passing into something altogether stranger, tenser, and ultimately unknowable. How to convey all this strangeness as if it was totally normal, while at the same time framing it in its own vanished wraiths? Despite my love of Middle English – all that supple, glottal music, like splashes of authentic mud – I could hardly write a whole novel in it. Much of what I was reading, however, had been translated over the last hundred years – from the Latin. So I hit on the solution: *Hodd* would be a translation from a soiled Latin manuscript, complete with footnotes and missing fragments, in the tradition of Horace Walpole's *The Castle of Otranto*.

Now I could look out from within the period. The peculiarly pragmatic poetry of the medieval vision was left undiluted. The linguistic restraint of this approach – I was determined to remain within the reduced lexical field of a monastic chronicler – liberated me. Dialogue would not be orally 'realistic'; incident would have to seem artlessly recalled... and the characters likewise. At last, after five years of wandering, I had smelled my way back.

Stella Tillyard

Stella Tillyard read English Literature at Oxford University. Her PhD on twentieth-century art criticism, completed in 1985, was published as *The Impact of Modernism* in 1987. In 1981 she became Knox Fellow at Harvard and subsequently taught English Literature and Art History there and at University of California, Los Angeles (UCLA). She moved to Florence, Italy, in 1993. *Aristocrats*, her biography of four eighteenth-century sisters was published in 1994, won the History Today Award, the Fawcett Prize and the Meilleur Livre Étranger and was made into a BBC/WGBH Masterpiece Theatre series in 2000. Two further biographies followed. In 2005 she became visiting scholar at the Centre for Editing Lives and Letters at Queen Mary, University of London, where she taught the history and practice of biography. Her first historical novel, *Tides of War*, is set against the backdrop of the Peninsular War.

Henry James famously disliked the historical novel; the reader, he complained, could always hear the creaking of the scenery. Besides, the modern mind could not erase enough of itself to get back to any past state of consciousness. 'It's all humbug', he growled and threw up his hands.

I think any writer of historical fiction will probably want to take this on and ask the question, Why a historical novel? What is it wanting to say? What, in other words, does the historical element deliver? It is easy, once plunged into the writing, to forget this, or not to ask the question at all, or feel that it doesn't really matter. Many people, after all, want to buy historical fiction. Is it for writers to ask why, or interrogate their own craft to death? But it nags at me, James's proscription, and, besides, it seems to me that any writer, whatever they write, needs clarity of purpose.

We know, or think we do, what the historical novel is not. It is not a way of telling history: we have historians to do that. It is not biography either, the telling of a life story. But already, matters are not so simple, especially now, when the historical novel is in one of its periodical moments of flowering. I have listened, covertly sometimes, on buses and trains or in libraries and cafes, to people talking about their reading, and it's obvious that many readers are happy to learn about the past, and about past lives, from historical novelists. 'Stop', I have wanted to say, 'It's fiction, and that means it's made up; it's not true'.

But this use made of historical fiction – that it offers a window into a lost world – is now one I don't think should be so easily condemned. In the first place readers manage a willing suspension of disbelief. They know and don't know that historical fiction isn't true, and that there is a boundary line somewhere, though it's not quite clear where, between history and fiction, and they are unworried by it. I no longer feel, as I sometimes did when I was exploring the boundary from the historical side, that that way madness lies. The past is out there in odd things we call facts, which, like the Higgs-Boson particle, we know to exist although we cannot see or feel them. History is the matter we make of those particles. We live in it and it in us; it changes its shape all the time as it moves through us. Just as any distinction between body and consciousness makes no sense, so no distinction between past and present really has any validity. History is us.

The past, then, is not the setting or the scenery; it is part of character itself. So the historical novel is always about the present, not just in the sense that the past is always filtered through a present consciousness, but also in the sense that the past makes us who we are. This is true at both a group or national level and for us as individuals. Our own sense of self is a largely historical narrative woven from ascertainable facts and all sorts of stories. So we are all historical novelists, existing in narrative, constantly telling and retelling past stories even as we experience the present.

In this sense I'd say there is really no such thing as the historical novel, though we will continue to categorise certain kinds of writing in this way. There is a novel set in the past or a novel set in the present; and there is just the novel, good or bad. What James complained about really was not so much the use of the past, but the use of scenery at all. James's scenery was firstly minimal and secondly usually symbolic. That is to say, James was not a realist, or not, in the end, a realist in the Anglo-Saxon tradition.

Here, I think, we are closing in on the nub of the question of what the historical novel can actually do. The English novel, or the novel in English, has always had a realist bias, and has never been strong on stylistic innovation or the depiction of great, abstract, forces. There is nothing in the English language tradition equivalent to the outpouring of allegorical, surrealist and linguistically experimental literature that came out of (mostly central) Europe between the two World Wars. Perhaps the only great, and recognised, English language novel that connects vitally to that tradition is *Tristram Shandy*, and my hunch is that it is rarely attempted by readers outside universities, and equally rarely finished. Similarly, many readers get more kudos than pleasure from *Ulysses*, let alone *Finnegan's Wake* – but then, *Ulysses* is really an Austro-Hungarian novel, and *Finnegan's Wake* arguably a French one.

Ironically – given the flapping scenery James so disliked and readers get so much from – I think this, perhaps, is where the historical novel comes in. Shorn of the need to place characters within a contemporary setting, which removes them from the general and necessarily sites them in the particular, the historical novel in English can actually tell stories that are universal, even archetypal. Rather like opera, with its often absurd sets and costumes, it can tell stories of forbidden love and callous betrayal, capricious fate and terrible revenge. Yes, *Carmen* is ridiculous, but it's also great.

Finally, a great historical novel is really, in the end, a great novel. Except in cases where its *raison d'être is* primarily to deliver ideas – we might (just) put *The Radetsky March* or *The Siege of Krishnapur* into this category – the scenery, after a few years, will fall away, leaving the characters to speak for themselves. How do we know that? Ironically, Henry James himself offers the proof. The book James dubbed, with exasperation and affection, 'the baggy monster', *War and Peace*, arguably the greatest of them all, is, though we often forget it, a historical novel.

Rose Tremain

Restoration (1989), set during the reign of Charles II, tells the story of Robert Merivel, an anatomy student and Court favourite, who falls in love with the King's mistress. The novel won the Angel Literary Award, the Sunday Express Book of the Year award and was shortlisted for the Booker Prize for Fiction. It was made into a film in 1996 and the sequel, *Merivel*, was published in 2012. Rose Tremain was educated at the

Sorbonne and is a graduate of the University of East Anglia, where she taught creative writing from 1988–95. Her publications include novels, plays and short-story collections.

History might be described as the accumulation of the known. But I take seriously the historical novelist's duty to surprise with the unknown. If the reader doesn't marvel a bit at what the writer has dared to invent, as well as by what she has discovered in her researches and set down, then that reader may quickly weary of the whole endeavour and decide to take refuge in history or biography to find out 'what really happened'. I have termed this weariness 'biographical unease' and I frequently suffer from it myself, when ploughing through the many fictionalised historical chronicles which come through my letter box year on year.

For this reason, I favour in my own work the invented protagonist as hero or anti-hero over the known historical character. The known characters may come into the story, but I like to see them always through the eyes of the fictional ones, so that they make take on a persona which transcends that which history has bequeathed to them. In my linked novels, *Restoration* (1989) and *Merivel* (2012), King Charles II has a profoundly important role to play in the story, but because he is only and ever seen through Merivel's eyes, the reader understands that this is one man's subjective perception of Charles II, in which he may become many different people: adored friend, father figure, imperious Caesar, fragile depressive, vile seducer, god. The question 'Did this really happen in Charles's life' is, thus, never the primary one to be asked.

To create this Charles, however, I spent long months researching his life. You can't embark on a fiction set in historical time without knowing that time very well. But as many authors – including Kipling and Graham Greene – have perfectly understood, the research has to undergo a process of alchemy or imaginative absorption before a lick of it touches the page. Kipling called this process 'riddling the fire' – letting the pallid, importunate flames of data be reduced to red hot coals by the power of the writer's imagination. Greene talked about the importance of 'forgetting' in the research process, so that the mind selects only what it remembers in a vibrant way and lets the rest drift away, unused.

books. That wasn't me, though: after reading my first historical novel at 14, I began scouring the history shelves at the City of London School to find out the truth – and I've been searching for it ever since.

Louisa Young

Louisa Young's novel, *My Dear, I Wanted to Tell You*, was shortlisted for the Wellcome Trust Book Prize and Costa Novel Award and won the Galaxy Audiobook of the Year Award. It tells the story of lovers and families separated during the First World War. With her daughter Isabel Adomakoh Young, she has written (as Zizou Corder) the bestselling *Lionboy* trilogy and *Halo*, a historical novel for children.

I've written four novels set in the present, three in the past and four in the future, five for children and six for adults. So I write historical novels, but I'm not a historical novelist. I don't want to be given one of those covers and put on that shelf – genre labels can't help but limit writers.

As a child historical fiction was about curiosity and wishing I'd been there. For *Halo*, which is set in Periclean Greece, I was sitting in Athens looking at the agora, thinking, wouldn't it be great to have a centaur as a friend? I read Geoffrey Trease, Roger Lancelyn Green, the *Puffin Book of Myths and Legends*, and the wonderful *I, Juan de Pareja*, about an African boy who was slave to Velasquez, and wanted to paint.

My first published book, which I wrote when I was very young, was a biography of my grandmother, the sculptor Kathleen Scott. During World War 1 she worked with Major Harold Gillies on the reconstruction of injured faces; I remember looking at photographs of the men undergoing the procedures and thinking, 'I'll come back to you.'

But for a novel you need more than one idea, you need several, which have to come together. The next idea came through an object, a preprinted field postcard I saw at the Wellcome in London. It starts: 'My dear,' and then blank for the name, and then, 'I wanted to tell you before any telegram arrives that I have received a slight/severe wound in my ... ' And the wounded man would fill it in as appropriate. I thought of being a 21-year-old Tommy in a casualty station, with a wound like the ones I saw in Major

Gillies' photographs – are you going to tell your family the truth, about the slightness/severity, or are you going to lie?

So many men didn't talk about the war. We are now able to be much more open than they were but we all know there are still many soldiers now who don't/won't/can't talk about what they've seen and done. Only in hindsight are we allowed to describe the suffering and the trauma.

Writers choose wars because they give you proper drama, real drama, death, separation, moral dilemmas. You can write about places but not for their picturesqueness. And you have that sense of immense gratitude to the individuals who fought, for example, Nazism, which triggers your thinking.

I prefer not to talk to individuals about their experience of what has become a historical period or event. I prefer to read, or to listen to other people's interviews. When you read something a witness has written, they have made their decision about what to tell the world, in the form of the anonymous reader. If I talk to them, they are giving me, personally, their story, which makes me far more directly responsible for how I use it. There are as many versions of an event as there were people there at the time – or more. I read history at university, I like to get things right. But even if you take evidence directly you are still only getting a version, and in the end you have to take responsibility for your own version. And I write fiction, so though I want to be accurate in general, in specifics – characters, in particular – I have to be free.

I make my characters articulate for modern ears, being careful because of the change in the meanings of words. You strike a carefully considered balance between what would have been said, what is beautiful and evocative, and what readers now will believe and understand by the language you use. You don't want too many 'what ho's' and 'topping, old man's'. When the book was read on the radio, the BBC took exception to my use of the word 'fuck.' They argued that there was no record of it being used before 1927. But it was in the nature of the word that it would not have been recorded, so that was its power. And one reader got very cross about the word 'nancy', and decided my cockney eighteen-year-old in 1914 was homophobic. If a reader wants to be anachronistic that's up to them, but I can't be.

Historical events give you the architecture of your novel. Your characters' personal experiences are bound to be affected by them, but it always seems rather forced when a story has to take on every important thing that happened; one individual can't be at every battle.

My theory is that history is speeding up. It seems faster because of technological efficiency, and also because we have been through things before, and there exists a certain familiarity of territory. We are culturally very practised at knowing what happens next.

Notes

1. From In 'Search of *Alias Grace*: On Writing Canadian Historical Fiction'. An address given at the Bronfman Lecture Series (Ottawa: November 1996), Smithsonian Institute (Washington: 11 December 1996), Chicago Library Foundations (6 January 1997), Oberlin College Friends of the Library (8 February 1997), City Arts & Lectures (San Francisco, March 1997). Reprinted in *American Historical Review*, Vol. 103. No 5 (December 1998) Reprinted in *Writing With Intent: Essays, Reviews, Personal Prose 1983–2005. 2005.* Carroll & Graf. New York. Reproduced by kind permission of the author.
2. William Sharp, *The Life and Letters of Joseph Severn*, London, 1892, p. 208.
3. It is also perfectly possible to do the reverse – to bring the historical narrative surprisingly and powerfully into the present by the use of anachronistic metaphors – as Christopher Logue does on occasion in his *War Music*.
4. Adapted by the author from her article 'Making The Dead Speak', published in the Wall Street Journal, 2012.
5. Excerpt from *Other Colors: Essays and a Story* by Orhan Pamuk, translation copyright © 2007 by Maureen Freely. Used by permission of Alfred A. Knopf, an imprint of the Knopf Doubleday Publishing Group, a division of Random House LLC. All rights reserved. Excerpt from *Other Colours: Essays and a Story* by Orhan Pamuk, translation copyright © 2007 by Maureen Freely. Used by permission of Faber & Faber. All rights reserved.

Part 3:
Write on

Planning

by Duncan Sprott

Finding your subject

William Golding said you don't find your subject, it's the subject that finds you. When it hits you there should be a Eureka! moment, with shivers down the spine. Writing any kind of novel is to be possessed, possessed, that is, by your characters, as if by a bunch of ghosts, and maybe that's how it should be, one of the vital ingredients of a novel, a bit of (divine?) inspiration.

If that Eureka! moment hasn't happened yet, there are a few ways of helping it along. The secret is to pretend not to be looking; and not to look too hard. Lurk in places where a meaty subject might reach out and grab you. Wander in overgrown graveyards, idly read the names on tombstones. Haunt the History section in your local library. Submit to the will of the universe by opening a few books at random. Loiter in the nearest museum or art gallery, sidle up to interesting portraits. Let your novel tap you on the shoulder.

Choosing a period

On the other hand, if that novel doesn't find you first, selecting the right subject *for you* may be difficult. You have the whole of History to range over. How do you decide what to write? And will what you want to do result in a viable, publishable book? Does the world need yet another novel about the House of Tudor, the female members thereof? What are the alternatives?

What then? A straightforward historical novel, or one of the sub-genres: historical mystery, historical thriller or historical romance? Virtual history?

Alternate history? Will it be serious literary stuff, like Ishiguro's *The Remains of the Day*, or Peter Ackroyd's *Hawksmoor*? Or something more popular, like Ken Follett's huge medieval blockbuster *The Pillars of the Earth/World Without End*? Or something inbetween?

Which period will be better (for you), Ancient, Medieval or Modern? Or will your book range across many time periods, like *Cloud Atlas*? And where (if, indeed, you have any choice), will you set your story? Chicago? Venice? Peking? Essex? Will your characters be well-known historical figures or unknown? Or totally fictitious? Or will you have famous names and made-up characters all mixed up? What will work best?

Some Pros and Cons

Prehistory

Cons

- The mists of time may well prove to be a totally impenetrable fog.
- Nothing, absolutely nothing, is known of prehistoric people's lives.
- Your research would consist of bones and pots and mammoth's teeth.
- We don't even know how prehistoric people spoke.
- Try writing a few chapters in grunts or click language. See how you get on...

Pros

- So little is known that you can make it all up: names, places, language, everything.
- Archaeology will help the reconstruction (at least you know what was on the menu).
- Where even the archaeologist must stop, the novelist can go on digging.
- A whole novel might emerge from a tantalising footnote in an archaeological journal.
- The *Proceedings of the Prehistoric Society* are waiting to be ransacked.
- Jean M. Auel (*The Clan of the Cave Bear*) and William Golding (*The Inheritors*) managed to write highly successful novels set in Neanderthal times, in deep prehistory.
- At the cutting edge, DNA-testing of ancient remains suggests a whole new world of untold stories from prehistory. Less may be more.

Antiquity
Cons

- Reconstructing antiquity will involve years of meticulous academic research.
- You must bust your way into the ancient mind, a foreign country indeed.
- Vast bibliographies for Ancient Greece and Rome may be impossible to cope with.
- For Ancient Egypt there is the added complication of the gods.
- And all the sources are in Latin, Greek, or Egyptian hieroglyphs.

Pros

- Classical scholars have already prepared the ground for you.
- Most ancient Greek and Roman (and Egyptian) texts are available in translation.
- The ancient mindset is not, in fact, impossible to penetrate.
- The constraint of what you don't know forms an interesting part of the challenge.
- What you don't know, you make up, informed by diligent but selective researches.

Dark Age (c.400–1000)
Cons

- The Dark Ages are not called dark for nothing. A blank page, if not a black one.
- King Arthur has already appeared in fiction. Can you not find a new old story?
- Nothing is known of this obscure period, nothing whatever.

Pros

- The Dark Ages were not as dark as you might think.
- The historical novel can shed light in places where the archaeologist cannot dig.
- King Arthur was not the only Dark Age king. Penda? Osric? Ethelfrid of Mercia?
- Where nothing is known, you imagine. That blank page may be a gift from the gods.

Medieval (c.1000–1500)
Cons

- Detailed information on medieval times is hard to come by, and fragmentary.
- Research may involve delving into original manuscripts that you can't read.
- You may need to hire a palaeographer to read your source material for you.

- Nobody knows quite how medieval people spoke or thought.

Pros

- You have the satisfaction of reconstructing a colourful/dramatic period.
- In many areas of medieval history there is plenty of information available.
- What information is available may already be in printed books and journals.
- The gaps in our knowledge of the Middle Ages are what makes it fascinating.

Modern 1500+

Cons

- Modern historical subjects may entail vast researches.
- The prospect of wading through a vast bibliography may be daunting.
- Research into recent history may be hampered by the unavailability of some records.
- Lytton Strachey said, it will be impossible to write a history of the nineteenth century because we know so much about it. The problem is having too much information.

Pros

- There is far more information available for the modern period.
- The research is easier, and the ground has already been prepared by historians.
- Buildings, portraits, letters and diaries all help in the reconstruction of modern times.
- The mindset of eighteenth- or nineteenth-century characters is not difficult to penetrate.
- Lengthy researches may not be necessary. You zoom in on a small area and select.

Historical characters

Cons

- The motivation of a real historical character is an unknown quantity, the psychology difficult to reconstruct.
- To penetrate the psyche of, say, Charlemagne, or Tarquinius Superbus, is not easy.
- Your subject may already have been fictionalised by 57 other writers.
- Worse, somebody else may already be writing a novel identical to yours.

Pros

- The constraint between the known and the unknown in a historical character is what makes the reconstruction rewarding to explore.
- You have a ready-made historical framework on which to base your story.
- A considerable amount of the research will have been done already, by others.
- Biographies and other printed books may help you to work faster.
- It's not impossible to find a new angle on a familiar subject.
- You may have an entirely different story to tell than the one known to history.
- A famous name is easier to promote, a useful hook for worldwide publicity.

Unknown historical characters
Cons

- It's more difficult to publicise and sell books about characters no one has heard of.
- It may be difficult to invent, say, a fourteenth-century peasant out of nothing.
- Unknown characters may be unknown because they never did anything of interest.
- Ordinary people's lives are less likely to have been researched before. In the absence of biographies, you will be starting from scratch, with no guarantee that you will find what you are looking for. And genealogical research can take a long time.

Pros

- What you can't find out, you can make up, based on your research.
- You are freer to invent details of character; you know your characters from the inside.
- You will feel more in control of characters you have invented yourself.
- This kind of character may 'ring true' whereas a more famous name may not.
- Many readers will think that ordinary people's lives are far more interesting.
- Half the fun of original research is that you are breaking new ground, not relying on secondhand information culled from other people's books.

Fictional characters in a historical framework
Cons

- Fictional characters may just not feel 'real'.
- Made-up characters may not quite fit into the period where you have stuck them.

- What is the point of putting made-up characters in history anyway?
- What matters, surely, is the real.

Pros

- It may be easier to occupy the minds of made-up characters and see through their eyes.
- It might be easier to put words into the mouth of an obscure fourteenth-century peasant than trying to guess how Pompey and Cornelia spoke to each other.
- Invented characters can be made to fit, adapted and altered, cut down or built up, made to do what you want them to do: it is more difficult to do this with historical characters.
- Fictional characters may end up far more convincing.

Unknown characters in a local historical setting
Con

- A local subject may only be of local interest.
- Even to the people who live in the village, local history can be very very dull.
- Regional or parochial matters will not engage a nationwide audience.
- It's impossible to turn a local subject into a book for the world market.

Pro

- In the right hands, local historical subjects can be interesting.
- Adam Thorpe's *Ulverton* (1992) and Richard Gough's (non-fiction) *The History of Myddle* (c.1700) are fine examples of local history made universal.
- Had anybody heard of Dorothea Brooke or Mr. Casaubon before George Eliot came up with *Middlemarch* ? It happens to be subtitled *A Study of Provincial Life*.
- The research is on your doorstep. You already have in-depth local knowledge. You know the landscape in which your characters live, the dialect they speak, and everything about the place. If you live on the spot, your research costs should not be astronomical.
- Emanuel Le Roy Ladurie's *Montaillou*, the microhistory of a Languedoc village from 1294–1324, shows that local history can have national and international significance.
- All history is, in some sense, local history.

Foreign and exotic?

Con

- Can you handle an extensive bibliography in French? German? Mongolian?
- You may have to learn a foreign language before you can begin writing.
- You may have to hire a budget-busting researcher or translator.
- Proper research may only be possible in Ulaanbataar.
- Extensive foreign travel is expensive.
- Nobody has ever heard of your characters; their names are unpronounceable.
- Such things are bad for publicity; nobody will buy your book.

Pro

- Exotic locations/subject matter might bring the sale of foreign and movie rights.
- You can make use of your experience of buzkashi in Upper Mongolia.
- You go there in your imagination; that's what fiction is all about.
- And the School of Oriental and African Studies (SOAS) library has an excellent Mongolian section...
- If you have to go to Ulaanbaatar, at least your research trip will be tax deductible.
- Your old friend, Prof. Battbold of Ulaanbaatar, will translate all the documents.
- You can build pronunciation into the text and include a glossary.
- For unpronounceable names, invent shortened forms, or use nicknames.
- Even if your characters are obscure, make them interesting and the book will sell.

Evaluation

In *Serious Creativity* – a book aimed not at writers but at businessmen – Edward de Bono devised eight categories for evaluating projects: Usable Idea, Good Idea but Not For Me, Good Idea but Not Now (Back Burner), Needs More Work, Powerful but Not Usable, Interesting but Unusable, Weak Value, and Unworkable. De Bono's eight classes might well be of use to novelists deciding what to write. De Bono also proposes a 'Cloud 9 File', for 'dreams' and future projects. Book-ideas might well sound great, valuable and workable, but not quite the right thing for you. Some ideas have fundamental impossibilites. You want a strong story, not a weak one, a powerful, usable story. If it's going to set the great book-reading public on fire that story will have to engage your own interest and enthusiasm first.

Historical research

by Duncan Sprott

> ❝ *The rules of the game: learn everything, read everything, inquire into everything... pursue the reality of facts across thousands of index-cards; strive to restore to these faces of stone their mobility and living suppleness.* ❞
> Marguerite Yourcenar, *Carnets de notes de 'Memoires d'Hadrien'* (1952)

Established wisdom for wannabe writers is 'Write what you know'. But historical fiction means writing what you DO NOT know – about a past that is irretrievable, beyond reach, about people you have never met. What you don't know, you can find out. And you are allowed to imagine.

Having made some decisions about subject and period, what next? How do you 'find out' about Alfred the Great, or Lambert Simnel, or Guy Fawkes's last meal, or the truth about Prince Albert and the Prince Albert?

You find out by reading, by making assiduous researches. Read on...

How much research?

How much research you do will depend on the complexity of your subject and period, on what kind of thing you are looking for, and on what level of detail you want. *How much* depends on you. If you can spin a story out of next to nothing and be convincing and historically accurate, you won't need to do much research.

If, on the other hand, your subject demands that you dive into a labyrinth of complicated manuscript sources, you can disappear for years. Most historical novels will not demand quite this level of research. All you need is the fuel to set your imagination on fire.

Research can be absorbing and exhilarating, but it's possible to overdo it. You don't want so much material that you can't use it all. The trick is knowing when to stop. The historian must remember his research; the historical novelist must forget it.

- Every writer evolves his or her own methods.
- There is no magical 'right way' to produce a publishable manuscript.
- The only wrong way is the one that doesn't end up with a finished book.

In his acknowledgements for *The Amber Spyglass*, Philip Pullman says 'I have stolen ideas from every book I have ever read. My principle in researching for a novel is "Read like a butterfly, write like a bee", and if this story contains any honey, it is entirely because of the quality of the nectar I found in the work of better writers.'

- For the historical novelist, the nectar is research.
- We are all borrowers, thieves in the night, terrible magpies.
- Everything is grist for the historical fiction mill.

Finding your direction

Knowing where you are going, what you are trying to do, that's the vital thing. So where is *your* idea going to? Where are you going? Do you know what you want to do? Or are you just going round and round in circles? How to establish a strong foundation on which to build? If a novel is going to go anywhere, certain vital ingredients have to be hauled into place first. There's no one way of doing this, no right or wrong way. But:

- You need a precise location, something manageable.
- You need a chronological frame within which to work, a time-span, and that must be manageable too. A story that covers a few days or weeks, or a couple of years, with a few main characters, will be easier than one that covers hundreds of years with a cast of thousands.
- You need a main character or characters, memorable, with memorable names

and traits. And your hero or heroine can't exist in isolation. They need a world that will revolve about them, a horizon, however limited: the microcosm that is your novel, the world in miniature. One house is easier to manage than the whole village; a village is easier than a town; a town is easier than a city, and a city than an entire empire, such as Rome.

● Although Flaubert wanted to write a novel that was about nothing at all (he never did write it) most novels need to be about something. Things should happen. And your characters may need some problem to deal with (conflict) – such as war, hunger, hardship, domestic troubles, some obstacle to be overcome, whether private and personal, local or national, something that threatens the status quo. Then comes the development of the conflict, complications, crisis, resolution. The separate strands of story need something to pull them together into a coherent whole. Characters have to interrelate and interlock; must somehow be involved with one another. If not, you may end up with a book of bits, or a bit of a book.

● You need a narrator with an overview of the whole story – maybe from the future looking back on the past; maybe mixed up in the story him/herself. Or an omniscient narrator who stands outside the story, like God, able to see and understand all that goes on in the minds of the protagonists – perhaps not so very different from you just being yourself.

● You have to collar the reader, as good as make him (her) your prisoner until The End.

Establishing foundations

> **"** In selecting – ask yourself, do these events add up to an involving plot, a good story? **"**
> Edmund White, 'Lost in the Funhouse'. TLS 19 May 2006

Somehow you have to find yourself a story that nobody else has told before. Ever. Or at least, a story that you can make your own. But *how* to find that story? And having found it, how to build it up? Cultivate a receptivity and openness to all possible sources of inspiration: books, of course, historical documents, of course (if necessary), but also take notice of the images that spring up in everyday life – people's faces, photos in newspapers, everyday twenty-first-century stories that might be projected back in time.

- Stare at people in the street, on trains, buses, planes (but don't get punched): they may come in handy as characters in your book. Wherever you go, gather up the details that strike you as interesting.

- Scrutinise the contents of museums for likely objects: knives, shoes, shields, helmets and jewels... Ransack art galleries for details of costume, faces in portraits, and a sense of the atmosphere of the past.

- Raid your own past. Make use of your family history, the dead, but don't forget the living (and don't forget to change them so they won't recognise themselves): these may be the only people in your entire life that you really know inside and out.

- Examine how your memory works. Think about truth and lies in your own family history, and how facts get changed. Think about truth and lies in the past. Your raw material is everything you have ever seen or heard of, every book you ever read.

- In the newspapers of the 1700s and 1800s it's the advertisements for lost dogs, escaped convicts and missing persons – complete with descriptions – that touch the heart and bring the past bouncing back to life. Such details might inspire half a dozen historical novels.

- All of the above will act as compost for the imagination.

- Listen, and the past will talk to you. (It sounds mad, but it's true.)

> Henry James said that a novel must above all be interesting — the story must be inherently involving, one you would want to hear the end of even in conversation.

> And since a novel aspires to be a work of art, its form must also be original enough and clever enough to capture the attention.
> Edmund White, 'Lost in the Funhouse'. TLS 19 May 2006

- You have to know every thing about your characters, including what they ate and drank, what they did all day, what were their hopes and fears, what made them happy or sad... You have to know their attitude to other people, how they treat animals, how they behave toward whores and queers...

● Take up temporary residence in your character's brain, penetrate his or her thought processes, until you know every last thing, down to the ins and outs of his sex life. If you know how he thinks, you know how he will act or react on any given occasion.

● Research is the passport that allows you to travel in time.

> ❝ Ideally perhaps one should, like the novelist, have one's subject under control, never losing it from sight and constantly aware of its overpowering presence. Fortunately or unfortunately, the historian has not the novelist's freedom. ❞
>
> Fernand Braudel, *The Mediterranean and the Mediterranean World in the Age of Philip II* (1949)

● If you want to write historical fiction, read some historical fiction. Forensic reading is needed: not reading fast but slow, taking time to notice how story works. Notice things like *precision*, and the handling of words; how the author has total control over them, makes them as good as march up and down at his command. Not one word out of place; not one word too many. And so tightly constructed that if one page is removed the whole story will collapse.

● Try re-reading your favourite historical novel; think about *why* it's so good.

● Try to re-read the worst historical novel you ever read. Think about why it is so bad, why it fails to work, what it was that made you want to throw it in the trash.

● Read some of the finest novels ever written: *War and Peace, The Leopard, The Memoirs of Hadrian, I, Claudius, Siddhartha,* timeless classics, that just happen to be historical novels.

● Read history like mad; whatever looks relevant to your subject. Plunge deep into your chosen period. Absorb whatever is necessary for you to write about it. Take reams of notes. Build a database. Make lists of questions that need answering before you can begin to write. Set about answering them by raiding every library you can find.

● Pay special attention to bibliographies. Make lists of books to be checked out. Keep a record of what you have read. Let your card index take over your life

– but don't forget that all this reading is just the facilitator for what you will write. Don't let the research become an end in itself.

- If you collect your materials from 20 books, or 120, that is called research; if you take everything from just one book, and you happen to quote from it quite a lot in your own book, word for word, that may be plagiarism, and could land you in trouble. Copyright law exists to protect not only *you* but also other writers, and is something that should not be ignored.

- For an overview of the fictional field, go to www.historicalnovels.info which lists 5,000 historical novels by period and location, time and place. How many novels already exist on your subject? Will there be room in a crowded market for your novel? Note the periods of history that nobody seems to have written about, ever. Find a gap, and fill it, and you've made a neglected subject into your own exclusive territory.

- A novel needs to convey a sense of place, needs atmosphere. If possible, visit the location you are writing about. Notice the landscape, whether it's flat; whether carriage horses might struggle to get up a hill.

- Notice things like rivers, ancient woods, the wind in the cornfields, natural sounds, what birds you see, the wildlife – Time does not change these things very much.

- Notice the houses from your period, the building style. Get inside if you can. Meditate on what it was like to live there.

- Check out the local museum – for weapons, notable local characters, costumes, portraits, ephemera from the past. Look inside the parish church for old funerary monuments, heraldry, and the tombs of notable parishioners.

- Root about in the graveyard: illegible inscriptions may have been transcribed and printed, in the record office. Look for hints and clues about what happened in this place. Listen to local people talking, for stock phrases, local accents and dialects.

- On the other hand, some writers prefer to stay away, and imagine the past instead.

- Cultivate the habit of writing down your thoughts. On the spot. Keep pen and paper within reach. Practise your art by filling that notebook with descriptions: landscape, weather conditions, sounds, faces in the street, facial expressions. Look hard at the way people move. Collect random bits of striking dialogue. If they're not useful now, these scribbled notes might be usable later on.

- Catch the dark and glittering jewels that spring out of your best nightmare (your subconscious will never stop working). Take the notebook when you go for a walk: it's when your mind is idling that it chucks out the best ideas. Grab them as they go by.

- Not only seize the day but seize the sunset; transfer it to 1381. Give your headache to Sophia, Electress of Hanover. Seize the death of your aged Uncle Charlie and apply it to Oliver Cromwell. Use everything.

Advice from experts

- The deeper you dig into your subject the more you will realise that there are others who have greater knowledge of it than you. While you might feel like writing the kind of book that can't be bothered to get things right, just for the hell of it, you might end up feeling pretty sick when *your* book is condemned in the Sunday papers as 'Preposterous'. There are a couple of short cuts to omniscience. One is to keep on researching, on and on. The other is to ask an expert.

- The Historical Novel Society or the Historical Writers' Association can link you up with other writers who have in-depth knowledge of your period and are willing to answer queries or share info: see www.historicalnovelsociety.org and www.thehwa.org

- Yahoo Groups comprises some 42,000 online forums. On the more serious side there are dozens of groups for specialised historical interests and arcane subjects (e.g. Historical Corsets, with 753 members...). If there is no Yahoo group on your subject, you can start one yourself. See www.groups.yahoo.com

Basic sources

Modern times 1500+

The info below should be useful in tracking down a *name*, at least, if you're looking for a real person.

- Most people in history leave behind a trail of documents in which they are mentioned: evidence of being born, married or buried, but there's often much more. All these documents are vital for the historical detective. Here are a few clues to follow:

- For well-known (and many lesser known) historical figures in the British Isles (and Ireland) check out 'DNB' – *The Oxford Dictionary of National Biography*. Also available online. There is also a *Concise DNB*. For Ireland see also *Dictionary of Irish Biography*.

- For Germany, see the *Allgemeine Deutsche Biographie* and *Neue Deutsche Biographie*; for France, *Dictionnaire de Biographie Française*; for Italy, *Dizionario Biografico degli Italiani*, and so on.

- For biographical details of well-known people in the recent past check *Who Was Who* (from 1897). For Europe, the out-of-date editions of *Who's Who in France*, *Who's Who in Italy*, *Wer ist Wer?* and *Who's Who in Germany*.

- *The Times Index* lists every name occurring in the newspaper from 1785 to date, and also covers *The Times Literary Supplement* (1902 onwards). Also check here for obituaries of notable people.

- For Royalty, see *Debrett's Peerage* (from 1769) and *Burke's Peerage* (from 1826) which list detailed genealogical information for all British kings and queens since 1066, their families and descendants. For European Royalty and higher nobility see the *Almanach de Gotha* (from 1763).

- For Peers, see *Burke* and *Debrett*, as above, for detailed family histories and glimpses of wonderful *stories*. Also online.

- The Parliamentary Archives provides access to the archives of the House of Lords, the House of Commons and to other records of Parliament. Also kept here are the private papers of e.g. Lloyd George, and several key sources for family history. Index online at www.parliament.uk/archives

● For MPs, see *DNB*, and *The History of Parliament*, an online (and ongoing) project to produce biographies of all MPs sitting in the House of Commons between 1386 and 1832. See www.histparl.ac.uk

● Hansard: Official reports of parliamentary debates exist from 1774 to date (though the early vols are not 100 per cent reliable). The Hansard of today, with full accounts of every speech, began in 1909. The US equivalent is the *Congressional Record*. Hansard also exists for Canada, Australia and many other countries.

● The Calendars of State Papers may turn up useful information. Many vols exist in print, including State Papers Venetian, Spanish, Foreign, Domestic, and Colonial.

● *State Papers Online 1509–1714* has rounded up all documents from the reign of Henry VIII through to Queen Anne. Also in the database are the Irish Manuscript Commission series of Calendars of State Papers Ireland, the manuscripts collection of Sir William Cecil, and much more. With some 3 million documents online this project has transformed and simplified the process of research: www. gale.cengage.co.uk (at present available via institutions only).

● Clergy, Church of England: For archbishops and bishops see *Burke* and *Debrett*. For other church dignitaries, deans, archdeacons, vicars and rectors, see *Crockford's Clerical Directory* (1858 to date). Graduate clerics may turn up in Oxford and Cambridge *Alumni* (details below).

● Clergy, Roman Catholic: Check Catholic Record Society publications for details of recusant priests. Vatican Archives are online at www.vaticanlibrary.va

● For Nonconformist clergy, go to Dr Williams's Library.

● The *Oxford Dictionary of the Christian Church* is stuffed with useful info and detailed bibliographies.

● Gentry: For info on Esquires, Gentlemen, and Ladies see *Burke's Landed Gentry*, *Burke's Irish Family Records*, and the *Gentleman's Magazine* (1731–1922). Also check *Burke* and *Debrett*.

● University Graduates: Foster's *Alumni Oxonienses* lists all known Oxford entrants from 1500–1886. Venn's *Alumni Cantabrigienses* does the same for Cambridge, from 1261 to 1900. Both give outline biographical info, where known, and both have databases online. Similar publications exist for e.g. St Andrews, Glasgow, Edinburgh.

● Professional directories: For military personnel attack the *Army List* (printed from 1740), *Navy List* (from 1782) and *Air Force List*.

- For doctors, the *Medical Register* (online, from 1858).

- For composers, *The New Grove Dictionary of Music and Musicians*.

- The Law: *The All England Law Reports* (1558 to date) give details of some 6,000 cases from the court system of England and Wales. *The All England Reprints Extension* added a further 3,000 important cases from 1861–1935. These constitute the premier English legal reports on proceedings.

- Schoolboys: There are published lists of pupils for all the major public schools (e.g. Eton, Harrow, Westminster, etc.), many minor ones (e.g. Cranleigh, Felsted etc.), and some grammar schools, all with dates, parentage, and career, if known.

- Schoolgirls, alas! do not make much of an appearance until the late 1800s.

- A valuable resource for people-hunting is *Sources for One-Name Studies and for other Family Historians* by Brian Wm Christmas. This comprises 2,500+ titles, from Abell's *Prisoners of War in Britain, 1756–1815* down to Young's *Annals of the Barber Surgeons' Company*.

- For ordinary folks: check provincial city and county newspapers (see British Library Newspapers, p. 191) – not indexed but you may strike lucky if you have a date to go on. Or dive into a random year and let serendipity play its part.

Early times

Where to start

Earlier biographical sources tend to be fragmentary and disjointed, but there is no shortage of *names*: even if the name is all that is known, these people *lived*, and their lives can be reconstructed. Below are some general works.

- For the earlier history of Britain look at the *New Oxford History of England*. For bibliographical info check any of the excellent *Cambridge History* series. The *Cambridge History of Iran* might lead you to Xerxes. The *Cambridge History of China* could fix you up with Sun Tzu, author of *The Art of War*...

Ancient Greece and Rome

- For prominent names in antiquity the most reliable starting point is the *Oxford*

Classical Dictionary (3rd edition), with countless bibliographical trails to follow, from Aesop to Zoroaster.

● The *Penguin Atlas of Ancient History* gives a useful overview of what's what at different periods. Also the *Timetables of History* and *The Timetables of Science*.

● Most ancient texts are available as Penguin Classics (e.g. Herodotus, Polybius), or in the Loeb Classical Library.

● The *Cambridge Ancient History* will lure you into deeper waters.

● The *Journal of Roman Studies* (JRS) and the *Journal of Hellenic Studies* (JHS) take you as deep into Classical archaeology as anybody can go (without making unpublished PhD theses your bedside reading).

● What fragments of biographical info survive on people in the ancient world have been rounded up in a succession of fat tomes. *Prosopographia Attica*, for example, has details of 16,000 Athenians in antiquity. *Prosopographia Imperii Romani* gives the lowdown on Imperial Rome. *Prosopographia Ptolemaica* contains the names of everybody known to have lived in Hellenistic Egypt (i.e. from Alexander the Great to Kleopatra VII).

● For all of the above books, and for Classics in general, the Joint Library of the Hellenic and Roman Societies, in London, is a vital resource.

● AWOL (Ancient World Online) has 1,000+ open access journals in Ancient Studies.

● BMCR (Bryn Mawr Classical Review) posts online reviews of new books in Classics.

● The British School at Athens has useful online databases: www.bsa.ac.uk and a library **(L)**

● See also the British School at Rome www.bsr.ac.uk **(L)**

Ancient Egypt

● For a useful guide to Pharaohs, see the *Complete Royal Families of Ancient Egypt.*

● For a good general history see Nicolas Grimal's *History of Ancient Egypt.*

● The *Atlas of Ancient Egypt* (Baines and Malek) gives a bird's-eye view of the political map over the ages.

● For the gods, go to George Hart's *Dictionary of Egyptian Gods and Goddesses*.

● The Egypt Exploration Society's *Journal of Egyptian Archaeology* will provide more detailed info than you can handle – and tantalising gaps to be filled by the imagination. To keep abreast with the latest developments on (or under) the ground, see the more accessible *Egyptian Archaeology* (EES, quarterly).

- *Kmt: A Modern Journal of Ancient Egypt* (USA) is lavishly illustrated and happens to review Egypt-themed fiction. All too often, the fictional focus is on Tutankhamun, or Akhenaten, as if these were the only two Pharaohs in Egypt's 4,000 year history. There are some 300 other kings and queens waiting to star in your novel.

- The Egyptologists' Electronic Forum (EEF) sends free regular email updates to subscribers: www.egyptologyforum.org

- Yahoo Groups has several Egypt-related mailing lists, e.g. Thoth-Scribe for Egyptology; Ta Seti for black African history. See www.groups.yahoo.com

Roman Britain

- You could seek out *Hadrian's Wall* (Breeze and Dobson) and follow the Romans on the ground.

- For Romans in depth, trawl the bibliographies in the Roman vols of the *Cambridge Ancient History*, the *New Oxford History of England*, or the *Penguin History of Britain*.

- The Roman Society journal *Britannia* will keep you up-to-date with current archaeological research.

- Or join the Yahoo groups mailing lists for Rome and Roman Britain.

- Julius Caesar, of course, is the principal contemporary authority.

Dark Age Britain

- We are not meant to call the Dark Ages 'Dark' any more, but the label is still a useful hook to hang things on, and more attractive than 'Sub-Roman Britain'.

- The Dark Ages means not only Arthur... who may or may not have existed, and whom we treat elsewhere, but also the Venerable Bede, whose *Ecclesiastical History* is packed with fragmentary battle reports, brief references to otherwise unknown kings and warriors, and tantalising bits of story.

- Seek out Guy Halsall's illuminating *Worlds of Arthur: Facts and Fictions of the Dark Ages* (2013) or the old war-horse, *In Search of the Dark Ages*, by Michael Wood. Then unleash the imagination.

Medieval Britain

Useful works.

- The bibliographies in the *New Cambridge Medieval History* (many volumes).
- The *Penguin Atlas of Medieval History* for an overview of the medieval world.
- Peter Ackroyd's *Foundation: A History of England*, with 16-page bibliography.
- Steven Runciman's *A History of the Crusades* and John Julius Norwich's *Byzantium*, though not new, can still take you deep into medieval history.
- Jonathan Sumption's *The Hundred Years War* and *The Albigensian Crusade*.
- For monks and monasteries see the works of Dom David Knowles.
- For *The Templars* read Piers Paul Read.
- And don't forget Emanuel Leroy Ladurie's *Montaillou*.

Wales

- For an overview of Welsh history see Geraint Jenkins' *A Concise History of Wales* (2007) in the excellent *Cambridge Concise Histories* series.
- For early Welsh legend see James MacKillop's *Dictionary of Celtic Mythology*.
- John Morris's *The Age of Arthur* deals with the period AD 350 to 650.
- A. D. Carr's *Medieval Wales* and W. Davies' *Wales in the Early Middle Ages* shed light on a little-known period.
- And don't forget the *Mabinogion*.

Scotland

- For a useful introduction see Michael Lynch's *Scotland: A New History*.
- For more detailed info, look up the *Oxford Companion to Scottish History*.
- The *Edinburgh History of Scotland* (4 vols) has extensive bibliographies.
- For medieval Scotland try Alan Macquarrie's *Scotland in the Crusades*.
- For the eighteenth century, see John Prebble's trilogy, *Culloden, Glencoe,* and *The Highland Clearances*.
- For eyewitness accounts of the Scottish past, see Louise Yeoman's *Reportage Scotland: History in the Making*.

Ireland

- Sean Duffy's *Atlas of Irish History*, or R.F. Foster's *Oxford History of Ireland*.
- For detailed info on historical figures see the *Oxford Companion to Irish History* and the *Dictionary of Irish Biography*.
- For early saga material, check out the *Oxford Companion to Irish Literature*.
- For Irish myth and legend, see James MacKillop's *Dictionary of Celtic Mythology*.
- For prehistoric archaeology, see Flanaghan's *Ancient Ireland: Life Before the Celts*.
- For the North, see Bardon's *History of Ulster*, and *The Narrow Ground: Aspects of Ulster, 1609–1969*.
- The *Dictionary of Ulster Biography* brings the story up to the present.

Online sources

In the brave new world of computer-based research you can look up anything you like online and have the answer to almost any question in a couple of clicks.

- Online research can turn up brilliant things, but (depending on where you look) some sites can be unreliable. Bear in mind that it is not difficult to latch on to some historical fact that is incorrect. Check all online dates and facts against some reliable printed source. Having said that, here are some useful (and reliable) websites:

- The Institute of Historical Research, University of London, has an online *Bibliography of British and Irish History* (BBIH) incorporating the former *London's Past Online* and *Irish History Online*. The complete database contains 530,000 records. Access is by subscription, or via a subscribing institution. See www.history.ac.uk/projects/bbih

- British History Online, is a vast digital library. See www.british-history.ac.uk

- Medieval Resources Online www.leeds.ac.uk/ims/med_online/medresources.htm

- Gale Databases provides access to an extensive library of digital archives, e.g. Archives Unbound: French Royal Acts 1256–1794; *National Geographic* complete (1888–1994); Nineteenth Century Collections Online (NCCO); the Burney Collection of seventeenth- and eighteenth-century newspapers); Eighteenth Century Collections Online (ECCO), and more, all available (for a fee) at www.gale.cengage.co.uk

- The E-Library at the London Library www.londonlibrary.co.uk gives access to many databases, including JSTOR (see below), *American National Biography*, George Washington Papers, the *Oxford DNB*, the *London Review of Books*, the BBIH, British History Online, British Humanities Index, Electronic Enlightenment.

- JSTOR (pronounced JAY-stor = Journal Storage) is a valuable online database with the complete texts of some 1,400 academic journals in 50+ disciplines (access usually via institutions) www.jstor.org

- The complete *Oxford English Dictionary* (OED) is online at www.oed.com
- The Encyclopedia Britannica is online (fee payable but free at some libraries), see http://www.britannica.com The famous 1911 edition (more detailed, so more useful to historians) is browsable free at www.1911encyclopedia.org
- The Columbia Encyclopedia is at www.encyclopedia.com
- Merriam-Webster is at www.merriam.webster.com
- Microsoft's Encarta encyclopedia is at www.encarta.msn.com
- For maps, local or worldwide, go to Stanfords: www.stanfords.co.uk/

Search engines

- Via Internet search engines you can hook up to the biggest libraries in the world.
- Google and Yahoo are the best known – but not the only – search engines.
- Others include AltaVista, Ask Jeeves, Excite, Hotbot and Lycos.
- If you still can't find what you want... you will just have to make it up. Or try Mimas, a research info site maintained by the University of Manchester, www.mimas.ac.uk/portfolio/current Among Mimas projects is an archives locator – www.archiveshub.ac.uk
- For access to the British Library's electronic tables of contents of journals and links to the texts, see www.zetoc.mimas.ac.uk

Online genealogy

- You can get quite a long way in genealogy without letting go of your mouse. With luck, and perseverance, you should find what you want. Most families can be traced back without much trouble to 1837, when civil registration began. Before that you must trawl through parish registers, which makes things more complicated, but by no means impossible.
- How far back can you go? 1800 will not be an unreasonable target, and then 1700, though it might take several years of research to get there.
- You will be lucky indeed if the family you seek is traceable before 1558 when parish records began, but don't expect to achieve it in a fortnight unless somebody has already done the research before you.

- The Society of Genealogists' Library has an extensive manuscript collection of family trees traced by its members.

- The rich leave better paper-trails than the poor. The same applies to the bad: the worse the crime, the greater the amount of info survives. Plenty of ordinary people in history are born but disappear without trace. Hunting a known, named historical figure will always be easier than tracing your own ancestors, though an unusual surname will help.

- In Scotland and Wales, few families except the wealthy are traceable in any connected way before 1700 simply because of haphazard methods of record-keeping, but plenty of individual names survive.

- Every record searcher comes, at length, to the same dead end – where the records fizzle out: genealogists call this 'hitting the wall'. When every source has been ransacked but you keep drawing blanks; when the trail just dries up, that's when fiction comes into its own. Or, at least, some deft use of conjecture. In any case, reading between the lines is what historical novelists train themselves to do.

Here are some useful places to begin online research:

- www.Ancestry.com will lead you to birth/baptism, marriage and death records worldwide; also to census returns, and many other vital documents – all online.

- The Genealogical Society of the Church of Jesus Christ of the Latter-day Saints – the Mormons – are the most assiduous genealogists in the world. Their International Genealogical Index (IGI) lists over one billion names culled from births/baptism, marriage and death records worldwide. The IGI may turn up what you are seeking, but it's also notorious for gaps. Use it as a starting point, but check the original register or record as well. IGI access is free of charge at www.familysearch.org For direct access to the online catalogue see www.familysearch.org/Search/searchcatalogue.asp IGI microfiches are also kept in county record offices.

- RootsWeb is the largest free genealogy site online, with forums, discussion groups, message boards and mailing lists. These are arranged by Surnames A-Z, USA States, International countries A-Z: see www.rootsweb.com

- *Genealogy: The Good Web Guide* (4th edition, 2005) by Caroline Peacock, will hook you up to you hundreds of websites.

- Cyndi's List is a trusted site with 300,000+ links to genealogical research sites worldwide: www.cyndislist.com

- The Federation of Family History Societies represents 150 family history societies; see www.ffhs.org.uk

- The Guild of One-Name Studies may be able to link you to one of the massive research projects being undertaken by their members re. the name you are hunting. One surname, worldwide, all occurrences, every record transcribed and indexed – that is the extraordinary goal. See www.one-name.org

- Check lists of local historical societies – county, city, or town – which often have useful publications, e.g. parish registers, and indexes of names in local graveyards. Tombstones often have valuable info that doesn't appear in parish registers, e.g. some reference to a place, or to wives, children and relatives. Many Monumental Inscriptions (MIs) have been transcribed and printed by local history societies.

- Local History Online lists all UK local history societies; see: www.local-history.co.uk

- If your quarry is still AWOL after a thorough search, check the records of the adjacent counties for *strays*. A groom born in Essex, for example, might have married a Suffolk wife, or shifted to London. For missing ancestors, emigration records may provide the solution.

Going offline

- Online research is great, but in the end, there is no substitute for browsing in a non-virtual library. You can't read everything; you can't hope to become overnight a world expert on a vast subject, but you can dip your toe in the water. You can find enough stuff to make your novel float, or fly. You could, in theory, write a historical novel without going anywhere near a library or an archive repository, but the more obscure the subject and the more remote the period, the greater the chance that you will need to consult a few original records, or at least check out what's there.

Libraries – UK

Public libraries

- In a gigantic research library you can wait hours for a book to be delivered (though ordering in advance can speed things up). Use the local library wherever possible.

- Most local libraries have a local interest section and can produce almost any book via Inter-Library Loan – though you may have to wait weeks for it to turn up (and if you want books from abroad you may have to pay a hefty fee).

- Your local library may have everything you need: an excellent history section, a comprehensive local studies department, and a cache of priceless nineteenth-century photos *of your characters*.

- There is little point seeking out original manuscripts if they have already been transcribed by experts and printed in a book (and you may find the entire book online).

- Working with archives can eat up a great deal of time and may mean travelling a great distance, which will add to your expenses.

- Check all printed sources before going anywhere near the archives.

Major libraries

The six Copyright Libraries are entitled to copies of every printed book published in the UK and the Republic of Ireland (the US equivalent is the Library of Congress):

- The British Library (BL), London, www.bl.uk The BL has some 150m items, including 25 million books. For direct access to the catalogue online go to http://catalogue.bl.uk

- The Bodleian Library, Oxford www.bodleian.ox.ac.uk

- Cambridge University Library, Cambridge www.lib.cam.ac.uk/

- The National Library of Scotland, Edinburgh www.nls.uk/

- National Library of Wales, Aberystwyth www.llgc.org.uk
- Trinity College Dublin Library www.tcd.ie/library

The catalogues of the Copyright Libraries are listed online by Copac, the National Academic and Specialist Library Catalogue, with 34+ million records from the national and main university libraries. See www.copac.ac.uk

University libraries

- Copac has merged the online catalogues of 70+ UK and Irish academic, national and specialist library catalogues, including the British Library, the Bodleian Library, Oxford, Cambridge University Library, the National Libraries of Scotland and Wales, Trinity College Dublin Library, and all/most other university libraries. See www.copac.ac.uk
- Reciprocal arrangements exist for graduates to make use of any university library (though if you are not an alumnus you may have to pay). Non-graduates engaged on serious research should be able to gain access to university libraries, though a letter of recommendation may be required. As a rule, the older and bigger the university, the better the library.
- At Oxford and Cambridge, in addition to the university libraries, individual colleges also have their own libraries and collections of manuscripts (e.g. the Pepys Library, Magdalene College, Cambridge).
- The older UK universities also hold collections of local material: books, manuscripts, maps and photographs.
- Contact the library in advance to make sure the materials you need are available.

For the complete list, search online. A few suggestions:

- Senate House Library, University of London www.senatehouselibrary.ac.uk
- Institute of Historical Research Library, University of London www.history.ac.uk
- SOAS Library, The School of Oriental and African Studies, University of London, has unrivalled collections on Africa, Asia and the Middle East; see www.soas.ac.uk/Library

Other libraries

- The British Library Newspaper Library has an unrivalled collection of 50,000+

newspapers, periodicals and magazines. Formerly at Colindale, North London, now at Boston Spa, West Yorkshire. Future access to the collection will be via microfilm and digital copies at the British Library, St Pancras, London, see www.bl.uk/collections/newspapers Also useful: the British Newspaper Archive Online, with 6 m+ searchable pages, see www.britishnewspaperarchive.co.uk

- The Bodleian Library, Oxford also has a substantial collection of newspapers. County record offices also have provincial newspapers from the eighteenth and nineteenth centuries.

- Guildhall Library, Aldermanbury, London EC2 (specialises in history of London) www.cityoflondon.gov.uk

- Westminster Central Reference Library, St Martin's Street, London WC2 (specialist reference library) www.westminster.gov.uk/services/library

- John Rylands Library, Manchester University (excellent local collections) www.library.manchester.ac.uk

- Mitchell Library, Glasgow www.mitchelllibrary.org (vast reference collection)

Subscription libraries

- The London Library is the biggest and best known, with one million books, 97 per cent of which may be borrowed in person or by post. There are also 750 periodicals and learned journals, and a complete run of *The Times* from 1785 to date. Membership includes access to a substantial E-Library, with the vital JSTOR. Impecunious scholars may apply for membership at reduced rates. See: www.londonlibrary.co.uk or www.elibrary.londonlibrary.co.uk

- Others include the 'Lit & Phil' in Newcastle, Bath Royal Literary and Scientific Institution, the Central Catholic Library, Dublin, and the Nottingham Subscription Library. For a complete list go to www.independentlibraries.co.uk

Special interest libraries

- British Library Sound Archive www.bl.uk/soundarchive
- BBC Written Archives Centre www.bbc.co.uk/heritage
- British Architectural Library, RIBA www.architecture.com
- College of Psychic Studies Library www.psychic-studies.org.uk
- Dr Williams's Library www.dwlib.co.uk (English Protestant Nonconformity)

- Egypt Exploration Society Library www.ees.ac.uk
  - Foreign & Commonwealth Office Library www.fco.gov.uk
  - Glasgow Women's Library (for and about women) www.womens-library.org.uk
  - Goethe Institute Library (specialises in German literature) www.goethe.de/london
  - Horniman Library, www.horniman.ac.uk (musical instruments and ethnography)
  - Joint Library of the Hellenic and Roman Societies www.hellenicsociety.org.uk
  - Lambeth Palace Library www.lambethpalacelibrary.org
  - Lindley Library, Royal Horticultural Society www.rhs.org.uk
  - National Art Library, Victoria and Albert Museum www.vam.ac.uk/nal
  - Royal Geographical Society Library www.rgs.org
  - Rural History Centre, University of Reading www.reading.ac.uk/merl/collections
  - School of Oriental and African Studies Library www.soas.ac.uk
  - Society of Antiquaries Library www.sal.org.uk
  - Society of Genealogists Library www.sog.org.uk
  - The Tate Library and Archive www.tate.org.uk/research
  - Wellcome Library www.library.wellcome.ac.uk (History of Medicine)
  - Westminster Reference Library www.westminster.gov.uk/libraries/westref
  - Wiener Library (History of Holocaust and Genocide) www.wienerlibrary.co.uk
  - The Women's Library, London www.thewomenslibrary.ac.uk (women's history)
  - Zoological Society of London Library www.zsl.org

Archives

UK – national archives

- The National Archives, Kew www.nationalarchives.gov.uk is the principal repository for historical manuscripts relating to England and Wales. Also army, navy and air force records, passenger lists (immigration and emigration) up to 1960 – see www.AncestorsOnBoard.com The catalogue has guides relating to particular subjects, e.g. slavery, and the transportation of convicts, and also has advice on tracing people, e.g. through birth, marriage and death certificates, occupations, adoption, etc. See www.nationalarchives.gov.uk/records/looking-for-person. For a direct link to the online catalogue go to www.pro.gov.uk/catalogues/default.htm

- The National Register of Archives is now part of the National Archives, Kew and accessible online at www.nationalarchives.gov.uk/nra The NRA contains info on the nature and whereabouts of manuscripts and records relating to British history – many of which are still in private hands. The Personal Index covers the correspondence and papers of 30,000+ notable figures from every field of British history.

- The Manuscript Department of the British Library is the major manuscript depository in England. For manuscripts in other libraries check the ARCHON (Archive Contacts) Directory at the National Archives site, www.nationalarchives.gov.uk/archon or the Historical Manuscripts Commission: www.nationalarchives.gov.uk/information-management/projects-and-work/hmc.htm

- For literary manuscripts (your novel may be about William Blake) see the Location Register of English Literary Manuscripts and Letters at the University of Reading, www.reading.ac.uk/library/about-us/projects/lib-location-register.aspx

- The Access to Archives project aims to put all UK archive catalogues on the Internet, see www.a2a.org.uk

Wales – national archives

- The National Library of Wales, Aberystwyth, holds some 25,000 manuscripts. Also books, archives, maps, photos, films. Here are records of Welsh landed gentry, manorial records, correspondence... from the medieval charters of the Cistercian Abbey of Strata Marcella to the scrapbooks of Freddie Welsh the boxer. See www.llgc.org.uk

- See also Archives Wales www.archiveswales.org.uk and Archives Network Wales www.archivesnetworkwales.info

Scotland – national archives

- National Records of Scotland. Based in Edinburgh. Access is free. See www. gro-scotland.gov.uk

- The National Register of Archives for Scotland will guide you re. the whereabouts of historical manuscripts. See www.nas.gov.uk with online catalogue. Many of the NRAS surveys are available on the NRAS OPAC at the National Records of Scotland.

- ScotlandsPeople is the official website for Scottish genealogy, with 90 million records. Pre-1855 old parish registers (OPRS), statutory registers of births, marriages and deaths, from 1855, Census returns 1841–1901, can all be accessed online. Also the testaments digitised by SCAN (see below). The online index is searchable free at www.Scotlandspeople.gov.uk

- ScotlandsPeople Centre, Edinburgh, provides a single base for genealogical research in Scotland. Fees apply. Website as above.

- Scottish Archive Network (SCAN) provides online access to the written history of Scotland, see catalogue at www.scan.org.uk for all Scottish testaments 1500–1901. The Index is searchable free at www.ScotlandsPeople.gov.uk (fees payable thereafter).

Nothern Ireland

Basic sources

- For biography see *Dictionary of Ulster Biography Online*, free access at www.ulsterbiography.co.uk
- Ulster Historical Foundation www.ancestryireland.com
- The Ulster Archaeological Society www.uas.society.qub.ac.uk

Archives

- Northern Ireland: Public Records Office of Northern Ireland, www.proni.gov.uk

University libraries

- Queen's University, Belfast www.qub.ac.uk/Lib/
- Ulster University Library, Coleraine www.library.ulster.ac.uk

Other libraries

- Linen Hall Library, Belfast – also Irish/Local Studies Dept. www.linenhall.com
- Belfast Central Library – also Ulster and Irish Studies Dept. www.belb.org.uk

Births, marriages, and deaths – UK

- The General Register Office (England and Wales) holds records of births, deaths, marriages, civil partnerships, stillbirths, adoptions in England and Wales (from 1837). See www.gov.uk

- GRO Indexes are searchable online at www.freebmd.org.uk

- Baptisms, marriages and burials before 1837 may be found in parish registers, which began in 1558. Since record-keeping varied in thoroughness, this may involve a lengthy and costly search, but many parish registers are available in print (the Society of Genealogists' Library has a large collection). County record offices have printed registers relating to their area as well as the originals, mostly on microfilm. For what is available, with dates and whereabouts, check the *Phillimore Atlas and Index of Parish Registers*; and the (more detailed) *National Index of Parish Registers*.

- For births and marriages check the IGI (see above, p. 187.)

- For elusive burials try the *National Burial Index*, 3rd issue on DVD (2010).

- For Scotland, births, marriages and deaths, see www.gro-scotland.gov.uk

- For Northern Ireland births, marriages and deaths, go to www.nidirect.gov.uk/gro

Wills – UK

- Wills can be a valuable source of information. In making bequests the testator often mentions his whole family by name, and the servants too. Earlier wills (e.g. sixteenth century) may have an inventory attached, itemising the deceased's goods and chattels down to the last red cow. Finding wills can be complicated: you may need expert guidance (see below).

- Wills 1858–present are kept at the Probate Search Room, First Avenue House, 42–49 High Holborn, London WC1. The National Probate Calendar, i.e. the index, is also available online.

- The National Probate Calendar gives info on wills and probate records, England and Wales, 1858–1966. Six million names are searchable online (for a fee) at www.ancestry.co.uk/probate

- For an up-to-date guide to wills see *Wills and Probate Records* by Karen Grannum and Nigel Taylor, published by the National Archives (2009).

- For Scottish testaments see above, p. 195

Local archives

County Record Offices

What can you expect to find?

- County Record Offices hold many records of great use, particularly the original parish registers from 1558, with details of baptisms, marriages and burials, and also the contemporary copies known as Bishop's Transcripts – useful if the original register has gone missing or is damaged.

- Census Returns for 1831, 1841, 1851 through to 1901.

- Judicial records: Sessions Rolls, for Quarter and Petty Sessions, lists of justices, indictments of criminals, depositions of defendants; jury lists, calendars of prisoners, and removal orders for paupers. The Order Books contain formal records of court proceedings.

- City and county directories (seventeenth to nineteenth centuries) with lists of nobility, gentry, clergy, shops and tradesmen.

- Records of bridges, highways and turnpike roads, canals, docks, railways, and gaols.

- Documents relating to police, vagrants and lunatics.

- Coroners' records, Enclosure Awards, Registers of Electors, Hairpowder Tax lists.

- Information on charities, freemasons, gamekeepers, jurors, parliamentary elections.

- Maps, estate records, papers of local landed families, diaries and letters.

- A card index of personal names, places, field-names, and copies of local newspapers.

- Most county records are now microfilmed and you will not get to see the original document unless the film is illegible. The important thing is to make an appointment a few days ahead of your visit, and *book a microfilm reader*. If you turn up on spec you may be turned away, regardless of how far you have travelled.

- All record offices have comprehensive collections of books relevant to their county.

- Archivists have vast local knowledge. They may take an interest in your project and make useful suggestions re your quest – if you ask – but they will not do the research for you.

- If you can't read a document, either swot up on palaeography or hire a record agent. It's not difficult to teach yourself to read medieval documents.

- Some county archivists will respond to brief written queries and supply photo-copies (e.g. of wills and inventories) at cost by post; the busier offices will refer you to a list of approved record searchers, who will find and transcribe whatever document you want, for a fee.

- Many authors recoil in horror at the thought of somebody doing their research for them. *Our advice is go yourself, if you possibly can.* Why? Because serendipity always turns up wonderful things you were not even looking for, things that a hired record agent might not notice. *You* are the one full of enthusiasm for your research project: you need to be on the case yourself.

- *The Oxford Companion to Local and Family History* has detailed info on records.

- The classic study of parish registers and other parish records is W.E. Tate's *The Parish Chest.*

- There are some 140 record repositories in the UK. The ARCHON Directory of Archive repositories lists 2,114 in England, Wales and Scotland (651 of them in London) but this includes libraries and organisations. To access the whole list, or to browse by region, with website links, email and phone contacts and street maps, go to www.nationalarchives.gov.uk/archon

Other useful organisations

Historic buildings and monuments — UK

- Ancient monuments, castles, palaces and stately homes open to the public are listed in full on the English Heritage and National Trust websites below. Detailed information on listed buildings can be obtained from the following:

- English Heritage (Historical Buildings and Monuments Commission for England) www.english-heritage.org.uk; National Monuments Record Centre, Swindon

- The Scottish equivalent is Historic Scotland www.historic-scotland.gov.uk

- Royal Commission on the Ancient and Historical Monuments of Scotland www.rcahms.gov.uk

- Cadw: Welsh Historic Monuments www.cadw.wales.gov.uk

- Royal Commission on the Ancient and Historical Monuments of Wales www.rcahmw.gov.uk

- National Trust www.nationaltrust.org.uk

- National Trust for Scotland www.nts.org.uk

Heraldry

- The herald offices have little-known but magnificent archive collections on genealogy and heraldry. Searches will be undertaken on your behalf, and since the heralds have no public funding they also charge magnificent fees.

- Many records, e.g. of heralds' visitations, have been published by the Harleian Society and contain valuable geneaological info on armigerous families.

- England (and Wales): College of Arms, London www.college-of-arms.gov.uk

- Scotland: Court of the Lord Lyon, Edinburgh www.lyon-court.com

Museums and galleries – England

> **❝** *Look at the same things again and again until they themselves begin to speak!* **❞**
> Charcot's advice to Sigmund Freud

Museums and art galleries will be useful for research, of course, but also for inspiration, revelation, brainwaves. There are hundreds to choose from in the UK and Ireland. Note that several have their own libraries **(L)**. Complete lists online.

England
London – museums

- British Museum www.thebritishmuseum.org
- Geffrye Museum www.geffrye-museum.org.uk
- Horniman Museum www.horniman.ac.uk
- Imperial War Museum www.iwm.org.uk **(L)**
- Museum of Childhood at Bethnal Green www.museumofchildhood.org.uk
- Museum of London www.museumoflondon.org.uk
- National Army Museum www.national-army-museum.ac.uk
- National Maritime Museum www.nmm.ac.uk
- Natural History Museum www.nhm.ac.uk
- Petrie Museum of Egyptian Archaeology www.petrie.ucl.ac.uk
- Science Museum www.sciencemuseum.org.uk

- Sir John Soane's Museum www.soane.org
- Victoria and Albert Museum www.vam.ac.uk **(L)**

London — galleries

- Courtauld Institute of Art Gallery www.courtauld.ac.uk **(L)**
- Dulwich Picture Gallery www.dulwichpicturegallery.org.uk
- National Gallery www.nationalgallery.org.uk
- National Portrait Gallery www.npg.org.uk
- The Queen's Gallery www.royalcollection.org.uk
- Royal Academy of Arts www.royalacademy.org.uk
- Tate Britain www.tate.org.uk
- Tate Modern www.tate.org.uk/modern
- Wallace Collection www.wallacecollection.org

TOP TIP

If you're writing about London, get hold of Ben Weinreb and Christopher Hibberts' wonderful London Encyclopaedia. Indispensable and detailed info, street by street.

Museums and galleries outside London

Here are a few stars. Search online for more.

- CAMBRIDGE: Fitzwilliam Museum www.fitzmuseum.cam.ac.uk
- Imperial War Museum, Duxford www.duxford.iwm.org.uk
- University Museum of Archaeology and Anthropology www.maa.cam.ac.uk
- Whipple Museum of the History of Science www.hps.cam.ac.uk/whipple
- LIVERPOOL: International Slavery Museum www.liverpoolmuseums.org.uk
- Tate Liverpool www.tate.org.uk/liverpool
- Walker Art Gallery www.liverpoolmuseums.org.uk/walker
- MANCHESTER: Imperial War Museum North www.north.iwm.org.uk
- Manchester Art Gallery www.manchestergalleries.org
- Manchester Museum www.museum.manchester.ac.uk
- OXFORD: Ashmolean Museum, Oxford www.ashmolean.org
- Museum of the History of Science www.mhs.ox.ac.uk
- Pitt-Rivers Museum www.prm.ox.ac.uk (anthropology and world archaeology)

Museums and galleries – Scotland

- Edinburgh: Museum of Childhood www.cac.org.uk
- Museum of Edinburgh www.cac.org.uk
- Museum of Scotland www.nms.ac.uk/scotland
- National Gallery of Scotland www.nationalgalleries.org
- National War Museum of Scotland www.nms.ac.uk/war
- Royal Museum www.nms.ac.uk
- Scottish National Portrait Gallery www.nationalgalleries.org

Historical societies and relevant organisations – UK

Academic journals can be difficult to penetrate; the journals of the county historical societies (not listed here, but worth tracking down) are less weighty. Together, they constitute a rich source of historical, genealogical and topographical information – like a vast encyclopedia of recherché knowledge about the past, where whole novels might be conjured out of a single footnote. Here is a selective list:

- Crimean War Research Society www.cwrs.russianwar.co.uk
- Egypt Exploration Society www.ees.ac.uk
- The Georgian Group www.georgiangroup.org.uk
- Hakluyt Society (for historical voyages/journeys of discovery) www.hakluyt.com
- Heraldry Society www.theheraldrysociety.com
- The Historical Novel Society www.historicalnovelsociety.org
- The Historical Writers' Association www.thehwa.co.uk
- Institute of Heraldic and Genealogical Studies www.ihgs.ac.uk
- Institute of Historical Research www.history.ac.uk/
- Military Historical Society www.milithistsocplus.com
- Navy Records Society www.navyrecords.org.uk
- Royal Geographical Society www.rgs.org
- Royal Historical Society www.royalhistoricalsociety.org
- Scottish Genealogy Society www.scotsgenealogy.com
- Scottish History Society www.scottishhistorysociety.org
- Society of Antiquaries of London www.sal.org.uk
- Society of Antiquaries of Scotland: www.socantscot.org

- Society for Army Historical Research www.sahr.co.uk/
  - Society for the Promotion of Hellenic Studies www.hellenicsociety.org.uk
  - Society for the Promotion of Roman Studies www.romansociety.org
  - Society for the Protection of Ancient Buildings www.spab.org.uk
  - Society for Psychical Research www.spr.ac.uk
  - Society of Genealogists www.sog.org.uk
  - Victorian Society www.victoriansociety.org.uk

Welsh journals

The National Library of Wales, Aberystwyth, has digitised the back numbers of 50 journals relating to Wales (not all of them in Welsh!) www.welsh-journals.llgc.org.uk

House history

Stately homes and country houses, with period furniture and portraits, are a vital source of inspiration. Many are open to the public and worth visiting to soak up the atmosphere of the past. Some of the grandest houses (e.g. Chatsworth) have an archive department, which will respond to queries about the collection. If the house you've hit upon happens to be in private hands, access may be impossible: write your politest letter and keep your fingers crossed – or use a different house as your model.

- *The Victoria County History*, see under county (1899, ongoing). VCH is not yet complete but has detailed info on churches, ancient monuments, historic houses, and landed familes – with comprehensive genealogies.
- See also *Burke's Guide to English Country Houses*, *Burke's Country Houses of* Ireland, Burke's *Country Houses of* Scotland, and *Country Life* (weekly from 1897).
- Nikolaus Pevsner, *The Buildings of England*. 46+ vols, by county, is the Bible of architectural historians and antiquaries. Pevsner also covers Scotland, Wales, Northern Ireland and (parts of) Eire.
- The RIBA Architectural Library may also be useful.

Topography

- Early editions of Baedeker (the Bible of every American tourist) are like time-capsules, preserving a picture of the world 1850–1900 with detailed info on everything of historical interest, plus meticulous maps and city plans (e.g. Venice, Damascus, Rome).

- The *Blue Guide* series gives detailed topographical and historical info on archaeological sites, temples, churches and other ancient monuments, e.g. in Greece, Egypt, Italy.

- The *Rough Guide* series is more hip but still includes valuable topographical information for countries you can't visit in person.

- The London Library has an extensive Topography section with worldwide coverage, all browsable on open shelves.

Picture libraries

- The famous Mary Evans Picture Library is still going strong, www.maryevans.com
- Getty Images has 80m still photos and 50,000 hours of film footage – www. gettyimages.com. Or try Google Images.
- All national museums have their own picture libraries. So do the National Archives, the British Library, English Heritage, the Hellenic and Roman Societies and many more.
- Check the British Association of Picture Libraries and Agencies, www.bpa.org.uk
- The world's biggest collection of images is flickr, www.flickr.com with some 6 billion photos and 51 millon registered users from 100+ countries. Most images are posted by private individuals and are therefore *copyright*. If you want a flickr picture on your dust jacket, ask the copyright owner first, and be prepared to pay.

Ireland (Eire)

Basic sources

- *Dictionary of Irish Biography* (DIB) online at www.dib.cambridge.org
- Irish History Online – bibliography of Irish history www.irishhistoryonline
- RASCAL (Research and Special Collections Available Locally – Ireland) is an electronic gateway to research resources.
- PADDI (Planning Architecture Design Database Ireland) covers historic buildings and architecture.

Archives

- Genealogical research in the Republic of Ireland has been described as all but impossible because the majority of records were destroyed in 1922. In truth, Irish research is not so difficult. What survives is kept in the National Archives in Dublin, the official state repository for the state records of Ireland.
- National Archives of Ireland www.nationalarchives.ie
- National Library of Ireland, Dublin www.nli.ie
- For the 1911 Census of Ireland online see www.census.nationalarchives.uk
- For Irish Family History Records go to www.familylink.com/ireland
- Ireland Genealogy Project www.igp-web.com

Local archives

- The ARCHON Directory lists 77 archive repositories in the Republic of Ireland; for the complete list see www.nationalarchives.gov.uk/archon

University libraries

- Trinity College Library, Dublin www.tcd.ie/Library
- University College Dublin Library www.ucd.ie/library

Museums and galleries

- National Gallery of Ireland, Dublin www.nationalgallery.ie
- National Museum of Ireland, Dublin www.museum.ie
- National Museum of Ireland – Archaeology, Dublin www.museum.ie
- National Museum of Ireland – Decorative Arts & History www.museum.ie
- Chester Beatty Library, Dublin www.cbl.ie

USA

Basic sources

- There are some mind-boggling statistics below on the number of books and manuscripts in the National Archives and the National Library of Congress. There is a whole world of archives waiting to be turned over, full of untold true stories from America's past.

- If the subject of your novel is a well-known *recent* historical figure, there should be something in print already, whether biographies, memoirs or letters. Search online for Bibliography, American History, or enter 'Bibliography Early American Naval History', and so on.

- For personal names, and obituaries, check *The New York Times* (from 1851, index and archive free online), also the *Washington Post* (from 1877), and *Los Angeles Times* (from 1881).

- For the general picture see Hugh Brogan's *Penguin History of the United States of America* or *A People's History of the United States: 1492 – Present* by Howard Zinn.

- The US equivalent of *DNB* is *American National Biography* (ANB) in 24 vols, with 17,400 entries. Also online, for a fee. The ANB's predecessor, the *Dictionary of American Biography* (DAB) is still useful. Also *The National Cyclopaedia of American Biography* with 63 vols and 60,000 entries. The NCAB is less scholarly than DAB and ANB (it doesn't cite original sources) but more comprehensive.

- For the twentieth century, check old editions of *Who's Who in America*.

- For presidents, see *Burke's Presidential Families of the United States of America*.

- The website based at Northwestern University, www.libraryspot.com will locate and link you to the online catalogues of public and academic libraries throughout the US and worldwide.

National archives

- The National Archives and Records Administration is the major US institution for manuscripts. Go to www.archives.gov for details of historic records of national and international significance, plus family history, genealogy, adoption records, federal census records, immigration, military and naturalisation records, ship passenger lists, city directories, newspapers, missing persons (and much more). The National Archives hold nine billion pages of textual records.

Local archives

- For state archives see www.archives.gov and go to Archives Library Information Center (ALIC) for details of every state repository from Alabama Department of Archives through Wyoming State Archives, with addresses, phone numbers and FAQ. To take one example, at New York State Archives you will find manuscripts and special collections, rare books, maps, atlases, prints and photographs. Also a Census Finder, Ellis Island passenger search, genealogical centre, ship passenger arrival books, land records, military service records, nationwide gravesite locator, help with tracing American Indian ancestors, and, of course, vital records – birth certificates, marriage licenses and death certificates.

Libraries

- Libraries in the USA tend to be big. Even the 100th in size (Massachusetts Institute of Technology Library) has three million books. Access to university libraries may be restricted to graduates: if you can't beat your way in, there are plenty of giant public libraries which may serve your needs just as well (see below).

Public libraries

The biggest public libraries are vast and there are 8,951 of them. Here are the top ten by size:

- Library of Congress, Washington (33 million volumes): www.loc.gov This the de facto national library of the USA, and the largest in the world, with 147 million items, including 33 m books and 61 m manuscripts. This is the American equivalent of the UK copyright libraries, entitled to a copy of every book published in the USA.
- New York Central Library (www.nypl.org) Second in size, with c.53 m items.
- Boston Public Library (23 million) www.bpl.org
- New York Public Library (15 m) www.nypl.org

- Public Library of Cincinatti and Hamilton County (9 m) www.cincinattilibrary.org
- County of Los Angeles Public Library (7 m) www.colapublib.org
- Detroit Public Library (7 m) www.detroit.lib.mi.us
- Queens Borough Public Library (6 m) www.queenslibrary.org
- Los Angeles Public Library (6 m) www.lapl.org
- Chicago Public Library (5 m) www.chipublib.org

Size, of course, is not everything. The best library is the one that has the book you want: always check your local library first.

University libraries

There are 3,689 academic libraries in the America. Here are the top five by size:

- Harvard University Library (16 million books) www.lib.harvard.edu
- University of Illinois Library (13 m) www.library.illinois.edu
- Yale University Library (12 m) www.library.yale.edu
- University of California, Berkeley, Libraries (10 m) www.lib.berkeley.edu
- Columbia University Libraries (10 m) www.library.columbia.edu

Other libraries
- Family History Library (FHL), Salt Lake City, Utah, is the genealogical arm of the Church of Jesus Christ of the Latter-day Saints (the Mormons). This is the largest genealogical library in the world, with records from 110+ countries. The total collection has 2.4+ million rolls of microfilm. For the IGI and other research see www.familysearch.org

Museums and galleries

America has some 17,500 museums and galleries to inspire you. Search online for complete lists. Here are 12 of the best:

- The Smithsonian Institution www.si.edu
- Cleveland Museum of Art www.clevelandart.org

- Field Museum, Chicago www.fieldmuseum.org
- Brooklyn Museum www.brooklynmuseum.org
- Museum of Fine Art, Boston MA www.mfa.org
- Frick Collection www.frick.org
- Guggenheim Museum www.guggenheim.org
- J. Paul Getty Museum www.getty.edu
- Metropolitan Museum, New York www.metmuseum.org
- New York Historical Society (American history museum + library) www.nyhistory.org/
- Museum of Fine Art, Boston, Massachusetts www.mfa.org
- National Gallery of Art, Washington www.nga.gov

Historical societies

- National associations: try the American Historical Association. Search online for the vast list of US historical associations and journals.
- There's also a vast number of state and local historical societies (Iowa has four, Kentucky has just the one, Indiana has 218.)

Canada

Basic sources

- The *Dictionary of Canadian Biography* (DCB) aka *Dictionnaire biographique du Canada* (DBC) exists in a 15-volume print version (ongoing) and is also online, free, at www.biographi.ca/index-e.html
- For general info and bibliography look at Robert Bothwell's *Penguin History of Canada* or Margaret Conrad's *A Concise History of Canada*.
- Or search online under Bibliography, History of Canada.

National and local archives

- Archives Canada, www.archivescanada.ca is the gateway to archival resources found in 800+ repositories across Canada. Whether you are hunting ancestors, tracking down Arctic explorers, Inuit tales and traditions, Canadians in the wars, or maps and photos, this site is the primary guide.

Major libraries

- The National Library of Canada is in Ottawa. www.collectionscanada.gc.ca
- John P. Robarts Library, Toronto www.onesearch.library.utoronto.ca
- University of Toronto Library (12 m vols) is Canada's largest academic library, ranking 3rd in North America, behind Harvard and Yale www.onesearch.library.utoronto.ca
- McGill University Library, Montreal www.mcgill.ca/library
- University of British Columbia, Vancouver www.library.ubc.ca/

Museums and galleries

There are 2,500+ museums and galleries in Canada for inspiration. Here are just a few:

- National Gallery of Canada www.gallery.ca
- Royal Ontario Museum, Toronto www.rom.on.ca
- Canadian Museum of History www.civilization.ca/history
- Montreal Museum of Fine Arts www.mbam.qc.ca
- Musée de l'Amérique Française, Quebec www.mcq.org/en/maf/index
- Royal Alberta Museum, Edmonton www.royalalbertamuseum.ca/

Australia

Basic sources

Is Ned Kelly really the only character in Australian history worth writing about? Sure, he is the only one that every English schoolboy knows. There is some updating to be done here...

- The pre-eminent publication on historical figures is the *Australian Dictionary of Biography* (ADB), with 12,000+ entries, available in print (18 vols), and online at www.adb.anu.edu/au
- For general history try Stuart Macintyre's *A Concise History of Australia.*
- Or Thomas Keneally's *The Commonwealth of Thieves.*
- For the story of transportation see Robert Hughes's *The Fatal Shore.*
- Or search online under Bibliography, Australia, History, for more possibilities.

Public libraries

- State Library of South Australia, Adelaide www.slsa.sa.gov.au
- State Library of Western Australia, Perth www.slwa.wa.gov.au
- State Library of Victoria, Melbourne www.slv.vic.gov.au
- State Library of New South Wales www.sl.nsw.gov.au
- State Library of Queensland www.slq.gov.au

Museums and galleries

For inspiration...

- National Museum of Australia, Canberra www.nma.gov.au
- National Gallery of Australia, Canberra www.nga.gov.au
- National Portrait Gallery, Canberra www.portrait.gov.au

- Art Gallery of South Australia, Adelaide www.artgallery.sa.gov.au
- Queensland Art Gallery, Brisbane www.qagoma.qld.gov.au
- Museum Victoria, Melbourne www.museumvictoria.com.au
- Western Australian Museum, Perth www.museum.wa.gov.au

New Zealand

Basic sources

All we seem to hear in the West is that New Zealand provided the landscape for the movie of *The Lord of the Rings*. Did nothing ever take place in that fabulous scenery that just happened to be real and historical?

- Getting started... The *Dictionary of New Zealand Biography* (DNZB) comes in a printed version (also available in Maori) and online at www.teara.govt.nz/en/biographies
- For general history see Michael King's *Penguin History of New Zealand*.
- An online search under Bibliography, New Zealand history, will turn up more titles.

Museums and galleries

Maori art, whaling, Antarctic exploration... Here are five suggestions:

- The Museum of New Zealand Te Papa Tongarewa, Wellington www.tepapa.govt.nz
- Canterbury Museum, Christchurch www.canterburymuseum.com
- Christchurch Gallery www.christchurchartgallery,org.nz
- City Gallery, Wellington www.citygallery.org.nz
- Dunedin Public Art Gallery www.dunedin.art.museum

Research plan – costing, time management, travelling

What will it cost?

- Writing a historical novel can cost as little, or as much, as you like. You might get away with no more than the price of ten reams of printer paper and a gross of biros (you don't *have* to work on a computer). If you make use of the library system and limit yourself to research online, writing a novel can cost next to nothing.

- On the other hand, if you buy a roomful of books, need access to fee-paying databases, private subscription libraries, and membership of half a dozen learned societies; if you need to hire record searchers, palaeographers and translators; and if you need to travel – then the writing of a novel could cost thousands of pounds or dollars.

- If you choose an exotic setting, your research trip may involve astronomical travel bills. One way round this is to go nowhere: take the interior journey instead; travel the highways of the imagination.

- Hiring a record searcher at £10 an hour might work out cheaper than making a long journey. Paying someone to carry out a brief search to see what records are available might make sense before undertaking an expensive trip yourself. Another time to hire an expert is when you get stuck – a difficult search might be completed more quickly by a professional.

- The plus side is that many of the expenses incurred in writing a book are tax deductible. Wherever your research takes you, keep a record of all expenses and keep all bills and receipts.

How long will it take?

- Every writer works at a different speed, and has a different method of going about writing a book. And different books demand different treatment, different means of attack.

- Some people can write a book in six weeks flat. Robert Graves wrote *I, Claudius* AND *Claudius the God* in eight months. It all depends on what sort of writer you are, what kind of book you want to write, how much research you feel you must do, and whether you find the actual process of writing dead easy or bloody difficult. How long it takes may also depend on whether you have just a few hours a day to spare, or are writing full-time. It should be possible to write a novel without too many historical complications in a year or two.

- Once your manuscript has been accepted by a publisher, be prepared to wait at least a year before publication – this allows time for editing, copy-editing, proof-reading, printing, distribution, dispatch of press copies for review, and for the generation of publicity.

Last minute questions

- If you are looking at a cast of hundreds of characters, spread over two or three centuries, ask yourself whether your story is going to be manageable? If you ever finish it, will any publisher want to print it? Will any reader want to buy it? Are you really on the right track?

- Expect a few false starts. The project you've embarked on may not, after all, be viable. You are bogged down in, say, the Holocaust and can't find the info that you need to make the book work. Be prepared to try something different.

- Changing the game-plan need not be the end of the world. The outline can go in a drawer. In a year's time you might think it's not so bad. Or you might find the missing link in the research that means you can go ahead after all.

- Most writers have more than one project in development at a time, something else in the pipeline, the next idea. Keep your options open.

- Nobody ever said writing a book is easy. It's the trials that make it interesting, and rewarding.

- It's impossible to use every fact gleaned from your researches: you have to SELECT, and SHAPE the material.

- First build your iceberg, then use the tip of it. Some icebergs are bigger than others.

- If you know in your heart and bones that you are on to a good story, keep going.

- Action.

Beginning

How to focus

> **There is absolutely no point in sitting down to write a book unless you feel that you must write that book, or else go mad, or die.**
>
> Robertson Davies

> **Genius = 1 per cent inspiration, 99 per cent perspiration.**
>
> Thomas Edison

- Writing a novel, particularly one based on historical research, is hard work. It won't write itself, and you can't write it all at once. In *Writing A Novel*, John Braine shared his mantra: 'A writer is someone who writes; a writer is someone who counts words.' Getting it done is about keeping going. Keeping going is about acquiring the habit of writing. If you wait for inspiration you may wait a long time. But you can train yourself up to be inspired between the hours of 9 a.m. and 5 p.m. Or 7–9 p.m. Whenever. The important thing is to keep up the habit of writing every day.

- If you can write 1,000 words a day (about three pages) and keep it up, you will have 7,000 words by the end of the week. Do this for two months and you have a novella-length manuscript (56,000 words). Four months at 1,000 words a day and you have the first draft of a novel 112,000 words long. That's nearly 300 pages in a printed book. So the answer to the question How Do I Write A Book? is this: you keep on writing. Hear the word of Robert Bach:

> **A professional writer is an amateur who didn't quit.**

- And if you type 2,000 words a day (about six pages) and keep on typing, your book will be written in eight weeks. Or, at least, the first draft.

- As for how long it should be, most novels weigh in at around 200–300 pages, or 80,000–120,000 words. Anything under 50,000 words counts as a novella (or a long short-story). Novels regularly exceed 300 pages, of course. In modern times anything over 1,000 pages is regarded as very difficult to publish (though in medieval China, novels might be as long as 2,000–3,000 pages...)

- There is no right or wrong way to write a novel. Everybody finds their own method of proceeding. It might suit you better to brainstorm your book 17 hours a day for three weeks, during your annual holiday (We hereby disclaim responsibility for your heart attack/divorce). You can't work all the time, and you probably shouldn't try. The times when you are not actually typing like a maniac are just as important as the times when you are.

> *A writer is not just at work when he holds a pen in his hand. He needs to allow the work to gestate.*
> A. N. Wilson, *Tolstoy*

- Remove all distractions – email, Internet, telephone (and, if possible, other people).

- You can lock yourself out of the web with Freedom Internet blocker.

- You can do the same for Facebook and Twitter with Anti-Social.

- Find out how you work best – what is your optimal time to write, how long you can write for without flagging, and what is the best place to work, whether the nearest Starbucks, the desk, the sofa, or propped up in bed.

- Make a habit of working at the same time, whether it's early morning, or late at night.

- Make yourself a schedule and stick to it. No cheating. Otherwise, no book.

- Sometimes you have to read books, but sometimes you read to avoid writing.

- Research can easily become avoidance, an excuse to put off writing Chapter 27.

- Some writers say that you should not try to write for more than three hours a day.

- You can train yourself to do more (say, if you have a publisher's deadline to meet).

- Try splitting the working day into two-hour or hour-long chunks.

- Schedule some proper breaks.
  - Exercise clears the mind. And provokes fresh ideas.
  - Spending all day with dead people can be... isolating.
  - Try to schedule some meetings with live people as well.

TOP TIP

DS Some people find it helps to work to music. For one thing, music drowns the noise of traffic. I often put myself into the novelist's equivalent of the poetic trance. A CD of Philip Glass String Quartets does the trick, same disc over and over again. Also Messiaen, John Adams, and Indian ragas.

Finding your voice

- Having gotten your ace subject and period, having done your research and decided on the trajectory of your story and who your characters are, who is going to tell the story? There are various options:
- Omniscient third person narrator.
- First person narrator.
- Partially omniscient narrator.
- Multiple narrators, each with a different perspective on events.
- Somehow, you must hold the reader under your spell for the extended period needed to read the book. For two radically different but equally captivating voices, look at J.D. Salinger, in *The Catcher in the Rye*, and Russell Hoban in *Riddley Walker*. In both these books it's the unique *voice* and the unique *tone* of the voice that take the reader prisoner.

How to get going

Drafting a plot

- Some writers just begin, haphazardly, and see where following their nose will take them, without any plotting. Fine, if it works.
- On the other hand, it might help to have an overview of the plot before you

start – so you can see where you are going. Otherwise it can be a bit like getting on the wrong bus.

- There's no right or wrong way to do this, but try writing the numbers 1–30 down the margin of a sheet of A4. These are the chapters. No. 1 is the start. No. 30 is the finish. Somewhere around No. 15 is the middle. No 5. might be the end of the beginning. Plot where the beginning of the middle will be, the middle of the middle, the end of the middle, the beginning of the end, the middle of the end, and the end of the end, then the very end. Add more subdivisions if you need more.

- Make diagrams to show the arc of the plot, how the momentum of the story will develop, and how you will keep it going: by means of successive conflicts and climaxes, followed by quieter interludes, lulls in the tension, then building up again, all leading on to the final resolution of the conflict.

- If the above seems difficult, try doing the same with somebody else's book first.

- Try thinking of the plot in musical terms, like a classical string quartet (Haydn, Mozart, Beethoven). It starts with exposition, setting the scene, mood and tone, medium pace: then it grabs your interest and takes off, pretty damn quick. Next come complicating factors, slowing-things-down factors, trouble, conflict; it moves on into the development, medium-fast, faster, then medium-slow; then comes a very slow movement, perhaps full of forebodings, and turbulence; this is followed by a zipping-along bit, swirling the listener inexorably to the end, and the resolution of the whole thing. This might not work if you are into Arctic Monkeys or Mumford & Sons, but you never know...

- During the weeks and months of writing, keep drawing and redrawing those diagrams that show the arc of the plot. Try juggling the sequence of events to heighten the tension. Try leaving out stuff that contributes nothing to the arc of the story.

- As Aristotle put it...for a proper plot you're going to need a beginning, a middle and an end.

- Are you going to start in the middle, like the *Odyssey*, and make use of flash-backs? Will you begin at the beginning? Or will you devise something clever with the time-scale, like the movie *Memento*?

- Sow your seeds early. Suggest what the principal theme is somewhere among the opening pages. If your book is about murder, for example, give some hint of murder near the start to signpost the way. Readers want to know where a book is going. Arouse their interest by the initial setting of the scene. Unfold the story by subtly alternating the revelation and the withholding of information. It's by creating suspense that you make readers urgent to know the outcome of the story and keep on turning the pages.

- Don't leave a battleaxe in the room unless somebody's going to use it.

Drafts

- Some writers (Graham Greene was a shining example) can write perfect publishable prose straight on to the page. Greene wrote at a steady 1,000 words a day, and – legend has it – would stop on the thousandth word, even in the middle of the sentence. Not everybody can emulate G.G.. Your first drafts may be a bit rough. It doesn't matter. What does matter is that you have captured some approximation of the story, which you can bash into shape; something to work on with the literary equivalent of hacksaw, hammer and nails. Then comes *sandpapering*, and *polishing*, and, in the end, with a bit of luck, prose that sparkles.

- So will your book be finished at the end of this period of hard labour? Maybe. Some books do just fall out of their creators' heads like taking dictation from the Almighty (e.g. the Book of Isaiah). Your book might fall in that category, but you'd be lucky.

- For most writers this initial phase represents the first draft. Now you have something to work on, you can go back and sort out the mess. Or at least, correct your spelling mitsakes, deal with the repeated places where where you have repeated yourself, and disentangle the thread of the plot.

- All writing is rewriting. That is, all *good* writing will have been through a lengthy process of redrafting and polishing. What you write can always be made better. No painting is ever finished, they say, only abandoned. The same applies to novels.

- If the first draft feels too long, cut. If too short, expand. If the plot is unbalanced, rearrange the furniture. Work on the dialogue, cutting and sharpening. Check every historical fact. This process of bettering might occupy you for a few months. Maybe more.

Practical stuff

- Fix up your document with wide margins (at least one inch left and right).

- Double-space the manuscript so that a whole extra line of print could be fitted inbetween. *You* need the broad margins and the spaces between the lines to scribble additions and corrections. Your friends need the spaces so they can write perky comments about your (lack of) logic. Copy-editors need room to mark up the manuscript for the printer. Repeat: Double. Space. The. Manuscript.

- Make it look right on the page. Begin each chapter with the first word flush against the margin. Indent your paragraphs thereafter. Don't write a novel that's laid out like a technical paper. You don't want a space between every paragraph. Save up the space to use for a major break in the narrative. Look at any published novel to see the standard layout, then follow that layout. Your manuscript should look as near as dammit how you want it to look in the finished book – spacing, paragraphing, gaps, italics, capitals, punctuation. That way, you stay in control of what is printed.

- Number the pages. All agents and publishers drop print-outs on the floor...

- If you're in this game for life, why not learn to type with more than two fingers?

- Some writers write straight on to the screen. Others write longhand and type up later. I do both, but I always print out the manuscript so I can see what I'm doing. I scribble corrections all over the page, then type in the changes. Then I print out and scribble again. This process goes on, on and on, until the book is finished.

- But the only right way to write is the way that works best for you.

TOP TIP

At the time this book was written, in 2013, the most popular software for organising a manuscript is Scrivener, available for PCs and Macs at http://www.literatureandlatte.com/scrivener.php. For US$40. In my experience, all the puffs for this programme are true. It really is a brilliantly helpful way to organise a large writing project and keep your research, your narrative planning, your notes, your dead darlings and your ideas for the next project organised and autosaved so you find them faster than your synapses fire. **CB**

- Study the art of the start. Watching the beginning of DVDs is not a bad way to do this. Spend some time in a bookshop reading the first lines of historical novels. When you've stopped laughing, make sure nobody laughs at yours unless you meant them to.

- Begin with something that will grab your reader's attention, something that will hook his/her curiosity, make them want to keep reading. Involve them from the start, from the first chapter, from the first page, from the first line, from the first sentence, from the very first word. If every chapter begins like that, then every paragraph (or quite a few of them), you may find you are cooking with gas. If, when you read the whole thing through, you move yourself to tears, you may be doing okay.

- *Save your work.* Remember to *back up.* Make a back-up disk. Don't let the ether swallow your manuscript. Some writers carry a back-up disc wherever they go, in case of house-fire, laptop thieves, literary burglars... Take all reasonable precautions.

Troubleshooting

> *There are known knowns; there are things that we know we know. We also know there are known unknowns; that is to say, we know there are some things we do not know. But there are also unknown unknowns — the ones that we don't know we don't know.*
>
> Donald Rumsfeld (2002)

What to do with a gap in your evidence

- You get around it by inventing. This is why your book is not history but fiction.

- All you can do is weigh up the facts and infer or deduce what might have happened.

- Progress is advanced by deduction, a judicious summing up of available evidence.

- What you do know will give you the confidence to know things about the unknown.

- When you know EVERYTHING about your characters and period, you will find that you begin to know even the things that nobody knows. This sounds mad but is true.

- Robert Graves spoke about the stage when you just *know* how something happened, even in the places where there is no evidence at all. Flaubert said that for the dedicated researcher, informed by the historical facts, everything he invents is true.

- If you can't decide which version of events to use, try building that doubt into the text, or give both accounts side by side, like Herodotus.

- Remember that info can be shunted sideways. We don't know what Alexander the Great ate for breakfast. But we do know that the ancient Greeks in general ate hot dough dipped in honey, or in neat wine, for breakfast. It's not unreasonable to assume that Alexander ate hot dough for breakfast too. If you proceed according to this slightly wacky logic, you are writing what is essentially the truth. It's as true as it can be.

- Speculate – on the basis of the evidence, the known facts. Apply simple logic. Draw logical conclusions. Idle speculation will probably result in a Big Mistake.

- Dealing with gaps should not, in fact, be a problem. Filling the gaps in history, making sense of the disparate parts, that is what historical fiction is all about.

Writer's block

- If you find you can't write, are struck wordless for days on end, what do you do? Somebody once said, 'Writer's block is just failure of nerve.' Concentrate, then, on keeping your nerve. Tell yourself you can do it, you will do it. Try Coué's system of auto-suggestion: 'Every day in every way my book is getting better and better.' (It does work.)

- If the blank page causes real trouble there are a few things that may help:

- Get away from the desk. Desks should be associated with working well, not with failing to work.

- Sleep on the problem. Your subconscious mind will, in the end, throw up a solution.

- Don't try to work all the time. Even three hours a day may be quite long enough.

- Try taking the evening off. And/or the weekend. Don't deny yourself holidays.

- Exercise keeps you fit, clears the brain, inspires fresh thoughts. Take a walk.

- Travel. Even short bus and train journeys can provoke amazing ideas.

- Watch movies set in your period of history. Spot the hysterical historical mistakes.

- Maybe you just haven't done enough research. Do you need to hit the library?

- A writing course might help. Talking through your literary problems with a professional can be therapeutic; so can discussing your novel with other students. See Writing courses page 256f.

- Some books, of course, never do come together. We've all written our fair share of 100pp of total nonsense. Maybe you have written a real turkey. Don't chuck it in the trash, though. Put it in a drawer. Even a turkey might be made to fly...

- Some books are complex and almost demand to go at their own pace. The reconstruction of a complicated period of history can be tough work. Your brain may take a while to figure out what really happened. Reconstructing the psychology of historical characters takes a lot of mulling over. You yourself may not be ready to take the book forward. It can be a good thing to let the book cook for a while, just leave it alone and do something else.

- At this stage, to find the answers you need to look within, within yourself. A book can begin almost to have a life of its own. It may take its own time to arrive at the finish. Every book is an interior journey, a kind of quest, to solve a problem, a personal question. It's possible to go too fast. In the middle of writing *War and Peace* Tolstoy took an entire year off to take stock and think about where his manuscript was going.

- Allowing time to reflect is vital.

- Cliché it may be, but Rome wasn't built in a day.

In the end, the way to proceed may be quite simple:

- 'A writer is someone who writes. A writer is someone who counts words'.
- Set yourself targets – hours, or days, or weeks for writing.
- Make a chart of your daily progress.
- Note the feelgood factor.
- Stick to the schedule.
- Allow for some breaks.
- Just keep going.

Exercises

by Celia Brayfield

We learn to be creative by creating. We learn to write by writing. Mostly, this appears to be a solitary learning experience. Writers with a gift for analysis might choose to deconstruct their process, discuss it with fellow writers or explain it to those just starting on their journey. They might find comfort in knowing that others face the same challenges and fascination in finding how different every writer is but, as the process is unique to every individual, it can't be taught in the same way as, say, physics. The professor does not indicate the required reading, deliver a lecture and grade a test.

For writers, there are no laws, no formulae, no experimental principles that always lead to the same result. A writer doesn't want the same result – they want something new, fresh, electrifyingly original; we each want our own result. And we each get to it in our own way.

About writing exercises

In teaching writing, a lecture is of limited use. It can stimulate thought, generate ideas and consolidate experiential learning. It can allow us to drink in the thoughts of a great mind. Authors can be rock stars – indeed, better than rock stars. I will cherish the memory of hearing Margaret Atwood more dearly than that of a Rolling Stones concert. But traditional academic teaching methods are not the most effective way to educate a writer, or any other artist.

Creative work is evoked, stimulated and nurtured. It thrives in an environment that is playful, in which what Martin Amis has called the ludic spirit is freely indulged, in which experiment is encouraged and confidence built. To expect creative work to be the reliable product of a certain spectrum of pedagogical input is mistaken. Ideas come forward in the mind's downtime, when you're walking, waiting for a plane or sitting on a train gazing out of the window, as J. K. Rowling was when 'this boy appeared in my head'. They bubble up from the unconscious depth of the mind.

Developing yourself as a writer

The first aim in the education of the writer is to feed that unconscious, to deepen the source from which inspiration rises. J. R. R. Tolkien described it as a cooking pot: 'Speaking of the history of stories and especially of fairy stories we may say that the Pot of Soup, the Cauldron of Story, has always been boiling, and to it have continually been added new bits, dainty and undainty.'[1]

I prefer to think of it as a well, into which everything you've ever read, or seen, or heard, or dreamed or imagined has filtered. The process can be conscious as well as unconscious – you can read widely and read well, you can observe, listen, daydream, seize experience wherever you can. In reading, there is a vast canon of world literature to choose from and it leads directly to our collective memory.

On that foundation, add the specialised selection guided by your personal taste, which eventually fines down to the period, the genre or the particular authors that interest you most. Consider a programme of optimum nutrition for your mind. Cut out the junk food, the pulp fiction, incoherent fanzines, soap operas, business reports, advertising leaflets and management jargon, as much as you can. For the historical writer there is the added challenge of reading research material, whose form and tone may filter into the novel and create pools of toxic exposition.

Your reading builds a foundation of forms, ideas, tropes and vocabulary which fuses with your instincts and your personal experience – and the result is inspiration. Which we don't always recognise. In her influential exploration of the practice of creativity, *The Artist's Way* (1992),[2] Julia Cameron advanced the idea of the *blocked creative*, which probably embraces all of us to some degree. So the second goal of creative education is to honour and recognise ideas.

The third aim in the education of a writer is to develop technique. Building a sand-pit for creative work is not the same as removing all discipline and treating everything produced with the rapture of a tiger mom receiving her child's first finger painting.

Another immensely influential work on the subject, *The Creative Habit* (2003)[3] by the choreographer Twyla Tharp, argues that artists train themselves to be creative simply through practice – ideally, daily practice. Technique is developed through the commitment to dedicate time and attention to writing and the courage to challenge yourself, try new things, step – indeed, live – outside the comfort zone.

The writer trains mental muscles, building neural pathways to process experiences, recognise ideas, observe the world and then to define, shape and express all these impressions in language. Technique grows with practice, and only with practice. In his often-quoted book *Outliers:The Story of Success* (2008), Malcolm Gladwell put forward the theory that the achievement of genius requires 10,000 hours of practice – and in his examples, it was intense practice, not a thousand hours of Sunday afternoons.

Writing exercises are valuable in each phase of a writer's development. They feed into the unconscious, offer a creative environment in which ideas can flourish and demand technical practice. Writing exercises are like the 30-second sketches an artist makes when learning to draw, the dancer's daily class or the scales a pianist practises. The only pressure is to perform the task, no other result is expected. They can be fun, even crazy – anything but the task-oriented, sit-at-a-desk-and-fill-a-page struggle. Don't wait anxiously for any result. It is a hard thing for very goal-oriented people to hear, but the creative process is organic and doesn't run to a timetable.

Exercises in historical writing

These exercises invite you to practise techniques that are particularly demanded in historical writing, although all the exercises in writing fiction that you can try individually or in a writing workshop will help you develop your work.

Voices

This is an exercise to develop dialogue for your characters. If you don't have a work in progress you can simply think of a historical character and ask yourself how their speech would have expressed their identity. If you like boxes, make two boxes for each item. Think about:

● What would make them swear — and what would they say?

● The people they loved — did they use pet names or terms of endearment?

● How did they say hello?

● And — the *Transactional Analysis* question — what did they say after they said hello?

● What was the worst insult they could think of?

● Thinking of Duncan's Ptolemies and their craze for Homer — did they quote a famous writer?

● How did they express surprise, or disbelief, or doubt?

● And pain — if they were hurt, what would they exclaim?

● Did they have a favourite proverb or a catch-phrase?

● And how did they say goodbye or take their leave of another person?

● You will build up a list of phrases that are historically accurate, and that's in the first column or row of boxes. Then, of course, in the second column you should write the revised expression as you intend to have it in your text, considering how accurate you want to be. For instance, in Elizabethan England an ordinary man, a farmer or a merchant, would swear by saying 'God's wounds', such a common tag that it was shortened to 'sounds' or 'zounds.' The word has been colonised in so many bad novels and history films that, accurate or not, it's almost impossible to use now.

EXERCISES

The setting shopping list

The setting, or the storyworld if you are thinking in terms of more than one medium for your work, is created from detail, and the detail comes from research. Not an overwhelming volume of detail. Just the telling detail. Here, from our guest contributors, are two shopping lists for the kind of detail that you may need.

This world I am creating, what did it look, sound, smell and taste like? Its inhabitants – men and women – how did they think, what did they read, what did they wear, what did they believe, what did they eat, what made them ill, what made them well, what were they ashamed of and how did they interact with each other? **Sarah Dunant**

This 'background' should include not only objects such as buildings, ornaments, food, clothes, artwork, weapons but also religion, philosophy, ideology, political organisation and even terminology. **Valerio Massimo Manfredi**

For this exercise, make your own shopping list. It will include obvious sources, such as the standard works on domestic life, medicine or architecture in the period. It can include less obvious sources, such as exhibitions, museums, pictures, locations, music.

Turn the list into something else — a research schedule or a mood/memo/pin board. Think of ways to surround yourself with these details, so that when you look up — like Gabriel Oak — there they will be, like Bathsheba Everdene.

What not to do: don't let this list take over your life, or your other research. Don't let it be an excuse to postpone writing. Don't chuck in a chapter because you don't know whether that coat had buttons or not. Lists are useful, and fun, but not a way to live.

EXERCISES

The object exercise

This is another way to come at the question of setting and detail, inspired by one of the chapters in *My Name Is Red* that is narrated by an object, in this case, a gold coin. In imagining the adventures of this coin, Orhan Pamuk takes what's almost an MRI scan of sixteenth-century Istanbul:

I've been well received in Istanbul. Young girls kiss me as if I were the husband of their dreams; they hide me beneath their pillows, between their huge breasts, and in their underwear; they even fondle me in their sleep to make certain I'm still there. I've been stored next to the furnace in a public bath, in a boot, at the bottom of a small bottle in a wonderful-smelling musk seller's shop, and in the secret pocket sewn into a chef's lentil sack. I've wandered through Istanbul in belts made of

camel leather, jacket linings made from checkered Egyptian cloth, in the
thick fabric of a shoe lining and in the hidden corners of multicolored
shalwars. The master watchmaker Petro hid me in a secret compartment
of a grandfather clock, and a Greek grocer stuck me directly into a wheel
of kashari cheese.

The exercise simply involves choosing an object from your
time and place and imagining its adventures. What would
happen to it in a day? Who would own it? Who made
it, was it sold, was it given, was it stolen? Think of the
people who would use it, covet it, treasure it. Think of
the worst things that could happen to it. Personalise the
object, give it feelings, ambitions, plans for its ambitions.

EXERCISES

The street view exercise

The inspiration for this exercise comes from Peter
Ackroyd's biography *The Life of Thomas More*, which
includes a passage in which the author imagines More as
a schoolboy walking from his home to his school, passing
workshops, shops, food stalls, the pump on the street
corner, the stinking ditch and so on. It's an exercise that
works on character and setting, as it should be written
in first person narration.

Ideally, you should have a map or a picture of one of
the locations of your novel, showing the area as it
was where your characters were alive. You may also
have Google Earth at your disposal, to show you the
topography today — much changed, of course, but still
helpful.

> Imagine one of your characters on a journey that they frequently make, and have them tell the reader what they can see. Or, imagine your character coming to a location as a stranger — what will strike them about the place, what will they notice? Remember to use all your senses in writing this description, so you'll think of what the character sees, hears, feels and touches, and even what they taste, the street food of the time.

Group exercises – interpretation and education

Historical writing has applications beyond the creation of publishable fiction. In this section are suggestions for workshops that can be organised to extend history lessons beyond the classroom or interpret a historical site or a museum exhibit. Writers are increasingly asked to apply their art in communities, as writers in residence, and this section draws on some of these initiatives.

Moderating a workshop for historical writers

Historical writing is such a complex process that writing workshops in this discipline need to be thoughtfully managed if they are to benefit all the participants. In addition to the ground rules you'd normally establish as a workshop leader, some extra issues need to be considered.

The first is the question of **accuracy versus authenticity.** It's particularly acute if you're working with a writer whose book is autobiographical or based on family history. They're the first to say, 'But it didn't happen that way.' This is your cue to engage the group in a discussion about historical accuracy and narrative construction. Does each writer want all the facts, or only the facts that fit the story? If the narrative demands one thing and the record tells a different story, which should the writer choose?

Use your own contributions to move the discussion towards a consensus and end with agreement that, while authenticity can be challenged, accuracy isn't an issue for the workshop. Agree not to waste time debating anachronisms – treat them like typos, unless the plot turns on one, in which case it must be debated.

You may well be working with **writers in different periods** – in one term, I had students writing about first-century Arabia, nineteenth-century France and 1960s Barbados in the same group. Students can feel completely thrown by the idea of critiquing writing about a time and place about which they know nothing. Of course, a great many of the potential readers for a historical novel will know just as little about the period of the book. So the workshop immediately tests the writer's skill in establishing the setting. Emphasise that the strength of the writing is what's most important.

Get a grip on **history lessons**. A workshop should feel dynamic, with all the participants engaged in discussing each other's work. But in a workshop with historical writers, those participants will be fascinated by their own research and very willing to pass it on. An outright ban is the only answer. History lessons are for the break.

EXERCISES

I was there

This is a group exercise which asks each individual member to imagine a historical event from the viewpoint of a different person who was there. It works well with both adults and children, and as a prose fiction exercise or a way of devising a short play. In schools, it can be used to confirm the learning of a period in history or to extend the interpretation of a religious event — Christian schools often take the Nativity or the Crucifixion as their prompt.

This exercise can be purely imaginative, in which case the first phase is to think about the event and decide whose memories you want to recreate.

You can take a written account of an event, extrapolate your cast from that and dramatise their accounts in first person narration or in monologues. To extend this exercise, the group can study the way in which a great writer has approached the same challenge.

Some notable reports:

- Plutarch's account of the last days and assassination of Julius Caesar

- Thomas Harriott's description of the British settler colony at Roanoke, *A Brief and True Report of the New Found Land of Virginia* (1588)

- Martha Gellhorn's reports to Harry Hopkins, the administrator of the New Deal's Federal Emergency Relief Association (FERA), on the condition of Americans suffering the effects of the Great Depression

- *Baghdad Burning: Girl Blog from Iraq* (2003)[4] by Riverbend, the young blogger who described 'ordinary' life in Iraq after the war that toppled the regime of Saddam Hussein.

Another approach is to choose a picture, preferably one of those narrative works that so often fall out of fashion. For a teacher taking a class to an art gallery or museum, this is an excellent way to focus students on the experience and help them to anchor it in their minds.

To use a picture as a prompt, start by identifying the figures in it and establishing the imperatives of each person — what their needs, ambitions or values might have been. If you have time, set this as a research exercise, but if you have only one teaching session, lead the opening discussion through these points and add the benefit of your own research to direct it.

If you set this exercise over a week or so, you can ask the writers to research their characters. If not, it would be helpful to provide some basic pointers. Decoding the painting in detail is not so important as suggesting the dynamics of the characters shown in it. If you chose the *Panorama in 12 Folds showing the last Mughal emperor of India, Emperor Bahadur Shah II, on his way to celebrate the feast of Eid in 1843,*[5] for instance, you would be faced with a vast procession led by richly caparisoned elephants. Your group could identify the Emperor himself on the first elephant and his heir under the howdah on the third elephant, and quickly find out enough to know that this Emperor was a Sufi sage and a poet, a devout but moderate Muslim who eventually became a freedom fighter in the Indian Rebellion. The immense wealth on display in the picture is in contrast to the Emperor's power, which by that time had dwindled to the rule of one city. Was he focused on the spiritual experience of Eid, or did he feel a sense of ancestral greatness passing? Or anger at the leaders of the East India Company, who had supplanted his dynasty?

What about a mahout, sitting behind the ears of the elephant, assigned to his mount for life, controlling the great beast with nothing but a pole? What of the servants with the fans and flywhisks, suffering in the heat, thinking of the feast to come? What of the soldiers, who would join the great uprising against the British a few years later? And the Emperor's heir — does he agree with his father's policies? You could extend the exercise to the artist himself, the British representative at the Mughal court, a scholar and diplomat more at home in India than in the land of his fathers.

Suggestions for more prompts:

- the bas-relief of Trajan's column in Rome

- The Bayeux Tapestry, scenes from the coronation of Harold or the Battle of Hastings

- *Queen Elizabeth Going in Procession to Blackfriars* (1600) by Marcus Gheerhaerts

- *Barbarians from the South* attributed to Kano Naizen, 1570—1616

- *Consecration of the Emperor Napoleon I and Coronation of the Empress Josephine* (1805—7) by Jacques-Louis David

- *Washington Crossing the Delaware* (1851) by Emanuel Leutze

- *Derby Day* (1856—8) by William Powell Frith

- *School's Out* (1936) by Allan Rohan Crite.

EXERCISES

Letters and love letters

This is an exercise in letter-writing, the pure epistolary form of literature. You might begin by considering the value of letters as, for centuries, the only form of historical record that was created by ordinary people, writing about their daily lives and often doing so for an audience of family, lover or friend only, without an eye on history.

A letter is full of intention, and written to be carefully read and considered. There is a talismanic quality about a letter — soldiers carry them into battle, families preserve them and hand them down through generations. Love letters are tied up with ribbon and kept with a pressed flower or a lock of hair, as if the intense but transitory feelings of the lovers can be preserved — our ancestors in the nineteenth century were particularly fond of the practice, but it predated them and continues to this day. Maybe Skype files will be cherished in the same way, but I find that hard to visualise.

You can ask your group to write as characters who're entirely imagined or to respond to letters they've read in the character of the recipient. In preliminary discussion the workshop moderator can draw out attitudes and experiences from the group. A collection of historic letters is a great talking point, if the curator will make them available. You may be working with letters in an archive, in which case you could invite your students to think about what had been excluded and what the writers themselves chose to leave out, as well as what has been preserved. Archives are often established for a specific purpose, so the motives of the original collector can also be considered.

If you choose to work with texts, there is a rich heritage on which to draw. Some of the most useful letters for the viewpoint of a writing group are not those from great writers or statesmen, but from ordinary people in extraordinary situations. Some particularly interesting collections of letters are:

- The Civil War Letters Collection, available from the University of Washington, online at http://content.lib. washington.edu/civilwarweb/index.html

- *Letters to Olga (1979—1982)* by Vaclav Havel [6] — a collection of the letters written by the Czech dissident writer to his wife from prison, where he could send only one letter a week.

- *The Letters of Mary Wollstonecraft to Gilbert Imlay.* In many editions published as *Letters Written During a Short Residence in Sweden, Norway, and Denmark* — the mother of modern feminism writing as a young woman whose husband is about to abandon her; her second husband, William Godwin, cited the letters as a reason he fell in love with her.

- *The Letters and Journals of Lord Nelson.* Again, many editions exist. Try to find one which includes both Nelson's love letters to Emma Hamilton and some of his official correspondence — the contrast between his formal and emotional writing is striking.

- *V-Mail: Letters from the Romans at Vindolanda Fort Near Hadrian's Wall* (2008) edited by Katharine Hoare. Written on small wooden boards, the Roman equivalent of postcards, by ordinary soldiers serving at the Scottish border.

- *Dear America: Letters Home from Vietnam* (2002) edited by Bernard Edelman. A particularly moving collection which includes biographical notes about the soldiers, many not yet 20 years old and many of whom died during the Vietnam War.

You may also wish to study some great epistolary novels. The form can be interpreted strictly, using only letters, emails, texts or tweets, or broadly, to include diary entries, press reports, advertisements and other ephemera — it can be fun to use a facsimile edition of a newspaper from a historic date, copied and cut up so that each writer in the group can pick one item to incorporate in a story.

As we live in culture saturated with messages, it's no surprise that epistolary novels are enjoying a moment in the sun at present. *In Our Time*, the cultural discussion programme hosted by Melvyn Bragg on BBC Radio 4, devoted an edition to the form in March 2007,[7] and this, and every programme in the series, is a great teaching aid for older students and adults.

Epistolary historical novels for workshop reading:

- *The Color Purple* (1983) by Alice Walker — beginning in the South of the US in the 1930s, this Pulitzer Prize-winning novel is told in the form of letters to God by a young black woman fighting to escape experiences of abuse.

- *Dangerous Liaisons* (1782) by Choderlos de Laclos. Two bored aristocrats in the last days of the Ancien Régime exchange accounts of pursuit and seduction.

- *Possession: A Romance* (1990) by A S Byatt[8] — a wonderfully complex novel, awarded the Booker Prize, in which two young scholars investigate the lives of two Victorian poets.

- *Dracula* (1897) by Bram Stoker. The classic gothic thriller, ancestor of successive generations of paranormal adventures, a valuable inspiration for modern fantasy writers.

Spirit and place

These are suggestions for workshops that are centred on a specific site, a street, house, castle or a battlefield. So many places have stories to tell: a beach in Normandy; an ancient trading route across the Sahara; a heather-covered mountainside in Scotland; a rubber plantation in Malaysia; an abandoned mine or railway track anywhere in the world.

There is a special quality of inspiration at a historic site. Despite the magic of Google Earth, there is nothing to beat standing on the spot where history was made, feeling the same wind on your face, the same earth underfoot. Often the scale of an event can't be appreciated until you have had the physical experience of its location. To stand on the edge of virgin forest in the Eastern United States is to feel the awe of the first Europeans who were confronted by this trackless and seemingly infinite green void; to stand on a ferry in Venice is to imagine Marco Polo returning from China, seeing the gingerbread architecture of the Doge's Palace with eyes that have gazed on the snows of the Himalayas and the emptiness of the Iranian desert.

Places can be eroded or built over, palaces fall down or are plundered for building stone, but an intact landscape is a truthful witness. As a child, I played on English beaches still littered with barbed wire, abandoned machine-gun posts and the concrete and iron fragments of tank traps. They told me more about the absolute fear of a Nazi invasion than my parents' carefully edited stories of the war years.

To use a place as a focus for a writing exercise, prepare the session carefully, assembling materials such as a map or plan, an old drawing or extracts from oral history of the site.

Give some thought to the physical demands of the task you intend to set your students. The first time I tried a location workshop, at Harlech Castle on the North Wales coast in November, one student wrote a haiku using only the word 'cold.' Not that experiences of cold, wet, exhaustion, altitude, suffocating tropical heat or the searing desert sun aren't valuable for a writer, but you don't want to make your group so miserable that they can hardly think.

Next choose a focus for the experience:

- Sensory — the classic exercise of using all the senses in a description always works well in a new environment. Ask your writers to describe the scene using what they've seen, heard, smelled, felt and tasted — and to supply what might be missing from their imagination.

- A Meeting — there is a natural drama in the occasions when significant historical figures met. Your writers can set the scene, imagine what was said and get into the minds of the speakers and spectators.

- Perspectives — if a conflict took place in the environment you're visiting, you can divide the group into two, and ask them to imagine an event from opposing sides, then write a report or a letter about it. A battle, a siege, a strike, a riot or an invasion can be re-enacted in written accounts.

- Windows — in a building, give each writer a window and ask them to write a description of what they would have seen out of it: a messenger? A war party? A long-awaited lover? The laundry maids pinning up wet washing, the dairy maid churning butter, the groom rubbing down a horse? A sailor coming home from the sea?

- Pages — in this exercise, ask your group to create some of the documents that would have been found in the place you are visiting. In a twentieth-century home this could include letters to or from absent members of the family, a young girl's diary, the shopping list for the day, a child's school homework, a recruiting leaflet, an advertisement for a car or a love note. On a tropical island you could suggest a sea captain's log, a naturalist's notes about the plants or animals, a missionary's sermon, a castaway's journal.

EXERCISES

Come dine with me

Our years are marked by ceremonial meals, at Thanksgiving, Christmas or Eid, for birthdays, funerals and Mardi Gras. Food seems to have a special significance at these times, when it becomes part of a ritual and eating evokes memories and associations. Preparing and sharing the food of a past time is a way of connecting with it, and a way of experiencing the life of that time. All you need to do for this exercise is choose the meal you want to recreate and, if time and equipment allow, get your group to collaborate in preparing it.

This exercise gets best results when the food or drink are palatable, but food memories aren't always of abundance and feasting. A retro high tea from wartime Britain, when the *weekly* ration for an adult was one egg, two ounces of butter and eight ounces of sugar, will soon persuade a writer that an iced birthday cake in this era was an impossible luxury.

Meals have an important place in fiction. They bring people together and put their wealth, or lack of it, on the table in front of them. Food traditions define cultures and span generations. Characters express love, lust and longing through food. For women, the preparation of food has been a sub-culture of its own all over the world for centuries, so that the hearth and the kitchen were, and still are in many cultures, a female state within a state.

Food motifs are so prevalent in literature that they've become clichés, like Oliver Twist's asking for more or Proust's madeleine memory. So re-creating a meal, while not a writing exercise on the page, is a legitimate way of supporting historical writing and one that offers an amusing break in a writing day.

The menu and the recipes will be a research exercise in themselves, but not a hard one since volumes have been written on the subject; a one-stop shop for historic recipes is *A History of Food in 100 Recipes*[9] by William Sitwell. With enough time, patience and kitchen space, you can extend the exercise to take in the way a meal prepared, for which *Consider The Fork* (2012)[10] by Bee

Wilson is an eye-opening guide. How did anyone beat egg-whites before the rotary whisk was invented?

Our ancestors chopped without chopping boards, peeled only with knives, plucked their own poultry and gutted their own fish. They cooked on charcoal braziers, hot stones, open fires, cast-iron ranges. After the preparation and cooking comes the eating, which was vastly different from sitting at a table like a citizen of the developed world in the twenty-first century.

The Romans reclined on couches; in Arabia, Turkey, the Maghreb and the Middle East the rich sat on divans and ate from communal plates on low tables; Europeans in the Renaissance sat on benches and, if they were poor, ate from wooden bowls and trenchers, while the rich fed from gold or silver plate; Regency dandies took tea from 'dishes', which look more like bowls to us; and the fork — well, the Egyptians used it, but the fork had a long and rocky road to worldwide acceptance and was almost excommunicated along the way at least twice. But that's enough history for today.

Notes

1. Lewis C. S. (ed.) op. cit.
2. Cameron, Julia. 1992. *The Artist's Way: A Spiritual Path to Higher Creativity*. USA. Penguin Group
3. Tharp, Twyla. 2003. *The Creative Habit Learn It and Use It For Life*.... USA. Simon & Schuster.
4. Riverbend. 2003. *Bagdhad Burning: Girl Blog from Iraq*. London, Marion Boyars Publishers Ltd; New edition (27 March 2006).
5. Available as a poster from the British Library or online from Wikimedia Commons at: http://en.wikipedia.org/wiki/File:A_panorama_in_12_folds_showing_the_

procession_of_the_Emperor_Bahadur_Shah_to_celebrate_the_feast_of_the_ per cent27ld.,_1843.jpg

6. Havel, Vaclav tr Wilson, Paul, Letters to Olga: June 1979 to September 1982) 1990. London. Faber & Faber.
7. In Our Time, Epistolary Novels, BBC Radio 4.http://www.bbc.co.uk/programmes/b00775dh
8. Byatt, A S. *Possession: A Romance*. 1990. London. Vintage.
9. Sitwell, William. 2012. *A History of Food in 100 Recipes*. London. Collins.
10. Wilson, Bee. 2012. *Consider The Fork: A History of How We Cook and Eat*. London. Particular Books.

Writing courses

How can they help? [DS]

- Nobody can teach you how to write. Period. A writing course won't teach you how to write either. But it can act as a facilitator: it can show you how to make the going easier. It can, for example, be useful to step back from your manuscript and see it from a different perspective, through other people's eyes; through fresh eyes – and that's what a writing course should help you to do. Above all, writing courses offer encouragement. It's always helpful to talk to professional writers, who will tell you if they think your work is brilliant, and if it's not, they should point out – gently – what you're doing wrong. Talking to other people on the course is also beneficial. So, moral support, supportive tutors and fellow writers, all this is valuable. And if you are stuck with your writing, can't see how to move forward, or don't know where to start, talking your literary problems through may be enough to solve them. Here are a few suggestions:

Writing courses – UK

- Many universities offer a Creative Writing MA, or a Creative Writing module as part of a first degree. The most famous UK writing course is run by the University of East Anglia.

- You may be able to find an online MA course. In place of meeting face-to-face, you email your tutors and talk on Skype.

- Or try a mentoring scheme:

  Gold Dust www.gold-dust.org.uk

  The Writer's Project www.thewritersproject.co.uk

- Creative Writing classes. Some local authorities still offer evening classes, usually with a local author as the tutor. Ask in your local library.

Many universities also offer Creative Writing as a single honours degree, or as part of a joint or combined degree. NAWE (the National Association of

Writers in Education, http://www.nawe.co.uk/), keep a full list of courses at all levels and, as the academic subject centre, also provide subject benchmarks and guidelines. The British Council http://www.britishcouncil.org/ also offers information and links to learning opportunities for writers in the UK.

Organisations – UK

- The Arvon Foundation runs residential creative writing courses tutored by well-known authors. See www.arvonfoundation.org Grants may be available.
- The Faber Academy offers evening and weekend writing classes in London. See www.faberacademy.co.uk
- The *Guardian* newspaper runs writing courses and masterclasses in London and Manchester. See www.guardian.co.uk/guardian-masterclasses/creative-writing-courses
- The Literary Consultancy will give you an honest and independent appraisal of your manuscript, for a fee. See www.theliteraryconsultancy.co.uk
- Curtis Brown Creative is the only agent-led creative writing school. See www.curtisbrowncreative.co.uk/writing-school/

The US has perfected the campus-based writing course, of which The Iowa Writers' Workshop http://www.uiowa.edu/~iww/ with 17 Pulitzer prizes to its credit, is the best-known. Consult The Association of Writers & Writing Programs – https://www.awpwriter.org/ – US based but international, for a directory of writing programs and sound advice to potential students. **CB**

Creative writing courses – USA

American universities have created a big business out of Creative Writing, from MFA programmes through to PhD level. For complete lists hunt online. Check the following:

- University of Texas at Austin
- New York University
- University of Michigan – Ann Arbor

- University of Wisconsin – Madison
- Florida State University

Creative writing courses – Canada

Check out the following for serious writing courses:

- Concordia University www.english.concordia.ca
- University of BC Creative Writing Program www.creativewriting.ubc.ca
- University of Guelph MFA Program www.uoguelph.ca
- University of Manitoba Creative Writing Program www.umanitoba.ca
- University of Calgary Creative Writing Program www.english.ucalgary.ca

Creative writing courses – Australia and New Zealand

- The Australasian Association of Writing Programs has rounded up some 50 university and other courses in Australia and New Zealand. See www.aawp.org.au

Ending

by Duncan Sprott

> *The novel is a long piece of prose that has something wrong with it.*
> Randall Jarrell

So what is wrong with yours? And can you fix it? (Yes you can. And you must.) How?

Read the manuscript, making lists of queries: things to be checked. Sort them out. Read the manuscript again... When the proofs of your book arrive you can make minor corrections, but it will be too late for major repairs. If you do have to make drastic changes at proof stage you may have to pay the printer's costs, so the final checks before sending the manuscript off should be your last go at tying up loose ends. Now dip into the Endgame below. Or maybe you should read it before you start.

Historical fiction from A–Z

Accuracy If you have set the manuscript out all wrong, and your spelling, punctuation and paragraphing are all wrong, don't expect any publisher to be interested. If you are dyslexic, ask somebody who is not dyslexic to check the manuscript for you.

Acknowledgements If you have received substantial help from experts, friends or colleagues, it might be good manners to thank them.

Adverbs Put the right verb in the right place and you won't need any adverbs at all. Far from adding punch, they may detract from the force of your verbs. Try deleting some.

Aeronautics What would make your story really fly? (Instead of just taxiing along the runway, going round in circles.) Does the book really take off as a work of fiction? Is it a mass of disjointed facts and undigested lumps of pure history? Is it really cooked in the middle?

Alliteration Caesar sojourned in the seaside city of Syracuse? Not advisable.

Anachronism The classic example is the striking clock in Shakespeare's *Julius Caesar*. (Striking clocks were known in China by circa 724 AD, but there were no striking clocks in ancient Rome.) Reviewers (and readers) love to pounce on this kind of thing. Remove all modern turns of phrase. You can't allow Ethelred Unraed to talk about 'downsizing'.

Archaism Have you overdone the archaic terms and phrases? And have you used them right? Will your readers understand your brilliant pastiche of Anglo-Saxon conversation?

Aristocracy If your novel happens to be teeming with lords and ladies, get their titles right. See *Burke* or *Debrett* for forms of address in modern times. Check up on historical forms of address: look at Chaucer, Shakespeare and Trollope, and so on, depending on the period.

Authority Mistakes in known historical facts will undermine an author's authority.

Author's Note If you have departed significantly from the historical 'truth' you should perhaps say so, and indicate where you left it behind. Equally, if you have stuck to the whole 'truth' and nothing but the 'truth' perhaps you should say this too.

Balance Have you got the right balance between dialogue and narrative? Between dialogue and description? Between the characters? Between the different events in the plot?

Bias Will your book be seen as racist, anti-black, homophobic, misogynistic, xenophobic, blasphemous or indecent? Take great care...

Capitals Cheshire cat but cheshire cheese, Julius Caesar but caesar salad. You may need to invest in the *Oxford Dictionary for Writers and Editors* and Judith Butcher's *Copy-editing*.

Characters Have you lumbered yourself with too many?

Checking When you are checking the manuscript you will often read what you think you wrote, not what is actually on the page. Writers' eyes love to play tricks. It's possible to read the same manuscript six times and still find appalling mistakes that you've overlooked.

Chronology A chronological table may help the reader through a complicated period of history. Keep it simple and clear, if you can.

Clarity Spell things out that might not make sense to foreign readers. Bear in mind that novels may be translated into several foreign languages. Will yours be untranslatable?

Cliché Just don't do it.

Consistency You say 'Perkin Warbeck died ten days later'. Check the dating. All references to time should coincide. Check all numbering systems, things like 'two years afterwards...' and 'Edward III had five sons and four daughters' (are you sure you haven't lost one or two?). Check that it's actually possible to travel from Rome to Byzantium in the time you have stated. If you want Julius Caesar to hold a conversation with Tiberius make sure they were both actually alive at the same time. In fact Tiberius was not born until two years after Caesar's death. Get this kind of thing wrong and the author's authority starts to unravel. Get it right and the reverse will apply.

> **TOP TIP**
>
> *Lionel Casson's* Travel in the Ancient World *can solve many problems with fictional journeys.*

Contents List If you list the contents, make sure that the chapter titles tally with the chapters in the body of the book. The same for chapter numbers.

Contradictions If Jane Seymour has green eyes on page 34 she must still have green eyes on page 245. If the road from Arelate to Glanum goes through open fields in January AD65, it can't be lined with lovely mature woods six months later. Apply rigorous logic. It is all too easy to make this kind of mistake: we all type too fast, get interrupted, forget what we're doing. You need eyes in the back of your head especially when you are tying up the manuscript ready for delivery.

Copyright If you have quoted someone else's work – say, from T.S. Eliot – check whether the work is still in copyright. You may need to get permission to quote. You do have to ask, and you may have to pay. You must obtain permission to quote from the work of another author unless he/she has been dead for over 70 years, though you may quote half a dozen words without permission.

Cuts Delete whatever is not vital to the telling of the story.

Dates Obviously you can't refer to years BC in a novel set before the birth of Christ. For ancient Greece try dating things according to the Olympiads (though this becomes rather dull reading, after a while). Or try referring to 400 years after Troy, or six months after Thermopylae – but watch out! because ancient Greek months do not quite behave like ours. For Rome you can use years from the founding of the city (AUC). Or you can say, 'When Caligula was on the throne...' and so on. This is probably how ordinary people in ancient history referred to time anyway. Consult Bickerman's invaluable *Chronology of the Ancient World* for details of calendars and chronography, and for complete lists of Olympiad years and Roman consuls. H.E.L. Mellersh's *Chronology of the Ancient World: 10,000 BC to AD 79* is also useful; companion volumes cover later periods.

Death There's a lot of death in history. So what do you know about dying? How long does it take to die from hemlock poisoning? How long to die of thirst in the desert? How long to die of plague? See Cedric Mimms' *When We Die* for what happens in death, from the onset of rigor mortis to the procession of fauna in the dead body (first to arrive are the blow-flies, last the maggots...).

Deletion Get used to crossing things out. This is called editing. If you don't do it yourself, your editor will do it for you.

Dialogue 'Have at thee for a foul caitiff!' Excess archaizing may put your readers off. Never write down what you would never say. Try reading dialogue aloud. Or ask someone else to read it to you. Your computer can also read your manuscript aloud (in American). If you don't like what you hear, wield the blue pencil.

Disclaimer Have you given a graphic description in your novel of your next door neighbour's face/private affairs/scandalous conduct? Will he recognise himself? Does he happen to be a millionaire with a penchant for legal action? It makes some considerable sense not to lay yourself open to being sued for libel in the first place. Protect yourself by including the usual notice: 'This book is a work of fiction. Names, characters, places, and incidents either are products of the author's imagination or are used fictitiously. Any resemblance to actual events or locales or persons, living or dead, is entirely coincidental.'

Drama/Suspense Can be fixed in many ways. Try leaving a trail of the subtlest hints, one by one, carefully placed, of what is to come in the future; faint flickers of suggestion that will make the reader wonder, and become urgent to know what happens. Look at the subtle way George Eliot sows her seeds one after another throughout the first 100 pages of *Middlemarch* regarding the character of Mr Casaubon; then she leaves you dangling while Casaubon and Dorothea go off to Rome for their honeymoon. Compare the cranking up of drama and suspense in a book like *The Da Vinci Code*, which has you turning the pages like crazy, simply panting to know what happens next.

Economy 'Say all you have to say in the fewest possible words, or your reader will be sure to skip them; and in the plainest possible words, or he will certainly misunderstand them.' (John Ruskin)

Editing 'The only art is to omit.' (Robert Louis Stevenson)

Emotion One way of involving or engaging the reader is to tug at the heart-strings. Have you engaged your readers' emotions? (It might be difficult to tell.) On the other hand will the story leave them cold and uninvolved? Or have you tugged at the reader's heartstrings a bit too much? Overdo it, and you may land your book in the category of slushy historical romance. Adjust the emotional balance if you need to.

Exclamation Marks!!! Moderation in all things!!! Even one is too many!!!

Facts We all begin with facts. Historical facts are like seeds: by applying a fertile imagination we make them grow. Then we transcend the facts.

Fiction Fiction can be perfect. History is not. In the back of *Havoc, in Its Third Year* (2004) Ronan Bennett says '...which brings me, lastly, to the acknowledgement every novelist working with history must make that when conflicts arise between historical fact and the demands of the novel we tend to settle them in favour of the latter. This is a work of fiction.'

Flashback Playing with the order of events is as old as Homer – the *Odyssey* begins with a gigantic flashback.

Food For food in antiquity see Andrew Dalby's *Siren Feasts*.

Foreign words 'Do not use a foreign word where a suitable English equivalent exists.' (George Orwell)

Fuck The first recorded instance is in 1278.

Ghosts If you are ghost-hunting, check the card index at the Society for Psychical Research, Marloes Road, London W8.

Glossary If you have crammed your novel with ancient gods and obscure practices you may need to provide a glossary of unfamiliar terms.

Grammar If in doubt, check in Gowers, *The Complete Plain Words*, or Fowler's *Modern Usage*.

History Have you transcended your research, or are you swamped by it? Too many dates? Too much information? Is your novel just a history book in disguise?

Humour The Past did have a sense of humour, though it seems to have been very different from ours. Whole books have been written about what the ancient Romans laughed at (e.g. Erich Segal, *Roman Laughter*, 1978).

Ice Cream was invented by the Romans.

Inconsistencies When you start fitting invented stuff into the nuts and bolts of history it doesn't always work. The whole business of dovetailing the fake and the real, side by side, needs careful attention.

Inner life Virginia Woolf said the real life is the inner life.

Inventions If you have made things up *passim*, double check that the invented bits fit beside the true. For example, you can't have Nelson at sea in 1769 when all the world knows he was at school in Norwich.

Itineraries You can easily tie yourself in knots if you use ancient names: make sure that if you say Cicero travelled from Terracina to Puteoli via Rhegium it makes sense. In fact, this example is like saying he went from London to Brighton via Manchester/New York to Washington via Los Angeles. Check all itineraries.

Language Too many long words? Follow George Orwell's rule: 'Never use a long word where a short one will do.' But if you need a long word, fine. Is the level of language appropriate to your readership? If your 'popular historical novel' is stuffed with jargon from archaeological journals you may not hook the popular audience you were hoping for. Have you used too many foreign words? Do your readers know the lingo? Will your novel appeal only to an academic audience? Is it so complicated that nobody can understand it? Is it really readable? And what about the other extreme? You set out meaning to write a literary novel, but your language is pure Enid Blyton...

Mannerisms, Personal Cultivate an acute self-consciousness. Ask yourself whether you are guilty of using pet phrases, repeating favourite words, tics of style. Alert friends, asked to read the manuscript with fresh eyes, will be delighted to point out such things.

Medical terms Ancient diseases, ancient cures... Check all references.

Military terms You should be okay with sinister-dexter, but what about the phalanx, *exeligmos* or *hypapistai*? *Clibinarii* and *catafractarii*? Check and double check.

Modernism Remove all noticeably modern words and phrases.

Money Will the reader understand your references to obols and hemi-obols, groats and pence, farthings and halfpennies, threepenny bits, florins, half-crowns, ten-shilling notes, sovereigns and guineas? And what about *sous, deniers, livres* and the *écu d'or*? Not to mention all the pre-Euro era currencies? Do you need a Note on Money?

Montbretia Named after the French botanist, Antoine-Francois-Ernest Coquebert de Montbret, who went to Egypt with Napoleon in 1798 and died there aged 20. Before that, this flower doesn't exist.

Names Boudicca or Boadicea? (Or Boudica?) St Petersburg or Leningrad? Beijing or Peking? Mao Tse-Tung or Mao Zedong? Marseille or Marseilles? If you are writing about Egypt in antiquity, have you used the modern Arabic name by accident or on purpose? And will you stick to Latin names which no one has ever heard of, like Mediolanum? Or opt for Milan, or Milano? Lugdunum, Lyon, or Lyons? Choose one style and stick to it.

Nautical terms Port – left, starboard – right. What about mizzen masts and fo'c'sle's? For antiquity see Lionel Casson, *Ships and Seamanship in the Ancient World*. For the rest, see Dear and Kemp, *The Oxford Dictionary of Ships and the Sea*.

Obscurity It's tempting to make maximum use of *The Penguin Dictionary of Historical Slang*. Unlike you, however, your readers may not have read it from cover to cover.

If Hilary Mantel had written *Wolf Hall* in total Tudor-speak, nobody would have understood a word. (See Hilary's remarks on dialogue in the Guest section, page 135)

On to Not onto. Kingsley Amis: 'I have found by experience that no one persistently using onto writes anything much worth reading.'

Pace/ Narrative Drive There are different speeds for page-turning, and different rates of turn for different bits of a book. Now fast, now slow, you vary the pace – like life, like music.

Plagiarism Not worth the trouble. Use your own ideas. And make sure you don't snitch ideas from other people's books by accident.

Plot Historical fiction has its own special problems. Your reader may know already, for example, that Julius Caesar was stabbed to death. You're going to have to do something pretty extraordinary to sustain the suspense and keep the reader with you. Everybody knows what happens to Napoleon in the end. In *War and Peace* Tolstoy keeps the reader's interest by deflecting attention elsewhere: we are desperate to know, not how Napoleon died, but who Natasha will marry.

Plotting Tighten your plotting. Get rid of what is not directly relevant to your story.

Poison For death by hemlock, arsenic, strychnine, etc, avoid stating exact quantities. (You need to keep your readers *alive*, so they can buy your next book.)

Politics Do you really need 40 pages expounding the political situation in 1485?

Punctuation The purpose of punctuation is to indicate a pause. Comma, semi-colon, colon, full stop: like a pause of one, two, three, four, in which number four is a complete halt.

TOP TIP

For punctuation look at www.shadycharacters.co.uk

Questions Ask yourself questions. In Xenophon's *Anabasis*, for example, why was Parysatis fonder of Cyrus than of Artaxerxes? Write as many possible answers as you can think of. The most likely answer will turn into the reason. Thus you get to work out what actually happened.

Quotations Check for accuracy. Also for copyright. Double quotes or single quotes? Is your system consistent?

Rabbits were introduced to Britain by the Normans. So no rabbit pie for Vortigern.

Readability Is it readable? How fast will the pages turn? Too fast? Too slow? Or just right? If you find it difficult to read yourself, what hope is there for the reader?

Repetition How many chapters have you started with the same word or phrase? Have you started six sentences in a row with the same word? How often do you repeat the same word in one sentence? In the same paragraph? On the same page? Are your repetitions really necessary?

Rhyme Unless it's 'quote some poetry' time, get rid of anything that makes it rhyme.

Ring of Truth Sometimes things that really are true will sound as if they're not. (Aristotle preferred plausible impossibilities to implausible possibilities.) The coincidences that happen in history, in real life, can seem corny in a novel. So what do you do? Avoid mentioning. Or rewrite, making a better, more convincing story. The false can be truer than the true.

Safety If you have given details of a medieval recipe, have you got the ingredients and quantities right? Even if you're a world authority on gunpowder, Greek fire, and ancient chemical warfare, avoid giving precise quantities of dangerous substances. Publishing contracts contain a safety clause whereby the author guarantees that 'any recipe, formula or instruction contained in the Work is not injurious to the user'.

Said Is better than added, commented, declared, pointed out, ejaculated.

Sentences, long Try reading things aloud. If you are panting for breath half way through a sentence, get punctuating. If a sentence needs to be long, okay, but it is not a bad thing to keep your sentences short. Though if every sentence is short you will get a staccato effect just as off-putting as the interminable sentences of Monsieur Proust. Vary the length. Find the appropriate balance.

Spelling Sort out: skilful or skillful, forbears or forebears, affect or effect, gaol or jail. Be consistent. Either use *judgment* or *judgement, civilised* or *civilized, realise* or *realize*, and so on, not both. See Judith Butcher's *Copy-editing* for further info about preparing manuscripts.

Style You can devote quite a lot of your time to rewriting and rephrasing and shortening. Rewrite sentences to give them punch. Short and sharp is good. Concise is good. No repetition is good. And not too many conjunctions.

Tics It's easy, when you're writing fast, to slap down all kinds of junk. We all have little phrases that we trot out in conversation, without really thinking: 'as it were', 'you know'. Everybody uses 'get' and 'nice' much too much in everyday speech. These things don't look so good in print, particularly if they crop up ten times on every page.

Title Have you got the right title? Is it memorable? Or pretty dull? Has anybody used your title before? Look it up on Google. Search on Amazon.

Tobacco First mentioned in 1507. Before that, NO SMOKING.

Tomatoes Not grown in Britain until the 1590s (when they were believed to be poisonous) but eaten widely in Britain by the mid-eighteenth century. The earliest mention of the tomato in North America is in 1710.

Time, Managing If you tell the story in real time you will never get to the end. Think of it in photographic (or cinematic) terms: you telescope some bits, or use a wide-angle lens, taking in a lot of ground in one shot: one year, ten years, half a century can be covered in a paragraph; then you zoom in and enlarge on other parts of the story, shooting, as it were, in close-up, capturing maximum detail. The whole novel works like this, alternating close-ups and long-shots. You vary the focus, you keep changing the lens through which you view your characters, just as you would if you were taking a photo or making a movie.

Variety Have you written 100,000 words all in dialogue? Fine, so long as you meant to. Marguerite Yourcenar managed to write *Memoirs of Hadrian* without letting any of her characters speak. Will *your* readers long for somebody to say something?

TOP TIPS

Very *'Substitute "damn" every time you're inclined to write "very". Your editor will delete it and the writing will be just as good'* Mark Twain

Writing *Want to know how writers write? See Writers at Work: The Paris Review Interviews Penguin, 6 vols. Also online at www.theparisreview.org*

Zip Tip *The Zip took off in 1918 when the US navy decided it would make an excellent fastener for flying suits. The name Zipper was coined in 1926. The zip fly caught on in 1937. Before that: buttons.*

● Copy-editors will check for all of the above, but even copy-editors can mistakes, and overlook things. It is the author's responsibility to get things right. Some copy-editors have been known to embark on a total rewrite of a scrappy manuscript. If you don't want this to happen to you, make sure you are writing with authority. Your agent/editor/copy-editor will probably not have a special knowledge of prehistoric cooking-places/everyday conversation among the Hittites/transport in thirteenth-century Turkey... But you ought to know what you're talking about. If not, reviewers – and readers – will be eager to tell you.

Lastly...

- With all these things in mind, read the manuscript several more times. It's easy to read what you think you wrote, rather than what is actually on the page. Editing on a printout may be easier than on the screen.

Is it really really finished?

- Somehow you have to fix things so that your book is not counted among the bad but the good. You can easily get so deeply involved in a book that you lose sight of what you're doing.

- Show your work to a friend whose judgement you trust. Urge them to apply rigorous logic and tell you the truth (not just what they think you'd like to hear) about your book. And that includes telling you it's not ready to go; telling you another draft should do the trick; and urging you to lock the manuscript in a drawer and forget all about it.

- At this stage in particular, then, fresh eyes are very important. Your friends will spot mistakes that you have no idea you have made: crass spelling mistakes, stupid howlers, idiotic repetitions, grotesque errors of fact, instances of haplography and dittography, ridiculous inconsistencies, verbs that don't agree with their subjects, plurals that should be singular.. Anybody who hammers away for months at a 100,000 word manuscript will make this kind of mistake. When you're satisifed that the novel is just perfect, move on to the next stage.

Getting published

Which means acquiring either an agent or a publisher. Preferably both.

Literary agents

- Do you really need an agent? YES YOU DO. Agents know the market for books inside out. They also know what a book is worth in terms of advances and worldwide sales. Agents are experienced in negotiating the best possible deal, will get you the best price for your book, and make sure you are not ripped off.

- An agent will handle all business negotiations and pass on to you (and chase up) all payments from the publisher. Agents are also geared up to sell foreign rights – i.e. Europe, America, and the Rest of the World – which can be a source of considerable extra income; they also deal with e-book rights, broadcasting, dramatic and movie rights. All these things require specialised knowledge of markets and trends.

- Many authors do survive without an agent, particularly in the beginning. These days, however, agents have more time than publishers to devote to editing: they will make editorial suggestions, perhaps help you to bash your book into better shape, or recommend a partial rewrite for promising material if it's not quite ready to submit.

- There is a price to pay for an agent's kind attentions, of course, and it varies from 10–20 per cent commission on all earnings (usually +VAT). Most writers would swear that it's worth every cent.

Finding an agent

Can be difficult... Some agencies receive 4,000 manuscripts a year but only take on four or five new authors. If you do get taken on, count yourself very lucky. Word of mouth may get you quite a long way. Network like crazy. Post stories online. Put yourself in places where agents or scouts on the watch for new talent can see you. Keep writing that blog. Somebody might notice and sign you up. (It has happened.) At the same time, if you're ready, try sending the manuscript off. See the *Writers' & Artists' Yearbook* for lists of literary agents in the UK, USA and worldwide, with contact details. Or hunt for listings online.

Submitting the manuscript

What to send?

Agents usually ask for a synopsis of the work and the first three chapters. This is standard practice. Having read your submission, the response will either be Thanks But No Thanks, or to ask for more. We recommend that you complete the entire novel to your own satisfaction before approaching an agent or a publisher. Suppose the agent lands you a publishing deal within a week. You sign the contract, trouser the fat cheque, advance to Cloud Nine. Great. But you still have to write the book. It may turn out that the book you thought you could write is impossible to finish, maybe through some historical problem. Or maybe some personal crisis will put an end to your freedom to write.... If you don't deliver the complete manuscript within a certain time you have to pay the money back. Hmm, you spent it already? End of dream. Beginning of nightmare.

Contacting an agent

Before you do anything, research agents – online. Basically, what agents want is a preliminary letter – some agents specify maximum 500 words – a CV, and an extract from your work – usually the first three chapters, or the first 50 pages, or 10,000 words maximum if your book has no chapters. All agency websites have different submission guidelines: look them up. Do what they say. Some ask for online submissions only. Others ask for paper submissions only, sent via snailmail. All say that if you do not send return postage your manuscript will be recycled.

- *No unsolicited manuscripts* means do not send anything unless they ask you to.
- Don't try to send the same manuscript to every agent or publisher at once.
- Work down the list, one at a time, and wait for the response. You may need patience.

The letter

- So, you start, like everybody else in the game, by writing a letter. It's not unlike a job application. Keep it short, no more than one page. Say a bit about your book, mention the title, even if it's provisional, say what it's about, why you think it deserves publication, and a bit about yourself and your qualifications for writing the book. If you happen to have a PhD in your period, for example, say so. If there are already 29 other novels on your subject, explain what will make yours stand out from all the rest, how it's different, why it's unique. Say where you think your book might fit in the market: is it literary or popular, aimed at young people or adults? Do you envisage an international audience (the book may be about France, or India). (Or do you see your book being read only by little old ladies living in the north of Scotland/ middle-aged farmers in deepest Texas?)

- Editors say they can tell from the preliminary letter whether they will want to publish your work. How? Because a letter reveals a great deal about you. It reveals whether you are sane or insane. It reveals whether you are a serious player or to be rejected pronto. It may reveal that you can't even write a short letter, let alone a book. The letter can make all the doors fly open for you; or it can make all the doors slam in your face. Even if it takes 17 drafts, get the letter right. Don't address it to 'Dear Sir or Madam' but to a chosen agent by name. Try to spell the name right.

- Look at the agent's lists of clients too, because that will reveal something of their interests (e.g. serious literary fiction or popular).

- Do your homework: don't bother contacting an agency that handles only non-fiction, or only children's books, or one that displays no interest whatsoever in historical fiction. Misdirected submissions lead to rejection. Hundreds and thousands of manuscripts may pass through an agent's hands in a year. They will find any excuse to turn you down.

- Fix all the above, and you stand a chance of getting somewhere. Don't let the horse stumble at the first fence. The second fence, somewhat higher, is the synopsis.

Writing a synopsis

- Keep it short-ish. Some agents specify maximum 1,500 words or two or three pages. You don't need to tell the whole story; stick to the main characters and events. Try to convey some idea of the narrative arc of the story, something of the plot. One agency asks for 'a sense of the plot, and an idea of where the story is going'.

- Just as the book itself should grab the reader's interest on the first page, if not in the first sentence, so the agent or publisher must be grabbed by the synopsis. Again, if it takes 17 drafts, so be it. Get it right, and wonderful things may happen. If you don't bother, nothing will happen except a rejection letter.

Handling rejection(s)

- If the agency response is positive and they want to see the whole manuscript, don't hold your breath. Turnaround times are not, on the whole, quick. But you might expect to hear back in six to eight weeks. If you wait six months, write a polite letter to ask what's happening.
- If the manuscript comes flying back by return of post, don't give up.
- And don't take it personally. Try again. Try a different agency. Keep on trying.
- Do ask yourself what might have provoked this brutal rejection of your master-piece. Is the storyline wrong/just too lacklustre/too convoluted? Is the layout crazy? Is the plot creaky and contrived? Is it a total non-starter? (All those things you were meant to have sorted out already...) Get some second opinions from friends if you still can't see what's wrong. (Maybe there was nothing wrong with it.) Do some rewrites if necessary. Then send the manuscript out again.
- Whatever you do, don't send your only copy of the manuscript. Things do get lost in the post.

Agency agreements

- If an agent does like your proposal and takes you on, the usual form is to exchange a letter outlining the terms of the agreement between you, which confirms what the agent will deal with, and what percentage will be deducted in commission. The next stage is for the agent to submit your work to a publisher.

Publishers

- Publishers will take care of all costs related to the publishing of your book from start to finish, including the editing, copy-editing, proof-reading, printing, binding, dust jacket (and fees for illustrations), distribution, marketing and publicity.

- Some publishing houses will still consider unsolicited manuscripts – i.e. stuff sent to them not by an agent but direct from the author. The stack of these unsolicited manuscripts is known as the 'slush pile', the stuff *from people they don't know*. It's not unheard of for publishers to accept novels from the slush pile, though many no longer accept unsolicited manuscripts at all.

- The slush pile was the first and last resort of the desperate and the mad. Stories circulate: one manuscript, thousands of pages long, turned up in a suitcase. Others look as if they have been slept on. Some actually smell.

- Whoever you send your manuscript to, never post it in anything less than perfect nick: that means *not* scribbled on by kids, *not* marked with coffee mug rings, *not* smeared with Marmite.

- Remember that if you forget to enclose return postage you will never see your manuscript again.

- These days publishers tend to prefer manuscripts to arrive via the filtering process of an agency. The agent will have met you and read your work and is excited about it. S/he can swear that you're not a total nut but an official Nice Person, not only a genius but charming, handsome/beautiful, photogenic, an eminently marketable property.

- Remember that some manuscripts are rejected 34 times before getting through the net and going on to win prestigious prizes. If your book is worth publishing, somebody, somewhere should pick it up. Eventually.

- Don't pay for your book to be published (self-publishing is a different matter). If your book is any good, somebody, somewhere will publish it – and they will pay you, not vice versa.

TOP TIP

Celia's advice:

1. Research agents – go to all possible events, spend a lot of time on Google, find exactly the right agent for you, and several back-up choices.

2. Go to the agent's website and look for submission guidelines.

3. Do what they say. Exactly. Not less, not more.

4. A beginning writer should complete the manuscript first, also write a one-page synopsis and CV.

Self-publishing and online publishing

by Celia Brayfield

Self-publishing. This is how the story goes. Once upon a time self-publishing was a last resort for the hatchers of literary turkeys. Then a writer called E. L. James self-published a book called *Fifty Shades of Grey*. The book was picked up by a mainstream publisher and became the sales sensation of the decade. At the time of writing, it has sold about 65 million copies in 37 different territories and it has revived the genre of erotic romance, which had been in decline since Jackie Collins was a debut novelist.

So if you self-publish your novel, this could happen to you, right?

Yes it could. If you just take care of a few features of the *Fifty Shades* story which readers tend to skip.

In essence, these features are the things that a publisher and agent might do for you if you had them – development, arithmetic and marketing. But then again, many publishers and agents don't do these things either. Any author who takes responsibility for these stretches of the path to publication will have an edge with the industry.

Development

This means getting your novel right. It does not mean believing that because your novel is *your* novel it *must* be right. One of the most successful self-published historical novelists, Libby Cone, interviewed on the blog site HistoricalNovelsInfo, described how she showed her book to a friend who had editing experience and, when the friend recommended she 'take a chainsaw' to the manuscript, she followed her advice.

'Not everybody understands, or takes, criticism. The most important words (here) aren't "agents" or "bloggers", but "friend" and "chainsaw". When my friend suggested a radical alteration, I trusted her judgement.'

So you should do everything you can to get feedback on your work, either before you approach literary agents or before you self-publish it. Your aim is to get honest and informed responses to your work from the sort of people who are likely to buy it. Bear in mind that, if you start sending your book to literary agents, you are very unlikely to get detailed or specific advice on it. On the other hand, any or all of the following may be helpful.

- A writing group – and if there isn't one in your area, you can start one. All you need is Facebook and a place to meet – coffee shops are good.

- A creative writing course – anything from a short course or evening classes to a PhD at a university where you will be tutored by a leading novelist. Read the section on choosing a writing course above.

- An online forum – some of these are moderated by publishers, who use them as a way of sourcing new authors. Visit Harper Collins' Authonomy http://authonomy.com

- A reading service – these tend to be expensive, but are typically run by professional editors or writing tutors. For a fee, they will read your book and write you a critique of it.

- Author development events. These are springing up all over, run by literary festivals, cultural non-profits, newspapers, publishers and literary agencies. They range through lectures by leading authors, masterclasses, speed-dating sessions with hungry young agents, short or one-off workshops, courses lasting several months and mentoring schemes.

- Development competitions. Again, often run by publishing outfits or online magazines such as *Zoetrope*. Authors post short stories or chapters online and the reading community votes on which writer they want to read more of. The winner of each session gets the whole work published. They may charge fees, which are quite low at the start but build up if you're winning.

- Fan-fiction sites. This was the route first taken by E. L. James, who posted early chapters of *Fifty Shades* on the *Twilight* fanfic site. Eventually those readers divided into those who liked the erotic content and those who hated it. The author then took the former group to her own website before getting her first publishing deal with the Australian indie publisher, The Writers' Café.

Arithmetic

Once you and your chainsaw-wielding friends or colleagues are happy with your novel, you can think about ways to self-publish it. Here are some options:

- Simply post the thing on a web site – not recommended unless, like E. L. James, you already have a following of readers or you can find a way to drive readers to the site and, ideally, make them pay to read.

- Approach a crowd-sourcing organisation like Unbound, who pre-sell your work and raise the money for publication from people to commit to buying it in advance. Unbound prefer authors who're already published or who have a very strong platform – see below.

- Pay around $800 minimum to an established publisher such as Authorhouse or Lulu. They will publish you in paper as well as online, and may offer you editorial, design and marketing advice. They may also be part of a distribution alliance that gets books into high street book shops.

- Publish digitally with a service such as Amazon's Kindle Books. This is free and allows you (at present) high royalties – but the unit price is very low. However, a low price makes you more attractive to readers.

Your budget is likely to be the determining factor in your choice, but you should also weigh up considerations such as whether you want a handsome physical volume at all, and, if you do, how effective your chosen publisher will be in getting the physical book on to Amazon or into shops and out to customers.

While you're making this choice, it would be instructive to check out independent publishers at one of the big publishing fairs, if your schedule and budget allow it. The world's major book fairs take place once a year in New York, London and Frankfurt, but many smaller events are also part of the schedule in specific markets, such as the Children's Book Fair in Bologna, Italy. At these you will find a whole section of indie exhibitors, with those who've joined together in distribution networks side by side. At slow times (first thing in the morning is usually slow) you can chat to the people on the stands. This is an ideal opportunity to compare your options and get a good understanding of indie publishing. If you're a student, book fair entry is usually free.

Look carefully at the contracts that self-publishing outfits want you to sign. This is where the need for arithmetic is acute, and the ability to think forward essential. You should consider:

- What they want, in terms of rights and commitment. There should be a clear and simple process for ending the contract when you want to, and a clear definition of what you own, including the original manuscript, subsequent drafts and the files from which the book itself is printed. The right to publish the book should not rest with the publisher after the end of the contract. The contract should also define ownership of rights in other countries and other media, including screen rights – if they want these, how good are they at getting screen deals? Never give up your copyright or, in the EU, your *droit moral* until a major American film producer offers you the price of a house to do so.

- The price of your book, who fixes it, how it is fixed and in what circumstances it can be discounted.

- Your royalties – what proportion of which price (recommended retail/ price received) comes to you, and when, and how this will be accounted. Don't be seduced by a big royalty on a price so high that you will sell few copies – authorship is a long game and at the beginning what you want is a lot of loyal readers.

- The printing or production cost – the sale price should be about twice this. Will you be liable for any other costs, such as design, marketing or distribution?

- The services available – copy-editing, design, publicity? Do you get a personal contact or editor? And what's the quality on offer here? How much experience do these people have, what's their track record? Research them – don't believe bland assertions such as 'We have an unrivalled success rate with new authors.'

Finally, read *From Pitch to Publication*[1] by Carole Blake, an internationally renowned literary agent whose guide to the publishing process should be on every author's bookshelf. If you're going to be your own literary agent, you might as well learn from the best.

Marketing

Whether you intend to find a traditional publisher or to self-publish your book, you will increase your chances of success by building a strong author platform and understanding the marketing process that will generate interest in your book and make people want to buy it.

An author platform means your presence in new media, coupled with your track record, public profile and connection to special interest groups. Suppose, for instance, you were a historical novelist called Verity Jones and you had written a novel about an animal rights activist in America in the 1890s. Your author platform might consist of:

- your Twitter account, @HackneyJones
- your Facebook account in the name of Verity Jones
- your Pinterest account featuring pictures of cab horses and other working animals in America in the 1890s
- your blog, High Steppin'
- your early career as a sports writer on Atlanta Intown
- your volunteer role as deputy secretary of the North Carolina branch of the American Hackney Horse Society
- your current role in the media department of Farming for the Future.
- the Creative Writing prize you won in college.

Through all these activities, you have built up a profile as someone with a special interest and engaged the attention of other people who share that interest. You may well have several thousand Twitter followers or blog visitors. Taken together, this platform is a strong one from which Verity Jones can interest people in her novel. As soon as she has a publication date she can begin to draw her community's attention, releasing pictures, tweeting news and comments on all matters animal, focusing her blog posts.

It takes time to build an author platform and there is no requirement for every author to engage in every potential part of the spectrum. While Twitter is a powerful medium, not everyone is given to one-liners. Writing a blog takes time, and if you're the father of four you may not have time. Those high-glamour careers that publishers find so appealing, in TV, journalism, stand-up comedy or acting, aren't for everyone. The key to the process is to create a coherent and focused public presence in a way that works for you.

- *What Not To Do* By all means get your friends to retweet, share and generally puff your book, but have some grace about it. Spamming your community with strident sales posts will simply alienate them.

With a profile to build on, think about actively marketing your book. The strongest and simplest option for a self-published author is to get a good review on a blog site – it was a review on dovegreyreader.com, managed by a former nurse in rural Devon, that caught the interest of Libby Cone's publisher. This ideally entails engaging in the site over months and building a relationship with their community through comments and interactions in response to the blogger's posts.

You can also send your book to traditional reviewers, although they're sniffy about self-published authors. Special interest publications may be more receptive. It may also be more productive to think of a newspaper or magazine feature linked to your book and try to place this. Think about media local to your story, as regional publications are hungrier for content than national. In a town where the tourists still enjoy carriage-rides through the park, Verity Jones could place a feature on the glory days of the cab horse. She would be well advised to take a positive approach to devising a story, as this is likely to play better than a negative focus – say on the cruel deaths such horses often suffered.

Physical marketing is hard graft but, if you have a gift for it, will increase your sales and also give you face-to-face contact with readers from which you'll be able to see from their happy shining faces how well your cover concept is working. If you have a physical book and your publisher has a good distribution service, you can approach bookshops and offer to give talks. As mainstream publishing has become more soul-less and commercial, independent booksellers with a creative approach have managed to build localised communities with imaginative events – they're the ones with dedicated shelves for indie-published volumes. The big bookshop chains aren't so author-friendly and may do little more than stick a poster on the door and sit you at a table to sign copies, but it's always worth exploring the manager's approach to hand-selling.

Self-published authors have set up stalls in almost any selling situation – a county show, state fair, farmer's market, pop festival, car-boot, garage or table-top sale. If your book is set in a period which attracts historical re-enactment societies, you could sell books at their events. If you have a connection with a place, a castle, battlefield, historic home or museum exhibit, you should be able to get your book into nearby shops and arrange a talk at the site, or in the local library. The local history society might like to host a talk, too. Literary festivals and book fairs often set out to attract authors selling their own books. Only experience will tell you whether you can make a profit after covering your travel costs and any entrance fee but it is certainly worth exploring all these options. At the least, you may meet a lot of great fellow authors.

Notes

1. Blake, Carole. 1999. *From Pitch to Publication: Everything You Need to Know to Get Your Novel Published*, Macmillan, London.

Acknowledgements

C.B.

My grateful thanks are due to:

Duncan Sprott for agreeing to be the best possible co-author.

Carole Angier and Sally Cline, our patient, helpful and inspirational editors.

My colleagues: Professor Tanya Krzywinska and Professor James Knowles at Brunel University, and Professor Gavin Cologne-Brooks and Professor Steve May at Bath Spa University, for their advice and guidance.

Bath Spa University for the leave to complete this work.

All our guest authors, for their excellent contributions and for generously accepting the Bloomsbury shilling.

Rachel Calder, the agent for this series.

Jonathan Lloyd at Curtis Brown, for giving this commission his blessing.

My daughter, Chloe Brayfield, for all the idyllic country weekends we didn't have.

D.S.

I am deeply grateful to all of the following for their help during the writing of this book:

Celia Brayfield for inviting me to be her co-author.

Carole Angier and Sally Cline.

Our wonderful guest contributors.

Rachel Calder, our temporary agent.

Deborah Rogers, my permanent agent.

James Harpur

M. J. Macgregor

The Rev. Dr. James D. Martin for advice on Scotland.

Dr. Simon Ollivant for advice on medieval bibliography (and Canada).

Eileen Gunn and The Royal Literary Fund for generous assistance in a computer crisis.

Geshe Pema Wangchuk.

Bibliography

Reflections 1
by Duncan Sprott

Assmann, Jan, *The Mind of Egypt: History and Meaning in the Time of the Pharaohs*, Harvard University Press, 2002.

Bloch, Marc, *The Historian's Craft*, Manchester University Press, Manchester, 1967.

Booker, Christopher, *The Seven Basic Plots: Why We Tell Stories*, Continuum, London, 2004.

Calvino, Italo, *Six Memos for the Next Millennium*, Jonathan Cape, London, 1992.

Carr, E. H., *What is History?* Pelican, 1971.

Doody, Margaret Anne, *The True Story of the Novel*, Fontana, 1998.

Dorsch, T. S. (ed.), *Classical Literary Criticism: Aristotle, Horace, Longinus*, Penguin, 1965.

Gaddis, John Lewis, *The Landscape of History*, Oxford University Press, New York, 2004.

Gay, Peter, *Freud for Historians*, Oxford University Press, New York and Oxford, 1986.

Krailsheimer, A. J. (ed.), Flaubert, Gustave, *Salammbô*, Penguin Classics, 1977.

MacKillop, James, *Dictionary of Celtic Mythology*, Oxford University Press, Oxford, 1998.

Mendoza, Plinio Apuleyo, and García Márquez, Gabriel, *The Fragrance of Guava*, Verso, London, 1983.

Murray, Katharine W., *Gates of Horn and Ivory*, Collins Biographical Histories, London and Glasgow, 2nd. edn, 1932.

Pelling, C. B. R., (ed.), *Plutarch: Life of Antony*, Cambridge University Press, Cambridge, 1988.

Plimpton, George (ed.), *Writers at Work: The Paris Review Interviews*, 4th Series, Penguin 1977. 1982 reprint.

—*Writers at Work: The Paris Review Interviews*, 6th Series, Penguin, 1985.

Said, Edward, *Orientalism: Western Conceptions of the Orient*, Penguin, 1995.

Savigneau, Josyane, *Marguerite Yourcenar: Inventing a Life*, University of Chicago Press, London, 1993.

Seymour-Smith, Martin, *Robert Graves: His Life and Work*, Bloomsbury, London, 1995.

Starkie, Enid, *Flaubert: The Making of the Master*, Penguin, 1971.

Steegmuller, Francis (ed. and trans.), *Letters of Gustave Flaubert*, Picador, London, 2001.

Sykes, Brian, *The Seven Daughters of Eve*, Bantam, London, 2001.

Warmington, E. H., *The Commerce of the Roman Empire and India*, 2nd edn, Curzon/Octagon, London and New York, 1974.

Wells, Spencer, *The Journey of Man: A Genetic Odyssey*, Penguin, 2003.

Yourcenar, Marguerite, *Memoirs of Hadrian* (with *Reflections on the Composition of Memoirs of Hadrian*), Penguin Classics, 2000.

Periodicals

Acocella, Joan, 'Becoming the Emperor', *New Yorker*, 14 and 21 February 2005.

Banville, John, 'The Prime of James Wood', review of James Wood, *How Fiction Works*, *New York Review of Books*, 20 November 2008.

Miller, Andrew, *The Guardian*, 29 June 2011.

Skidelsky, William, 'It's time to stop this obsession with works of art based on real events' *Observer*, 23 January 2011.

Wagner, Erica, 'Back to the future', *The Times*, 1 November 2000.

White, Edmund, 'More history, less nature', *Times Literary Supplement*, 5 July 2003.

—'Today the artist is a saint who writes his own life', *London Review of Books*, 9 March 2005.

A Short History of Historical Fiction
Gilgamesh to Rome by Duncan Sprott

General

de Groot, Jerome, *The Historical Novel*, Routledge, Abingdon, 2010.

Doody, Margaret Anne, *The True Story of the Novel* (1997), Fontana, London, 1998.

Forster, E. M., *Aspects of the Novel* (1927), Penguin, 1976.

Hook, Andrew (ed.), *Sir Walter Scott: Waverley* (1814), Penguin 1972, 1985.

Lukács, Georg, *The Historical Novel* (1962), Penguin, 1981.

Moore, Steven, *The Novel: An Alternative History*, Continuum, London, 2010.

Watt, Ian, *The Rise of the Novel: Studies in Defoe, Richardson and Fielding* (1957), Pimlico, London, 2000.

The Epic of Gilgamesh

Booker, Christopher, *The Seven Basic Plots: Why we tell stories* (2004), Continuum, London, 2005.

George, Andrew (ed.), *The Epic of Gilgamesh*, Penguin Classics, 1999, 2003 reprint.

Rice, Michael, *The Power of the Bull*, Routledge, London and New York, 1998.

Sandars, N. K. (ed.), *The Epic of Gilgamesh*, Penguin Classics, 1960.

Ancient Egypt

Assmann, Jan, *The Mind of Egypt*, Harvard University Press, 1996, 2002 paperback.

Lichtheim, Miriam, *Ancient Egyptian Literature*, Volume I: The Old and Middle Kingdoms, 1975 pb; Volume II: The New Kingdom, 1976 pb; Volume III: The Late Period, 1980.

Parkinson, R. B., *The Tale of Sinuhe: And Other Ancient Egyptian Poems* (1997).

Simpson, William Kelly (ed.), *The Literature of Ancient Egypt: An Anthology of Stories, Instruction and Poetry*, Yale University Press, New Haven and London, 1972.

Tait, John (ed.), *'Never Had the Like Occurred': Egypt's view of its past*, UCL Press, London, 2003.

Homer

Fowler, Robert (ed.), *The Cambridge Companion to Homer*, Cambridge University Press, Cambridge, 2004.

Gill, Christopher, and Wiseman, T.P. (eds), *Lies and Fiction in the Ancient World*, University of Exeter Press, Exeter, 1993.

Hammond, Martin (trans. and ed.), Homer, *The Iliad: A New Prose Translation*, Penguin, 1987.

Latacz, Joachim, Windle, Kevin, and Ireland, Rosh, *Troy and Homer: Towards a Solution of an Old Mystery*, Oxford University Press, Oxford, 2004.

Janko, Richard, 'Go away and rule', *Times Literary Supplement* 15 April 2005 – review of Joachim Latacz et al., *Troy and Homer* (Oxford University Press, Oxford, 2005).

Herodotus

Burn, A. R. (ed.), *Herodotus: The Histories*, revised edn, Penguin Classics, 1972, 1988 reprint.

Gill, Christopher, and Wiseman, T. P. (eds), *Lies and Fiction in the Ancient World*, University of Exeter Press, Exeter, 1993.

Gould, John, *Herodotus*, Weidenfeld and Nicolson, London, 1989.

Levi, Peter, *The Pelican History of Greek Literature*, Pelican, 1985.

Warner, Rex (trans.), *Thucydides: The Peloponnesian War*, Penguin Classics, 1959.

Xenophon of Athens

Miller, Walter (ed.), *Xenophon* [of Athens]: *Cyropaedia*, 2 vols. Loeb Classical Library (1914), Harvard University Press/William Heinemann, Cambridge, Massachusetts, and London, 1983.

The Greek Alexander Romance

Reardon, B. P. (ed.), *Collected Ancient Greek Novels*, University of California Press, Berkeley and Los Angeles, 1989.

Stoneman, Richard (trans.), *The Greek Alexander Romance*, Penguin Classics, 1991.

Apollonius of Rhodes

Green, Peter, ' "These fragments have I shored against my ruins": Apollonios Rhodios and the Social Revalidation of Myth for a New Age' in Paul Cartledge, Peter Garnsey and Erich Gruen (eds), *Hellenistic Constructs: Essays in Culture, History and Historiography*, University of California Press, Berkeley and Los Angeles, 1997.

Morgan, J. R., and Stoneman, Richard (eds), *Greek Fiction: The Greek Novel in Context*, Routledge, London and New York, 1994.

Rieu, E. V. ed., *Apollonius of Rhodes: The Voyage of Argo*, Penguin Classics, 1959.

Virgil

Fagles, Robert (trans.), *Virgil: The Aeneid*, Penguin Classics, 2007.

Knight, W. F. Jackson (ed.), *Virgil: The Aeneid*, Penguin, 1956.

Lucan

Graves, Robert (trans.), *Lucan: Pharsalia*, Penguin, 1956.

Little, Douglas (ed. and trans.) *Lucan: Pharsalia: The Civil War*, University of Otago Press, Dunedin, New Zealand, 1989.

Plutarch

Pelling, C. B. R. (ed.), *Plutarch: Life of Antony*, Cambridge University Press, Cambridge, 1988.

Beowulf to King Arthur by Duncan Sprott

The Dark Ages

Alexander, Michael (trans.), *Beowulf: A Verse Translation* (1973), Penguin Classics, revised edn, 2001.

Heaney, Seamus (trans.), and Donoghue, Daniel (ed.), *Beowulf: A Verse Translation*, Norton & Co., New York and London, 2002.

Wood, Michael, *In Search of the Dark Ages*, BBC, 1988, 2006 reprint.

Medieval Icelandic historical fiction

Magnusson, Magnus, and Pálsson, Hermann (trans.), *Njal's Saga*, 1960, 1976.

Magnusson, Magnus, and Pálsson, Hermann (trans.), *Laxdaela Saga*, Penguin, 1969.

Moore, Steven, *The Novel: An Alternative History*, Continuum, London, 2010.

The Arthurian Legend

Archibald, Elizabeth, and Putter, Ad (eds), *The Cambridge Companion to the Arthurian Legend*, Cambridge University Press, Cambridge, 2009.

Cooper, Helen (ed.), *Sir Thomas Malory: Le Morte Darthur: The Winchester Manuscript* (1998), Oxford World's Classics, Oxford, 2008.

Cowen, Janet (ed.), *Sir Thomas Malory: Le Morte d'Arthur*, 2 vols., Penguin, 1986.

Halsall, Guy, *Worlds of Arthurian Fiction: Facts and Fictions of the Dark Ages*, Oxford University Press, Oxford, 2013.

Hatto, A.T. (trans.), *Wolfram von Eschenbach: Parzifal*, Penguin Classics (1980), 2004.

Kibler, William W., and Carroll, Carleton W. (trans.), *Chrétien de Troyes: Arthurian Romances* (1991) Penguin, 2004.

Stone, Brian, *Sir Gawain and the Green Knight* (1959), Penguin Classics, 2nd edn, 1974.

Thorpe, Lewis (ed.), *Geoffrey of Monmouth: History of the Kings of Britain* (1960), Penguin Classics, 1978 reprint.

Vinaver, Eugène (ed.), *Sir Thomas Malory: Works*, Oxford University Press, Oxford, 1971.

Le Morte d'Arthur to Wolf Hall by Celia Brayfield

Achebe, Chinua, *Things Fall Apart* (1958), Penguin, London, 2001.

Atwood, Margaret, *Alias Grace* (1996), Virago Press, 1997.

Austen, Jane, *Northanger Abbey* (1818), Barnes & Noble Classics, 2005.

Bagnyon, Jehan, *Le Roman de Fierabras le Géant* (1497), *L'Histoire de Charlemagne (Parfois Dite "Roman de Fierabras")*, Droz, France, 1992.

Barker, Pat, *Regeneration* (1991), Penguin, London, 1997.

Beck, Ian, *The Secret History of Tom Trueheart, Boy Adventurer*, Oxford University Press, Oxford, 2006.

Byatt, A. S., *Possession*, Chatto & Windus, London, 1990.

De Cervantes, Miguel, *El Ingenioso Hidalgo Don Quixote de la Mancha* (1605 & 1615) *Don Quixote*, Wordsworth Classics, Hertfordshire, 1992.

Chevalier, Tracy, *Girl With a Pearl Earring*, Harper Collins, London, 2000.

Clavell, James, *King Rat* (1962), Coronet, London, 1984.

Cookson, Catherine, *Kate Hannigan* (1950), Corgi, London, 2008.

Cooper, James Fenimore, *The Last of the Mohicans* (1826), Penguin, London, 2007.

Cornwell, Bernard, *Sharpe's Eagle* (1981), Harper, London, 2011.

Dumas, Alexandre, *The Three Musketeers* (1844), Wordsworth, Hertfordshire, 1992.

Dunant, Sarah, *The Birth of Venus,* Virago, London, 2003.

—*In the Company of the Courtesan,* Virago, London, 2007.

—*Blood and Beauty,* Virago, London, 2013.

Dunnet, Dorothy, *King Hereafter,* Hamlyn, London, 1982.

Eco, Umberto, *The Name of the Rose* (1980), Vintage, London, 2004.

Eliot, George, *Middlemarch: A Study of Provincial Life* (1874), Wordsworth, Hertfordshire, 1993.

Faulks, Sebastian, *Charlotte Gray,* Vintage, London, 1998.

—*Birdsong,* Vintage, London, 1993.

Fayette, Mme de la, *La Princesse de Cleves* (1678), Pocket, France, 1998.

Forester, C. S., *The Happy Return* (1937), Penguin, London, 2011.

Fowles, John, *The French Lieutenant's Woman* (1969), Vintage, London, 2013.

Frazier, Charles, *Cold Mountain,* Hodder & Stoughton, London, 1997.

Golon, Anne, *Angélique: The Marquise of the Angels* (1956), Pan, London, 1972.

Graves, Robert, *I, Claudius* (1934), Penguin, London, 1975.

Gregory, Philippa, *The Other Boleyn Girl,* Harper Collins, London, 2001.

Hardy, Thomas, *Tess of the d'Urbervilles* (1891), Wordsworth, Hertfordshire, 1994.

Harris, Robert, *Enigma* (1995), Arrow, London, 2009.

—*Fatherland* (1992), Arrow, London, 2009.

—*Pompeii* (2003), Arrow, London, 2009.

Hartley, L. P., *The Go-Between* (1953), Penguin, London, 2004.

Heller, Joseph, *Catch-22* (1961), Vintage, London, 1994.

Heyer, Georgette, *Regency Buck* (1935), Arrow, London, 2004.

Hollinghurst, Alan, *The Line of Beauty,* Picador, London, 2004.

Hugo, Victor, *Les Misérables* (1862), Wordsworth, Hertfordshire, 1994.

Kunzru, Hari, *The Impressionist,* Hamish Hamilton, London, 2002.

Lampedusa, Giuseppe Tomasi di, *The Leopard* (1958), Trans. Colquhoun, Archibald, Vintage, London, 2007.

Lewis, Matthew Gregory, *The Monk* (1796), Wordsworth, Hertfordshire, 2009.

Maclean, Alastair, *The Guns of Navarone* (1957), Harper Collins, London, 2004.

Mailer, Norman, *The Naked and the Dead* (1948), Harper Perennial, 2006.

Mantel, Hilary, *Wolf Hall*, Fourth Estate, London, 2009.

—*Bring Up The Bodies*, Fourth Estate, London, 2012.

Malory, Thomas, *Le Morte d'Arthur* (1485), Wordsworth, Hertfordshire, 1997.

Manning, Olivia, *Fortunes of War* (1960), NYRB, New York, 2010.

McEwan, Ian, *Atonement*, Jonathan Cape, London, 2001.

Michener, James A., *Tales of the South Pacific* (1948), Ballantine, New York, 1994.

Miller, Madeline, *The Song of Achilles*, Bloomsbury, London, 2011.

Mitchell, Margaret, *Gone With The Wind* (1936), Pan, London, 2013.

Montserrat, Nicholas, *The Cruel Sea* (1951), Penguin, London, 2009.

Morpurgo, Michael, *War Horse* (1982), Egmont, UK, 2006.

Morrison, Toni, *Beloved*, Chatto & Windus, London, 1987.

Ondaatje, Michael, *The English Patient*, Bloomsbury, London, 1992.

Pamuk, Orhan, *My Name is Red* (1998), Faber, London, 2011.

Plaidy, Jean, *Murder Most Royal* (1949), Pan, London, 1966.

Pushkin, Alexander, *The Queen of Spades & Other Stories* (1833), Trans Myers, A. Oxford University Press, Oxford, 1997.

Radcliffe, Ann, *The Mysteries of Udolpho* (1794), Oxford University Press, Oxford, 2008.

Remarque, Erich Maria, *All Quiet on the Western Front* (1929), Trans. Murdoch, Brian, Vintage, London, 1994.

Rushdie, Salman, *Midnight's Children* (1980), Vintage, London, 2006.

Schlink, Bernhard, *The Reader* (1995), Phoenix, UK, 2008.

Schwarz, Liesel, *A Conspiracy of Alchemists*, Del Rey, London, 2013.

Scott, Walter, *Waverley* (1814), Oxford University Press, Oxford, 2008.

Sholokhov, Mikhail Alexandrovich, *The Quiet Don* (1928), Penguin, London, 1970.

Sidney, Philip, *The Defence of Poesy* (1579), Penguin, London, 2004.

Solzhenitsyn, Alexander, *August 1914* (1971), Trans. Glenny, Michael, Penguin, London. 1974.

Thomas, D. M., *The White Hotel,* Gollancz, London, 1981.

Tolstoy, Leo, *War And Peace* (1869), Trans. Maude, Louise & Aylmer, Wordsworth, Hertfordshire, 1993.

Tremain, Rose, *Restoration,* Hamish Hamilton, London, 1989.

Vonnegut, Kurt, *Slaughterhouse Five, or The Children's Crusade,* Delacorte, US, 1969.

Walpole, Horace, *The Castle of Otranto* (1764), Wordsworth, Hertfordshire, 2009.

Waters, Sarah, *Tipping The Velvet,* Virago, London, 1998.

Winsor, Kathleen, *Forever Amber* (1944), Penguin, London, 2002.

Winterson, Jeanette, *The Passion,* Grove, London, 1997.

Woolf, Virginia, *Orlando, A Biography* (1928), Wordsworth, Hertfordshire, 1995.

Young, Louisa, *My Dear, I Wanted to Tell You,* Harper Collins, London, 2011.

Plays

Marlowe, Christopher, *The Massacre at Paris* (1593), Forgotten Books, UK, 2008.

Shakespeare, William, *Richard III* (1592), Oxford University Press, Oxford, 2008.

Non Fiction

De Groot, Jerome, *The Historical Novel,* Routledge, New York & London, 2010.

Gladwell, Malcolm, *Outliers: The Story of Success,* Little Brown, New York, 2008.

Lukács, Georg, *The Historical Novel* (1937), Merlin, London, 1962.

Radway, Janice, *Reading the Romance: Women, Patriarchy & Popular Literature* (1984), University of North Carolina Press, USA, 1991.

Whitaker, Robert, *The Mapmaker's Wife: A True Tale of Love, Murder and Survival in the Amazon* (2004), Bantam, London, 2005.

Some useful books

Ackroyd, Peter, *Foundation: A History of England, Vol. 1,* London, Macmillan, 2011.

Bachelard, Gaston, *The Poetics of Space*, Beacon Press, Boston, 1994.

Bardon, Jonathan, *A History of Ulster*, Blackstaff Press, Belfast, 2001.

Bickerman, E.J., *Chronology of the Ancient World*, revised edn, Thames & Hudson, London 1980.

Bloch, Marc, *Feudal Society*, 2 vols, Routledge & Kegan Paul, London, 1965.

Bothwell, Robert, *The Penguin History of Canada*, Penguin, 2008.

Bourke, Joanna, *An Intimate History of Killing*, Granta Books, London, 1999.

Breeze, David J., and Dobson, Brian, *Hadrian's Wall*, 3rd edn, Penguin, London, 1987.

Brogan, Hugh, *The Penguin History of the United States of America*, Penguin, 2001.

Cambridge History of Iran, 7 vols, Cambridge, 1968–89.

Casson, Lionel, *Ships and Seamanship in the Ancient World*, Princeton University Press, Princeton, 1971.

Caunce, Stephen, *Oral History for Local Historians*, 1994.

Christmas, Brian Wm., *Sources for One-Name Studies and for other Family Historians, A Selected List and Finding Aid*, Guild of One-Name Studies, 1991.

Cobb, Richard, *Death in Paris 1795–1801*, Oxford University Press, Oxford, 1978.

Connolly, S. J. (ed.), *Oxford Companion to Irish History*, Oxford University Press, Oxford, 1998.

Conrad, Margaret, *A Concise History of Canada*, Cambridge University Press, Cambridge, 2012.

Cross, F. L., *Oxford Dictionary of the Christian Church*, Oxford University Press, Oxford, 1971.

Cunnington, C. Willet and Cunnington, Phillis, *Handbook of English Costume in the Eighteenth Century*, Faber, London, revised edn, 1972.

Dalby, Andrew, *Siren Feasts: A History of Food and Gastronomy in Greece*, Routledge, London, 1995.

Dear, I. C. B., and Kemp, Peter, *The Oxford Companion to Ships and the Sea*, 2nd edn, Oxford University Press, Oxford, 2006.

de Bono, Edward, *Serious Creativity*, HarperCollins Business, London, 1996.

Donaldson, Gordon (ed.), *Edinburgh History of Scotland*, 4 vols, Edinburgh. 1974–96.

Duffy, Sean, *Atlas of Irish History*, 2nd edition, Gill & Macmillan, Dublin, 2000.

Emmison, F. G., *Archives and Local History*, Methuen, 1966.

Flanaghan, Laurence, *Ancient Ireland: Life Before the Celts*, Gill & Macmillan, Dublin, 1998.

Foster, Joseph, *Alumni Oxonienses 1500–1886*, Parker & Co, Oxford, 1888–92.

Foster, R. F. (ed.), *The Oxford History of Ireland*, Oxford University Press, 1989.

Freud, Sigmund, *The Interpretation of Dreams*, Penguin, 1991.

—*The Psychopathology of Everyday Life*, Penguin, 2002.

Gay, Peter, *Freud for Historians*, Oxford University Press, New York, 1986.

Goffman, Erving, *The Presentation of Self in Everyday Life*, Penguin, 1975.

Gooder, Eileen A., *Latin for Local History: An Introduction*, Longman, 1986.

Grieve, Hilda, E. P., *Examples of English Handwriting 1150–1750*, Essex Record Office, 1966.

Grimal, Nicolas, *A History of Ancient Egypt*, Blackwell, Oxford, 1992.

Grun, Bernard and Simpson, Eva, *The Timetables of History: A Horizontal Linkage of People and Events*, 4th edition, Simon & Schuster, 2005.

Hart, George, *A Dictionary of Egyptian Gods and Goddesses*, Routledge, London, 1986.

Hey, David, *Oxford Companion to Local and Family History*, Oxford University Press, Oxford, 1996.

Hornblower, Simon, and Spawforth, Antony, *The Oxford Classical Dictionary*, 3rd edn, Oxford University Press, Oxford, 1996.

Hoskins, W. G., *The Making of the English Landscape*, Penguin, 1991.

Hughes, Robert, *The Fatal Shore*, Vintage, 2003.

Humphery-Smith, Cecil R. (ed.), *Phillimore Atlas and Index of Parish Registers*, 3rd edn, Phillimore, 2003.

Hutchinson, Peter, *Games Authors Play*, Methuen, London and New York, 1983.

Hyland, Anne, *Equus: The Horse in the Roman World*, Yale University Press, 1990.

Ison, Alf, *A Secretary Hand ABC Book*, Berkshire Books, 1996.

Keneally, Thomas, *The Commonwealth of Thieves: The Story of the Founding of Australia*, Vintage, 2007.

King, Michael, *The Penguin History of New Zealand*, Penguin NZ, 2003 repr.

Knowles, Dom David, *Bare Ruined Choirs: The Dissolution of the English Monasteries*, Cambridge University Press, Cambridge, 1976.

—*The Religious Orders in England* (3 vols), Cambridge University Press, 1948–59.

MacKillop, James, *Dictionary of Celtic Mythology*, Oxford University Press, Oxford, 1998.

Mellersh, H. E. L., *Chronology of the Ancient World, 10,000 BC to AD 79*, Helicon, Oxford, 1995 reprint.

Morris, John, *The Age of Arthur: A History of the British Isles from 350 to 650*, Weidenfeld and Nicolson, London, 1973.

Ladurie, Emanuel Le Roy, *Montaillou: Cathars and Catholics in a French Village, 1294–1324*, Scolar Press, London, 1978.

Ladurie, Emanuel Le Roy, *The Peasants of Languedoc*, Illinois University Press, 1974.

Lowenthal, David, *The Past is a Foreign Country*, Cambridge University Press, Cambridge, 1985.

Lynch, Michael, *Scotland: A New History*, Pimlico, London, 1992.

—*The Oxford Companion to Scottish History*, Oxford University Press, Oxford, 2011.

Macintyre, Stuart, *A Concise History of Australia* (Cambridge Concise Histories), 3rd edn, Cambridge University Press, Cambridge, 2009.

McEvedy, Colin, *The Penguin Atlas of Medieval History*, Penguin 1961, 1969 reprint.

Mimms, Cedric, *When We Die*, Robinson Publishing, London, 1998.

Mortimer, Ian, *The Time Traveller's Guide to Medieval England: A Handbook for Visitors to the Fourteenth Century*, Bodley Head, London, 2008.

—*The Time Traveller's Guide to Elizabethan England*, Bodley Head, London, 2012.

New Cambridge Ancient History, Second Series, 14 vols in 19 books, Cambridge University Press, Cambridge, 1970–2005.

New Cambridge Medieval History, 7 vols, Cambridge University Press, Cambridge, 1995–2005.

New Cambridge Modern History, Second Series, 14 vols, Cambridge University Press, Cambridge, 1957–79.

New Oxford History of England, 12 vols, Oxford University Press, Oxford, 1995–

Norwich, John Julius, *Byzantium,* 3 vols, Viking-Penguin, 1988–95.

Partridge, Eric, *The Penguin Dictionary of Historical Slang,* Penguin, 1972.

Pevsner, Nikolaus (ed.), *The Buildings of England,* 46 vols, Penguin, 1951–74; revised and updated editions, Yale University Press, ongoing.

Plumb, J. H., *The Death of the Past,* Macmillan, London, 1969.

Prebble, John, *Glencoe: The Story of the* Massacre, Martin Secker & Warburg, London, 1966.

—*Culloden,* Martin Secker & Warburg, London, 1961.

—*The Highland Clearances,* Martin Secker & Warburg, London, 1963.

Read, Piers Paul, *The Templars,* Phoenix, London, 2003.

Ribeiro, Aileen, *Dress in Eighteenth Century Europe 1715–1789,* Batsford, London, 1984.

Ross, Anne, *Pagan Celtic Britain,* Routledge, London, 1967.

Rodger, N. A. M., *The Safeguard of the Sea: A Naval History of Britain 660–1649,* Harper Collins, London, 1997.

—*The Wooden World: An Anatomy of the Georgian* Navy, Naval Institute Press, London, 1986.

Runciman, Steven, *A History of the Crusades,* 3 vols, 1952, 2nd edn, 1978.

Smith, Philippa Mein, *A Concise History of New Zealand,* Cambridge University Press, Cambridge, 2nd edn, 2011.

Steel, D. J., et al., *National Index of Parish Registers,* 12 vols, Phillimore/Society of Genealogists, 1966–98.

Stewart, A. T. Q., *The Narrow Ground: Aspects of Ulster 1609–1969,* Faber, London, 1977.

Storey, R. L., Mellersh, H. E. L., and Williams, Neville, *Chronology of the Medieval World: 800 – 1491,* Helicon Publishing, Oxford, 1994.

Tate, W. E., *The Parish Chest: A Study of the Records of Parochial Administration in England,* Cambridge University Press, 1946. 3rd edn, revised, Phillimore, 2010.

Venn, John, and Venn, J. A., *Alumni Cantabrigienses, from the Earliest Times to 1900,* 10 vols, Cambridge, 1922–53.

Weinreb, Ben, and Hibbert, Christopher, *The London Encyclopaedia,* Macmillan, London, 1983.

Welch, Robert (ed.), *The Oxford Companion to Irish Literature*, Oxford University Press, Oxford, 1996.

White, Hayden (ed.), *Metahistory: The Historical Imagination in Nineteenth Century Europe*, Johns Hopkins University Press, 1975.

Wilson, A.N., *Tolstoy*, Hamish Hamilton, London, 1988.

Yeoman, Louise, *Reportage Scotland: History in the Making*, Luath Press, Edinburgh 2000.

Zinn, Howard, *A People's History of the United States: 1492 – Present*, Harper Perennial, 2005.

Genealogy

Grannum, Karen, and Taylor, Nigel, *Wills and Probate Records*, National Archives, 2009.

Osborn, Helen, *Genealogy: Essential Methods*, Robert Hale, 2012.

Peacock, Caroline, *Genealogy*, The Good Web Guide, 2002. 4th edn, 2005.

Wagner, Antony, *English Genealogy*, Clarendon Press, Oxford, 1960.

Writing

Allott, Miriam, *Novelists on the Novel* (1959), Routledge, London, 1975.

Blake, Carole, *From Pitch to Publication: Everything you need to know to get your novel published*. Macmillan, London, 1999.

Braine, John, *Writing a Novel*, Eyre Methuen, London, 1974.

Burchfield, R. W., *The New Fowler's Modern English Usage*, revised 3rd edn., Oxford University Press, Oxford, 1998.

Butcher, Judith, *Copy-editing: The Cambridge Handbook for Editors, Authors and Publishers*, 3rd edn, Cambridge University Press, Cambridge, 1992.

Carey, G. V., *Mind the Stop: A Brief Guide to Punctuation*, Penguin, 1983.

Economist Style Guide, The Profile Books, 2005.

Forster, E. M., *Aspects of the Novel*, Penguin, 1976.

Gowers, Sir Ernest, *The Complete Plain Words* (1954), Pelican, 1977 reprint.

Marsh, David, *Guardian Style*, Guardian Books, London, 2007.

Mittelmark, Howard, and Newman, Sandra, *How Not to Write a Novel*, Penguin, 2009.

Oxford Dictionary for Writers and Editors, The, Oxford University Press, 2000.

Siegal, Alan M. and Connolly, William G., *The New York Times Manual of Style and Usage*, Times Books, New York, 1999.
Whale, John, *Put it in Writing*, Dent, London, 1984.
Wood, James, *How Fiction Works*, Vintage, London, 2008.

Index